Friendship is unnecessary, like philosophy, like art....It has no survival value; rather it is one of those things that give value to survival.
—C. S. Lewis

Getting from
ME to We

*I just want someone to play with me.
I want a friend. I don't have any friends.*
—Clara, aged 4

Getting from ME to We

to

How to Help Young Children Fit In and Make Friends

Shonna Tuck, M.A., SLP

Woodbine House

Published in the United States of America by Woodbine House, Inc.,
6510 Bells Mill Road, Bethesda, MD 20817. 800-843-7323. www.woodbinehouse.com.

Library of Congress Cataloging-in-Publication Data

Tuck, Shonna L.
  Getting from me to we : how to help young children fit in and make friends
/ Shonna L. Tuck, M.A., SLP. -- 1st ed.
      pages cm
  Includes bibliographical references and index.
  ISBN 978-1-60613-269-2 (pbk. : alk. paper) 1. Adjustment (Psychology)
in children. 2. Child development. 3. Friendship. I. Title.
  BF724.3.A32T83 2015
  155.4'192--dc23
                                                                2015023676

Manufactured in the United States of America

10 9   8   7   6   5   4   3   2   1

For Simon, Maya, Elliott, and yes, you too, Teddy
—you are loved immeasurably.

Also for B and the recess that changed everything for me.

Getting from...

Me	to	We
Self-directed	⟶	Includes others
Self-directed	⟶	Listens to others
Self-directed	⟶	Watches others
Tuned out	⟶	Tuned in
Rigid play	⟶	Flexible play
Me, NOW!!!	⟶	Me later, you now
Conflict with force	⟶	Solves conflict with words
Out in the hallway	⟶	Stays in class
Parallel play	⟶	Cooperative play
Sidelines	⟶	Included
No one to play with	⟶	Someone to play with

Table of Contents

Part 2.
Taylor-Made Tools for Recess Success

Introduction

It's hard to believe that in this preschool class full of two-year-olds busy at play, at least three of them will struggle with friendships through-out school. All around are children with bright eyes, tousled hair, and big smiles. They are all unique and beautiful. There are fearless explorers, me-ticulous builders, creative innovators, and sensitive caretakers. They express who they are completely without thought or the baggage of fitting in.

Fast-forward three years, to the same classroom, with the same kids. Now five and in kindergarten, they are all still beautiful and full of promise, but now there is a clear, unspoken social hierarchy. Kindergarten and the pri-mary school years are set up to teach children how to follow routines and how to socialize with other kids. It's set up for those who can do that.

This book is for the kids who can't. Yet.

Kids like A.J.

He hops down the steps of his school bus with his Hot Wheels backpack swinging and a grin that takes up most of his face. At four, he's tall for his age, and with his shock of red hair, he's hard to miss. He rounds the corner into the yard just as the bell rings. With a loud whoop and his heart racing, he opens his eyes wide with alarm when he realizes that everyone has already lined up. It is clear that he is determined to get to the front of the line NOW! He sprints over and elbows his way in.

"Hey! Move!" he demands. A couple of the kids shout, "Stop it, A.J. We were here first."

He keeps jockeying for front position, ignoring the increasingly loud protests from the other kids. Until, with one more whack on the legs from his backpack…he finally makes it. Front-of-the-line victory.

He turns to the kid behind him, seeming to ignore the irritated and angry faces of the other boys, and says, "Hey! I got a new spark effects Hot Wheel—see!" One child reluctantly acknowledges that it is pretty cool. The others give him dirty looks as they are hustled through the doors into the noisy junior kindergarten room.

Once there, having had enough of the line butting from A.J., one of the boys tells the teacher. A.J. overhears and is outraged. "Naw! I did not!—I was there first! He's always trying to get me in trouble. Anyway, Dante hit me." (Not really true; Dante's backpack, unbeknownst to him, kind of bumped A.J.'s leg.)

A.J. is embarrassed, feeling cornered and self-righteous.

"Now, boys, if you two can't get along you'll both have to go in the thinking chair to cool down," the teacher says. "Do you need to cool down a bit or can we move on to circle?" Dante chooses circle.

A.J. experiences the world more intensely than most kids and cannot change gears as quickly. "Why do I have to go to the thinking chair when Dante hit me?

"I was first!" (In his mind, yes.)

The class is now quiet. Everyone is watching the scene unfold like clouds gathering right before a thunderstorm. The teacher now feels she has no choice but to send A.J. to the thinking chair.

But he won't go.

Burning with self-righteous anger, he starts yelling "NO! NO!" He then knocks the chair down, which gets him sent to the principal's office. Again.

By 10:00 a.m., with red, blotchy cheeks and eyes swollen from crying, A.J. returns to his class, which is now bubbling with conversation, as his classmates have broken off into pairs and small groups during free play.

He walks over to a couple of boys who are building bridges out of wooden blocks and says, "Hey." He feels awkward and unsure of what to do now that his classmates all seem engrossed in their own games. The two boys keep playing, oblivious to A.J. standing there wanting to play too. A.J. squirms and becomes increasingly agitated. He hesitates and then dives in saying, "I'm back," and pulling a goofy face. The boys glance up but keep talking to each other and building, absorbed in what they are doing.

A.J. pulls his Hot Wheels car out of his pocket. He shouts, "Timber! Wham!" and smashes it into the bridge.

The boys cry out in indignation and start chasing A.J., who is now laughing and feeling like at least now they are all playing together.

A.J. has no friends, but it's not by choice.

Here's the thing. A.J. is a loving, enthusiastic, generous little boy, but he's already struggling with making and keeping friends, and he's not even in first grade yet. These negative interactions compound with interest over time until things sort themselves out. Or, more likely, don't.

As a parent reading this, you may be worried about your young one but wondering where to begin. The bottom line is this: "What does your child need to gain a sense of belonging in their school community and, more specifically, what does your child need to make friends and turn things around?"

At ten years old, A.J. can more often than not be found in the school hallway. He is a quiet, fidgety, foot-tapping, deep-sighing, angry kid. At recess, he hangs out with one other boy.

When the other kids in the schoolyard see A.J., they quickly look away. They are afraid, and he knows it. A.J. now has a friend, but not one who brings out the best in him.

At seventeen, with only two weeks until high school graduation, A.J. has missed so much school that despite having scraped by academically, he may not have met the required number of in-class hours to graduate. He is a party boy who frequents the park at break and comes back smelling of pot with red-rimmed eyes. He has had some minor scrapes with the law, including a vandalism charge that wasn't proven in court. The people he spends the most time with do much more damage than knocking down wooden block bridges when they want attention. A.J. now has lots of "friends," all with their own history of living life on the margins. His story, like those of so many others, is that of a young person whose train has gone off the rails and shows no signs of it getting back on.

What could have been done in kindergarten to change his path?

Zack is just four years old when he breaks the door window leading into his class. The principal hauls him down to the office and immediately calls his mother. When she arrives and surveys the damage, she asks a pertinent question: "What was a four-year-old doing in the hallway, by himself and unsupervised?"

Zack wouldn't sit in the thinking chair. He couldn't sit during circle time. He didn't know how to play with the other kids, so he was put in the hallway to "think about what he had done."

In the car, his visibly shaken mom asks Zack why he was put in the hall. He said he kicked Brody.

Seeing that Zack understood the initial problem, his mother probes further. "Why did you break the window?"

Zack's answer surprises her. "Because I knocked and knocked and yelled to come get me, and nobody would come."

While he has trouble paying attention during circle time and doesn't always do the cutting and pasting that is asked of him, his biggest challenge is in interacting with the other kids. During free play, he grabs toys, hits kids, and runs away laughing. He says pretty disgusting toilet words, and he often hovers around kids who are playing, without saying or doing anything. He is a child with a short fuse—quick to hit, cry, and tantrum.

Zack has no friends.

Fast-forward six years.

In fifth grade, Zack is the proud recipient of that week's starfish award for excellent school citizenship. Zack has two or three kids that he hangs out with all the time.

In high school, Zack is a solid B student. He plays in the concert band, runs track, and has a group of three friends that he has hung out with since seventh grade. He also has held down a summer job and is getting his driver's license, though his parents have some trepidation because he remains a risk taker.

What happened to Zack that didn't happen to A.J.?

When Ashley tries to play with the other girls in her kindergarten class, they run away. Ashley runs after them, thinking that she is part of the gang. She works very hard to catch up—and when she finally does, they scream, "Ew! Get away!" She laughs like she is part of the joke, but, painfully, she doesn't realize that the other kids are laughing at her not with her. During free play, she stands near the group of girls at the sand table just watching, chewing on her sleeve—a sleeve that has a tattered, soaking wet bottom.

Although she may or may not realize it, Ashley has no friends.

Neither does Kate. But unlike many kids with these types of social challenges, she doesn't make a lot of noise, break things, or draw attention. She simply plays with Legos by herself, quietly on the floor. The same Legos that she's been playing with in the exact same way every day for the past eight months.

Maybe you think that these kinds of stories don't happen in your child's class. If so, you're sadly mistaken. There are kids like A.J., Zack, Ashley, and Kate in just about every classroom.

According to the U.S Census Bureau, there were 36.2 million elementary school–aged children in 2008 (Davis, J., Bauman, K. 2011). If we add together the incidence of just autism (1/68) and ADD/ADHD (11/100) alone there are 4,514,140 children who could meet the criteria for having one of these diagnoses in America (CDC, 2015).

Now, include other classifiable issues that are known to have potential social skills ramifications such as anxiety disorder, depression, nonverbal learning disability, social pragmatic disorder, oppositional defiant disorder, speech-language learning challenges, and so on. That means that on average, each elementary classroom will have *at least* three children who markedly stand out from the others—and not in a good way. Add to the obvious three a few more whose challenges are subtle like Kate's but still contribute to struggles with making and keeping friends, and it becomes clear pretty quickly that this is a widespread societal issue.

It's as if a game of friendship musical chairs is going on in each classroom in each school, but the social playing field is at least three chairs short.

Whether or not classmates have formal diagnoses, kids respond to differences and have already decided by kindergarten who is included and who is not. Classmates have already started to determine who is to be ignored, shunned, and bullied and who is motivated to become a bully.

By ninth grade, those kids on the sidelines are now often harassed or are just ignored because they've strived to disappear. These marginalized, vulnerable people often respond to years of abuse or social neglect in negative, maladaptive ways, which only compounds damage. Now, being left without a seat in musical chairs feels more like social Russian roulette.

Could you predict which kids in preschool would be the ones left standing? Is your child one of them?

How Can Adults Help?

While we as parents, professionals, and educators would like for these kids to just magically "grow out of it," the reality is that many don't figure out how to find a place to belong in school. If your child is struggling to make friends at four, what makes adults feel reassured that everything will be fine by age eight or twelve, when the rules are even more complicated and subtle?

Helping early is critical.

Think about it. While no child is exempt from some struggle, and, of course, some kids have a tough time early on figuring out on their own how to make and keep a friend or two, how much preventable struggle is okay? Some kids accumulate years of negative experiences with peers and teachers that could have been avoided or at least lessened. The physician's mandate is to "Do no harm." But sometimes inaction is what is harmful, like a lie by omission.

If you have concerns and want to do something to prevent bigger problems later, then what are the things you need to be looking for as a parent, educator, or professional so that you can advocate for the children you are worried about?

To start, if you recognized elements of the children in the examples above in your own child, it is important to consider the underlying issues that might be at the root of these problems. Information is power, and an assessment by a specialist can provide important information. Figuring out why your child is struggling socially can give the adults who want to help clearer insight and more specific tools to help.

However, sometimes these challenged kids who struggle early in school do not easily fit into established categories, and underlying issues are tricky to figure out. Perhaps an evaluation is not easily available, or maybe issues are just challenging enough that adults are paying attention, but mild enough that the school isn't prioritizing your child's assessment. Perhaps you are dealing with a really long wait list, or maybe you are just plain unsure. Do we just throw our hands up in despair? Absolutely not.

Wherever you are in exploring why your child is struggling with making and keeping friends, we adults can figure out where breakdowns in social communication occur and what the next steps should be.

So, whether your child has an underlying diagnosis, or you are wondering if he or she will later require a specific diagnosis, or you are just gathering information and watching, the *skills* your child needs to be able to make friends will be the same.

The differences will be in where your child's abilities fall on the social skills development ladder, how hard it will be for him or her to climb higher rungs, and how long it will take.

It will not, however, change the structure of the ladder and the steps needed to get to the top.

This book provides a model to identify and intervene for these at-risk children from ages three and a half to seven. This age range is a critical time in which most kids move from playing independently to playing cooperatively.

The more cooperative and dramatic play a child participates in at a young age, the stronger that child's abilities become in the area of social perspective taking. Dramatic play gives kids a chance to think with someone else's thoughts and feelings. Strong social perspective taking, or the ability to "walk in someone else's shoes," is a good indicator that children will be able to "read" other children and have the tools that will help them get along well within their peer group.

How to Use This Book

In writing this book, I drew on twenty years of observation, my studies of the research, and my experiences providing intervention as a speech-language pathologist working with young children and their families.

All of the stories cited are true and the children referred to are real, though details have been modified to protect the identities of the people described. While the children in this book come from a variety of backgrounds and upbringings, they all had one thing in common: they had struggled ever since they first started interacting with peers.

Many of the children described had language abilities that were in the average range on paper, but they were missing crucial elements in the functional *use* of the language they had. Some of them had trouble coordinating their thoughts in more abstract, complex ways. It was as if they just couldn't seem to pull together what they knew to make and keep friends—kind of like sitting in the car without keys to make it go.

Drawing from research and identifying what socially successful children do from infancy to the second grade, I attempted to deconstruct social skills to best identify the key elements needed to successfully interact with peers. Each major element is represented as a rung on a ladder.

The first rungs begin for most children in infancy; the last rungs are more developed by about seven years old—an age when classroom social hierarchies are more clearly defined and most children have already developed a solid foundation of social interaction skills.

After reading this book, you will be able to identify:

- where your child is on the social skills development ladder
- how to set goals to help fill in gaps and help your child learn to make and keep friends
- how and when to support your child during play
- how your child's play preferences can help or hinder making and keeping friends
- what to watch for and how to help your child be able to participate fully at recess

If you are unsure how to get your child to engage and play with you, or if your child runs away or gets irritated when you join in, then the first three rungs on the ladder will be of particular interest to you:

- **Rung #1: Joint Attention**
  This is where the magic of moving from being self-directed toward true interaction and sharing experiences begins.

- **Rung #2: Emotional Awareness**
  In this chapter, we will explore how and when children learn to recognize emotions in themselves and others and the impact on social interaction.

- **Rung #3: Imitation**
  Here you'll learn how imitation in play helps your child to be included by other children, helps your child pay attention to others, and gives him or her access to being allowed to stay in play with other kids.

- **Rung #4: Early Perspective Taking**
This is where children learn that other people think and feel too and that those thoughts/feelings may even be different than their own. This is a major shift from an egocentric, literal world-view toward a more inclusive, flexible one. This change forms the basis for being able to see things from another's point of view, which accounts for being able to "read" social dynamics.

- **Rung #5: Later Perspective Taking (Theory of Mind)**
Theory of Mind ability builds on your child's understanding that others have different ideas and knowledge, which informs their unique perspectives. Helping your child develop theory of mind will support understanding of why others may behave the way they do and how to adapt his or her own behavior based on who he or she is playing with.

- **Rung #6: Narratives**
Your child most likely has challenges with narratives if you and your child enjoy playing together in a variety of ways, but it's hard to follow your child's train of thought in conversation, your child changes topics in conversation abruptly, or leaves out information crucial for friends to follow his or her ideas. Helping children describe their experiences in an organized way with appropriate inclusion of necessary details so that the listener can follow their ideas is crucial to be included in play with others.

- **Rung #7: Conflict Resolution/Executive Function**
When young kids fight, well-meaning adults often intervene by saying, "Use your words." Of course kids need to learn to verbally deal with conflict, but it can be very difficult for many children. If your child has all of the skills developed on earlier rungs but persistent challenges organizing and expressing his or her thoughts during heightened emotional situations, then you will find your child's skills at this level.

At this point, it is important to consider that while the ladder image gives the appropriate sense of how skills are built up, child development is not always quite so neat and tidy. Some children will have developed just enough of the foundational social skills needed to reach more complicated upper rung skills, but they may continue throughout life to need to reinforce lower rungs that relate to paying attention to others (e.g., joint attention, emotions/nonverbal communication, and imitation). Some children may be a bit more rigid in their approach to life and will need ongoing support for flexible thinking (imitation, perspective taking, conflict resolution) in order to build and maintain friendships. Still others may struggle with intense and immediate responses to social situations and will need a great deal of extra learning in the areas of emotional recognition, perspective taking, and conflict resolution.

The ladder image, in essence, then, is a guide to help you understand the foundational skills your child needs to make and keep friends and to help you identify strengths and areas needed for growth. It is not necessarily a one-way ticket to social success—but it may be a means to visit and revisit skills as needed to support your child's ability to make and keep friends. You may need to go up and down the ladder many times depending on social demands placed on your child; some days your child's social skills may hover around the bottom, but on other days, or with different kids, he or she can handle higher social rungs. Compared to other children, your child may need more people at the bottom keeping the ladder steady and stable as he climbs, or his rungs may be spaced further apart. This metaphor can and should be individualized to your child's specific and always-changing needs.

In later chapters, we will explore how the ways your child prefers to play can potentially affect his ability to make and keep friends, discuss what makes kids "cool" in the schoolyard during the younger years, and finally look at what your child needs to be ready for recess with friends.

What Does Speech-Language Therapy Have to Do with It?

As you make your way through the book, you'll notice frequent references to speech-language therapy and to the professionals who provide it: speech-language pathologists, speech therapists, and clinicians. For ease of writing, I am using these terms interchangeably to describe a person who has obtained at least a master's degree specializing in communication disorders and is registered with his or her appropriate overseeing association. However, you should know that not all people who call themselves "speech therapists" have as much training as a certified speech-language pathologist.

Differences in terminology aside, you will see that many of the kids profiled in this book received assistance from a speech therapist. Does that mean that your child should have speech-language therapy if he or she is struggling with social skills? Not necessarily, but you may want to find out if your child would benefit from therapy. There is more information about speech therapy in the last chapter of the book. For now, you should know that speech therapists who specialize in pediatrics can assess and provide intervention for pretty much anything that interferes with communication, whatever the underlying cause—whether it is spoken, written, or read. They can assess and treat problems in the following areas:

- oral expression: grammar, formulating complete sentences, organizing spoken language so it makes sense and vocabulary
- understanding language: following spoken instructions, understanding vocabulary, key words/concepts, auditory processing of language, etc.
- social interaction ability: interpreting body language, functional use of language with another person, etc.
- clarity of speech, articulation, speech-sound coordination challenges (verbal apraxia), etc.
- voice/resonance issues (e.g., sounding too nasal or "stuffed up")
- stuttering
- reading (readiness, decoding, and comprehension)
- writing (formulating coherent thoughts, organizing them on paper) and so on.

If you want to read more about what a speech therapist does, the associations that regulate the profession in North America have excellent summaries and information for parents and professionals. In Canada, it is Speech-Language and Audiology Canada (SAC), and in the United States, it is the American Speech-Language-Hearing Association (ASHA). The Resources section provides contact information for these organizations.

Your Crucial Role

Before launching in, it's important to pause for a moment to emphasize the single, most significant thing that you can do to help your child make friends right now.

Play with him or her! Get your child away from the TV, away from the video games; get yourself up off the park bench. Aim for at least ten minutes of uninterrupted, child-led fun time every day for the two of you. This does not mean time spent teaching your child what to do and how to do it, nor is it time for correcting behavior or setting up rules. This is special time to *do* something, anything, that you and your child enjoy together. This playtime does not focus on the "right way" or the "wrong way." You need to go for the smile, the laugh, and the sharing of the experience.

Your child begins life learning pretty much everything from you. With the love and commitment you have for your little one, you can get down to his or her level and demonstrate what it means to play. The goal is to feel how much fun it can be to play together.

A gentle, loving adult play partner can model skills that help children fill in gaps that they are struggling with on their own. In this way, you are helping prepare your little one for similar social situations when he or she is with far-less-forgiving peers.

So, take a deep breath and break out the play dough. Here we go!

Part 1
Social Climbing:
Seven Rungs to Making Friends

RUNG 1

Seeing Me Seeing You
Joint Attention

Joint Attention

Raven lived in a shabby, geared-to-income apartment complex with her teenaged mom and an often-absent father. At just five months old, she had no awareness that the common room she was in this morning was the scene of a drug-fuelled police hostage takedown just a week before. Her "normal" included breathing air so polluted with cigarette smoke that it smelled like fumes from an exhaust pipe. Her normal involved never leaving this building that was so dimly lit that it always looked like it was evening.

In this common area, on the main floor, some mothers had gathered at the urging of their caseworkers to learn about how to connect and communicate with their babies and toddlers.

The purpose of this meeting was to educate these moms about the importance of talking to their infants and toddlers. The goal was to help at-risk mothers understand that they have the ability to be their young children's best teachers because they love them and are with them most during the critical early years before school. There is an abundance of research supporting that academic success is predicated on vocabulary size and that children develop vocabularies based on the number of words they hear from their primary caregivers during the crucial years of infancy to kindergarten (Weisleder & Fernald, 2013).

It was clear that this group of women drinking coffee and chatting had hard lives and that it wasn't going to be easy for an outsider to reach these women—suspicion was written on their prematurely lined faces. Conversation stopped, and an uncomfortable silence marked the beginning of our time together.

After introductions, we talked about how babies naturally love and seek out their mom's face and how that powerful connection and relationship makes mothers their most important teachers.

We then explored the idea that babies do talk, just not with words—that they communicate through crying, eye gaze, body movements, smiles and laughs, etc. Understanding that communication exists beyond just words can help parents learn to recognize and tune in to the cues an infant is giving and forms not only the basis of a relationship, but also the foundation for a child to understand the power of communication. It's this understanding that helps children grow to learn that language is important and to become motivated to use it.

After establishing that all of the moms present had extensive experience with crying babies, they were then asked to consider why babies cry. One mom spoke up and said, "For the first three months, Piper cried all the f*&#@' time. The only way she would stop was if I put *Jeopardy* on."

The other moms laughed and were encouraged to consider what Piper's mom had done right. That is, although it took her a while to figure out what Piper needed because she didn't have words to tell her mom, it was because her mom tuned in to Piper, watched her carefully, and acted like her baby's crying was communicating a need that she figured out that *Jeopardy* was the answer.

"Drove me freakin' nuts trying to figure that one out. I would walk her around for hours. Try a bottle, change her diaper, nothing," Piper's mom said.

Sometimes you might be dealing with something "special" like colic that can make it hard to guess what will help your baby feel better. However, the important thing is that your baby gets the message over and over that when she cries, you act to try and help her feel better. That crying is your baby's first attempt at communicating with you.

The young moms were then asked how they could tell when their baby was about to cry. One mom said, "My baby starts breathing really fast and his lip starts goin' like this." (The woman showed a rapid in-and-out motion.)

Someone blurted out, "That's so cute!" and the mom laughed as if to say, "Doesn't always feel too cute." But it was easy to tell she was proud of her little boy.

Everyone agreed that watching closely is the most important thing to do in order to pick up messages that their baby is sending. It can be very empowering to watch for clues from infants and satisfy their unspoken requests. In addition, the relationship between looking at their babies and watching for what they might be trying to communicate connects a parent and child. Essentially, one of the most important things a parent and child do is learn to "read each" other by watching closely.

The fun part began with the women getting down on the floor, sitting face-to-face with their babies, and just looking at each other. Most mothers couldn't resist making silly faces to get their child to smile.

Each mom was given a rattle and was instructed to shake it and wait to see what signs her baby gave to indicate that he wanted it to happen again. Everyone was laughing and doing really well except a hunched-over woman in a deeply stained sweatsuit. She sat silently in the corner, her tangled hair still holding a pillow indent shape on one side.

"It's not working," she whispered without looking up.

After we made some light small talk and exchanged names, Mary tried shaking the little rattle in front of her baby Raven's face again.

No response.

Raven's eyes could best be described as dead. She barely blinked. This beautiful, pale, silent little baby was "gone." There was no reaction. No joy. Just this flat expression.

Mary shrugged, her own face passive. "She's not sick or anything. She's always like this."

It is hard to imagine a more shocking image than an infant so detached and unanimated. Physically, Raven appeared healthy, but it turned out that her unresponsiveness was a product of a mom overwhelmed by severe depression. This depression was so complete that it prevented her from attending to Raven's needs. Raven had stopped crying long ago because no one responded. She had stopped checking and looking for faces that didn't respond.

The Children's Aid Society eventually stepped in and placed Raven in care until the mother could climb her way out of her pain.

The Importance of Making Connections

A powerful and simple truth was shown that day. *We are born to connect.*

Babies connect by looking at us looking at them and acting. Babies learn that they are valuable and that they can change their environment by crying and having that cry responded to.

Clearly, Raven's situation is an extreme example of how things can go wrong, but it illustrates the importance of simply looking at each other and having someone respond when you need them. This attention to each other is at the core of what it means to be in a relationship with a caregiver, and sets the stage for having relationships with others.

The power of this reinforcing connection occurs over time and is cumulative.

If you are like most parents, you may be thinking Raven's story is all very interesting, but you didn't need Children's Aid Society to remove your child, and you probably remember responding to the thousands of cries your child made for diapers gone wild, throwing up in the crib, and runny noses. So, what does this story have to do with your young child making friends? Everything. There are many, many children out there who have not fully developed joint attention even though other milestones happened at expected times.

Signs of Difficulty with Joint Attention

Joint attention is the first rung of the ladder that measures our social skills development, and children use the skill first with parents and caregivers and then with peers. Signs that an infant or child is not developing joint attention include not bothering to look for and at a caregiver's face, not crying to show that he needs something and, perhaps, a flat, non-expressive face.

Preschoolers who lack or have not fully developed joint attention can look like children who don't often seek out others. They may not ask for things with words, gestures, or pointing and are almost too independent. A child who hasn't fully developed joint attention generally pursues activities that are self-directed, doesn't show or point out things that are interesting to him, and often demonstrates limited eye contact.

In kindergarten and during the primary school years, a child who lacks joint attention may seem to be always moving, not following the classroom routine, not really interacting with the teacher, and being disruptive or non-compliant. The child may also appear extremely passive, may not initiate socially or otherwise, and may not look at others or survey the classroom to watch what is happening.

Many children who go on to struggle with connecting with others in the classroom need more work on joint attention skills. With this in mind, it makes sense that anything—a neurological difference, an underlying learning difficulty, an environmental problem, or any combination of these that interrupts this joint focus during the critical early years of development—will, in the future, affect that child's ability to communicate socially. The degree and duration of the interruption of this communicative "flow" will determine in large part how disengaged a child is.

In Raven's case, her lack of responsiveness was due to her mother's severe postpartum depression, but there are many reasons a child may have challenges with joint attention.

Whatever the reason, when children do not demonstrate joint attention, somewhere along the line their ability to engage with others has been interrupted. This means that when a child has trouble socially noticing others, his motivation to pay attention to another person has not been fully developed.

How impaired a child's social communication will be depends on what interrupted this natural process and to what degree. This, in turn, determines how much extra learning will be needed to grow these skills.

The Benefits of Strong Joint Attention Skills

Joint attention is a crucial foundational skill that must be in place for us to connect with others. Kids who show strong joint attention with their parents are more socially competent with peers, are included by classmates more, and have reduced hyperactivity and reduced distractibility when interacting with other children (Meek et al., 2012).

But that's not all. Strong joint attention is linked to better executive functioning at eighteen and thirty-six months than in children with poor joint attention (Vaughan Van Hecke et al., 2011), and executive functioning is strongly correlated to school and social success (Ursache et al., 2012).

Better friendships, stronger connection with others, more inclusion at school, better potential for academic success—this joint attention sounds pretty good! But it's not always easy for kids to develop.

Consider Ravi. He was a little boy who missed that early face-to-face interaction and had not learned to pay attention to nonverbal communication—not because his parents didn't attempt to engage him, but because he was born wired not to seek it. In contrast to kids like Raven, Ravi had problems that couldn't be traced back to environmental deprivation. His tendency to turn inward was innate.

Ravi's parents and grandma came into the clinic for a speech/language assessment with worry clearly etched into their faces. "We have been seeing a private therapist working on Ravi's receptive and expressive language, and he is making some progress," his dad, Mr. Varma, said in very articulate, lightly accented English. "But he continues to struggle at school."

Ravi apparently needed spoken instructions to be repeated many times and was not sitting through stories or circle time. After his case history was taken, Ravi was tested to better understand his language development to see if difficulties in these areas might explain his social and academic challenges. He had an overall language profile of mildly delayed comprehension and expressive language (spoken words). This profile did not explain the degree of challenge that he apparently was experiencing at school with making friends and following spoken instructions.

After an hour and a half of intensive testing, Ravi continued to present as a very compliant little guy. When asked a question, he answered it—but offered up nothing more. When asked to point to something, he did. He was perfectly behaved, did everything asked, and actually seemed to enjoy sitting in his chair doing everything asked of him. He was an evaluator's dream and not at all typical of children seen in a speech-language pathologist's office. He was more focused on the testing pictures than he was on the person asking the questions.

To see how Ravi did socially, his father was encouraged to play on the floor as he would at home and interact with his son. His dad cleared his throat, clearly uncertain, and seemed disarmed by the request. At this point, it became a distinct possibility that there were some cultural differences related to adult roles and playing with children that made this request awkward.

When asked what he and his son liked to do at home to spend time with each other, Ravi's father said, "Well, I work quite late, so I read him books at bedtime, and we do some workbooks for his language development together."

Obviously, Ravi's father was very supportive of his son's academic development, but perhaps Ravi's inexperience with playing with toys may have been a contributing factor to his atypical social presentation. When Mr. Varma was asked which toys Ravi liked to play with at home, there was a very long pause. "He does like the movie *Toy Story,* and he has a Buzz Lightyear that he likes to go like this." (He demonstrated a flying gesture.) "He enjoys to line up his cars. He mostly likes to play by himself, and gets very angry with me if I ask him what he is doing."

The private school that Ravi attended had a strong academic focus, which meant not much exposure to play, and it was perhaps not the best fit for a socially at-risk child like Ravi.

Now it was time to be concerned.

See, Ravi was three and a half, and, up to this point, had initiated very little *spontaneous language*. In therapy speak, that means interactions that he started versus interactions that were formatted for him. Ravi was a master waiter. He would wait for the other person to speak and then copy or echo what that person said. When his dad said, "Wheee, Buzz is flying," Ravi would mimic his dad and say, "Buzz flying." However, not once when Ravi was playing with Buzz would he say, "Buzz flying" on his own without a model to copy.

Ravi was also very object/picture focused, and he seldom looked at the therapist testing him.

By two years old, most children will initiate communication with familiar people a minimum of five times per minute (Chapman, 2000). By three and a half, they initiate communication for a wide variety of reasons such as asking for something, protesting, asking questions, showing and commenting, and even teasing. Also, by three and a half, most kids play together cooperatively, have complicated pretend play, and even participate in some simple games with rules.

Something was not adding up, and it appeared to be more than just language development.

When the school was contacted, his teachers reported, "Ravi is a lovely little boy who likes to do his own thing. He likes exploring items and is learning to put things away when he is finished. He is a quiet and observant boy who is a little dreamy in the classroom. " Hmmm....What was sometimes challenging for the teachers was that they often had to repeat instructions and "get in his face" for him to comply when those instructions were outside of his daily routine.

Because Ravi was keeping up academically, was not a big disturbance behaviorally, and followed the routine, his teachers did not see his lack of relationships as problematic.

When asked if he had any friends at school, the teachers praised his independence. When pressed to find out if he was even interacting with the other children in the class, they described him as not really seeking others out for help or company. At recess, he preferred to walk along the edges of the playground, not even watching the other kids to see how and what they were playing.

So, is this sort of lack of engagement a problem?

It's one thing if a child has developed all of the skills to be able to participate appropriately with classmates, to interact, and to make friends but *chooses* not to. It is quite another when a child has no idea how to navigate social relationships and has opted out of social society at age three and a half. With Ravi, we were clearly dealing with a much more complex issue, and one that required more information.

The next time Ravi came to see his speech therapist, it was to better gauge his functional, social use of language. He sat on the floor with a toy house and the therapist waited expectantly to see what he would do.

He picked up the furniture and people and then lined them up, not looking at his play partner even for a second. Even when he was provided a model of doing something else like putting a toy bed in the house, he continued to line up the furniture.

Thinking that maybe he would do better with a different toy, his therapist gave him a variety of things to play with. He lined up the cars and then he lined up the farm animals.

Trying to add a new element to his play, his speech therapist took an animal and modeled for him the cow eating hay in an exaggerated silly way, and he laughed. He then looked at her and back at the hay.

This was the first example of joint attention he had demonstrated in three hours. The first time he actually *shared* an interaction. The therapist did something silly that grabbed his attention...he noticed...looked at her... looked at the toy...and then back at her to see what she would do.

Ravi may have understood words at around a three-year-old level, he may have spoken words at the three-year-old level, but his *social use* of language and communication ability had been halted at infancy. Of course he didn't play with other kids yet—he didn't appreciate why people are motivated to communicate in the first place.

Somehow, somewhere, his development of joint attention had been interrupted. The questions were "why?" and "what do we do about it?" If someone didn't begin working on joint attention now, the gulf between Ravi and others would get wider and harder to bridge.

Ravi was then paired with another little boy to work on social use of language. The other little guy was a bit further down the social path than Ravi: he had joint attention but preferred to not imitate or include a friend in his play.

As therapy progressed, Ravi's parents began to see that their son was missing some foundational skills but was making significant progress. They pursued a psychological assessment that ruled out autism, but he was diagnosed with mixed expressive/receptive language disorder. This essentially meant that Ravi had some trouble with understanding spoken words and generating spoken language. That alone did not qualitatively capture the social component to Ravi's profile—meaning things like not engaging with others, not really looking at a communication partner, and not playing with toys like other kids his age.

There was obviously a "more" quality to Ravi's ability to communicate that simply wasn't easy to tease out. At this point, his parents decided to focus on determining where Ravi was with communicating functionally with peers and what was holding him back and then build his skills up one rung at a time.

Mr. and Mrs. Varma began playing more with Ravi, trying to get him to notice what they were doing and basically enticed Ravi into looking and discovering that interactions with someone can be a lot of fun. Ravi's parents had to play some silly games and find exciting activities to get Ravi out of his very focused way of playing and into something they could all do together. While it was still hard to get Ravi to look at them and notice, he started to do so more and more.

More Eye Contact Means More Joint Focus and Shared Experiences

When you have to work extra hard to get your child to look at you, professionals may refer to this as "lacking eye contact." If your child has difficulties with eye contact, you are most likely going to find that his joint attention is affected. In other words, if your child doesn't look at his communication partner, it will be harder for him to pick up on cues from his partner and be able to share the experience. You often hear about this in conjunction with children with autism, but it can also occur with children with sensory sensitivities without autism—as turned out to be the case with Ravi.

Whatever the reason, if a child doesn't visually check with his communication partner, his social skills development will be affected. That's because he is not attending to and subsequently receiving, practicing, or recognizing others' perspectives when experiencing things. So much communication happens with our eyes and face.

If you have a child like Ravi, you will need an entry ticket into your child's world so that with a bit of adjustment, you can create more space for yourself and your child to interact. The bottom line is that you want your child to find *you* much more interesting than his toys.

Maybe your child has a special passion for a particular kind of toy, which makes it hard for you to join in. It can be tempting to leave him to it and get the dishes done. But we know that it is important to interact with children while they are playing so that their social skills can get stronger through practice and they can learn to understand the value of communication. Nathan's story, below, illustrates how parents can use a child's passion to improve his social engagement.

Nathan was all things Thomas the tank. He watched Thomas on TV, read Thomas books, wore Thomas jammies, and was only interested in playing with Thomas trains and the roundhouse. Nathan "strongly" preferred (screamed and cried) to play with these trains his way, which was kind of repetitive and did not allow for others to join in. His parents were rightly concerned that his rigid play was restricting him from interacting with peers and with them.

Now a word about playing the same way all of the time. All kids can be strong-minded about how things need to be done about just about everything. Sometimes they express their opinions frequently and dramatically, which can be part of typical development. This behavior becomes a problem when it is so frequent and long lasting that it restricts joint attention and play is no longer shared. That was the case with Nathan.

In an attempt to manipulate the environment to maximize opportunities for Nathan to include others in play, his parents were encouraged to get a container with a lid. They found a sweet, metal train holder box that had compartments in it. It had a Thomas picture on the lid, and, best of all, was hard to open. This hard-to-open part was key to getting Nathan to notice his parents because he needed their help to open it. His parents got some brand-new trains and kept them and some others in the box, which one of them held on their lap.

Nathan's parents opened the box when he asked them to, offered him a choice between two trains, and then waited expectantly for him to fleetingly look/acknowledge/communicate a preference, before they gave him the train that he was interested in. Once he made a choice, his parents closed the container until next time, took a train for themselves, and copied what Nathan did on the track.

By holding what Nathan really wanted, and being the means to get what he wanted, his parents made Nathan dig a little deeper and learn to ask them for what he wanted. This meant that now he was no longer doing his own thing: he was now checking with, and including, his parents before acting.

Nathan allowed his parents to stay and participate because they were doing what he liked to do. Not once did his parents tell him or need to tell him to "look at me" to get him to check with them. He realized for himself that looking up at them to see what was happening would give him the toy he needed. That is the learning we strive for—the kind that comes from the child's own motivation and growing understanding. Not because someone tells them to do it without the child understanding why.

It would be so nice at this point to say something along the lines of "and then Nathan beautifully and graciously included his parents in play every day in all activities…spontaneously moving toward cooperative play with peers, and is now, at thirty, an engineer for Amtrak and happily married, etc."

Nope. The reality was that he initially resisted the intrusion—a lot. But slowly, with persistence, kindness, and love, he was won over. His parents were convinced too because their little boy began to include them more and more. They copied Nathan's actions (e.g., if he pushed his train over the hill, they pushed their train over the hill). He took a train out of the case his parents held (which they then quickly shut and locked), and then his parents got their train ready to let Nathan lead them to where they needed to go.

Nathan began to appreciate how fun it could be to play with his parents. The play moved from being one-sided and self-directed to having a more back-and-forth quality to it (turn taking) like a conversation. He was now more frequently checking to see which trains his parents had and what they were doing with them. Most importantly, they were sharing the experience and enjoying each other.

That, of course, is not the end of the story. Nathan remained pretty rigid in his interactions and play preferences. His peers were not so willing to go along with everything that he asked for. But Nathan was now having many more positive experiences with other kids and was also learning more about imitation by watching his parents imitate *him*. Imitation is an important component of social success with peers that will be explored more deeply in chapter 3.

Joint Attention Fosters Communication and Language Development

Maybe you have a child who is not only self-directed, but is also so independent he doesn't really need to talk to get what he wants. If so, then you might see yourself in Bao's family.

Bao was a quietly self-directed little preschooler who needed support for developing joint attention and language in general. His parents came to the speech and language clinic for an assessment to find out whether his exposure to three languages was the reason he wasn't really talking much yet.

It quickly became apparent that Bao did not yet understand that if he communicated by looking with his eyes, attempting sounds or words, or pointing that he would get what he wanted. He hadn't developed an understanding of the power of requesting because he didn't really share experiences with others yet. If you were thinking at this point that he was lacking joint attention, you would be right.

When another person tried to sit with him, he would move and avoid it. He soon moved away to the floor and so his therapist followed. At first they sat across from each other, but soon the therapist found herself on her side, and then practically lying on her belly to engage him. No matter how she tried to position herself, she couldn't make eye contact. Bao was just so purposefully focused on the toys rather than the person trying to play.

The challenge became to find an activity that would capture Bao's attention enough to keep him from leaving and be so interesting that he would tolerate another person's presence. The "hook" ended up being a bin of bubbly, warm water and a cup for him and his mom to share. When he poured, his mom was instructed to say "pour" and take the cup. She then lifted it up pretty high above their heads so that he would look up. The minute he glanced upward, she said "pour" and let the water come down in an interesting way.

The point of this exercise was to create an opportunity to share and experience a fun activity. With a lot of repetition and expectant, well-placed pauses, the hope was that Bao might begin to ask the therapist to pour, either by reaching/pointing, making a sound, or even attempting a word.

It was obvious that he was really enjoying himself, and he began to show that he wanted his mother to pour again by looking at her, smiling, and wiggling his body. His mom was asked to watch him carefully for communication clues and interpret these nonverbal communication actions as requests and do what he wanted her to do. The more Bao requested, the more he got what he wanted and began to recognize the power and value of communication. Within a couple of weeks, he even started using words to ask for a wide variety of activities to continue.

The reality is that many kids who are stuck at the establishing joint attention phase don't yet get *why* we communicate in the first place. This understanding typically begins with kids learning to request things from others. To help with this major hurdle, the first steps are to do the following:
1. Share really fun, repetitive activities with your child.
2. Pause expectantly at the most exciting point to show your child you expect something from him.
3. Watch for any verbal or nonverbal communication that your child wants you to do the fun thing again.
4. Then do what your child wants…over and over again.

Communication Temptations

You may also want to try using communication temptations to capture the attention of particularly hard-to-engage kids. The idea of manipulating play and environment to maximize shared communication originated with Amy Wetherby and Barry Prizant, clinical researchers who developed a list of toys and activities that are super exciting but require the help of another person to start and keep going.

One example is blowing up a balloon and then either letting the air go out on your child's stomach, or just letting go and allowing the balloon to fly around the room. This is sure to get many children's interest and attention. What makes this activity particularly powerful is that most young kids can't blow up a balloon themselves and will need some help. Enter wonderful you!

This activity encourages joint attention, eye contact (especially if you bring the balloon up to your face before you let it go), and requesting from you. You reinforce that when your child engages with you, he gets what he wants.

Other examples of communication temptations include using wind-up toys, yo-yos, Jack-in-the-boxes—anything that is super fun, only lasts for a few quick turns, and requires your help.

Remember that joint attention is closely related to goals associated with getting your child to ask for what he wants and simply sharing a pleasurable experience.

Sharing an interesting activity that your child needs your help with will allow him to come out of his self-oriented world and draw you in to the activity. You'll know that this is happening when your child begins to look at you, laughs, smiles, protests when the activity stops, and asks for you to do it again. In other words, you'll know that you are helping your child develop joint attention because your child will be including you in the activity.

Quick Guide to Establishing Joint Attention

In a nutshell, here is how to establish joint attention games and routines:

- Begin by sitting face-to-face while holding an exciting toy. Show your child what it does, and then hand it over.
- Wait with animation and expectation for your child to request help from you.
- Remember that this request can be done verbally or nonverbally.
- If he doesn't request, and it looks like you might lose his attention, put the toy or activity into action in front of him. Then wait again saying, "Help" or "Blow the balloon?" or whatever makes sense for what you are doing. Once your child has had a turn, then you take a turn.

You are waiting for your child to request from you somehow that he wants you to do it again. Remember, in the beginning, some kids may communicate that request just by glancing up at you.

If your child doesn't make eye contact much, then you can draw his focus to your face by bringing the very interesting object up near your eyes. Do it again and again with the same toy, and then move on to other toys when you think he is ready.

When your child asks or indicates to you that he wants it to happen again, you are sharing the experience together, and that means a shared focus.

Toys, Activities, and Games for Joint Attention

Here are some more great joint attention, high-interest toys, activities, and games:

For Younger Kids:
- wind-up toys
- balls of all shapes and sizes with lights or bells, etc.
- bubbles
- Jack-in-the-box
- ball runs with hammers to pound the balls in
- pinwheels
- balloons (be extra careful with this activity, as there is choking potential if not carefully supervised)
- blankets for pulling your kid on
- blankets for swinging your kid in
- props for playing peek-a-boo, blankets, silky scarves, long tunnels, big cardboard boxes, IKEA tents

For Older Kids:
- Hexbots and track for it to go on (Hexbots are little motorized "bugs" that your child can have go through an obstacle course)
- Hot Wheels and simple racetracks or homemade ramps out of 2x4 pieces of wood
- Marble works: plastic tubes that you assemble into a roller coaster for marbles
- Stomp rockets—you stomp and the rocket soars

Sensory Play Is High Interest Too

Sensory play refers to activities that engage the senses in a fun way. Many children find sensory play very motivating and enjoyable. Here are some ideas:

Water Play

Fill a large plastic container a quarter of the way full with water and drop in a couple of empty containers. Don't add too many toys, or your child won't need to share items and take turns with you. To expand, you can experiment with:

- different temperatures, (e.g., add some ice cubes)
- food coloring
- different-sized containers

For Younger Kids:
- scoops and containers from the kitchen
- water wheels to pour on
- boats/submarines to take turns with

For Older Kids:
- You can put other toys inside the plastic container (e.g., Hot Wheels for a car wash or dolls for a "spa")
- Take turns putting different sea creatures in the water
- Take turns letting toy mermaids swim
- Take turns dropping marbles into paper cups to see which one will sink first

Sand Play

You don't necessarily have to use sand...especially if your child has a tendency to put things in his mouth. Those under-the-bed, plastic storage bins on wheels can be a wonderful place to put interesting sensory items to explore—especially in the winter when everyone is cooped up inside.

Instead of sand, you could try:
- rice
- corn meal
- raw lentils or beans
- corn starch mixed with a bit of water (called "goop") (mess alert!)
- pompoms

For Younger Kids:
- Use a scoop and take turns scooping and dumping; include front end loaders and dump trucks
- Fill containers of various sizes with lids—little empty spice containers, Tupperware, etc.

For Older Kids:
- Bury high interest toys (e.g., dinosaurs, pirate treasure, mermaid jewels, magic items, etc.) to give your child an opportunity for heightened interest as he looks for and discovers the surprises. (Using a paintbrush to dig like an archaeologist can be fun.)
- Create little sand condos for ants or bugs

- Make a maze and then put water in—you can block some tracks and watch to see where the water goes.
- Same idea but add boats

Just make sure that for these activities you are holding the most important pieces to encourage your child to request. Think about it—if you give everything to your child, then he doesn't need you to participate and can play his game by himself.

Also, be sure to take turns copying your little one. If he dumps sand into a pile, then you take his scoop and you dump sand on his pile …then stop, holding the scoop…wait expectantly for him to show that he wants you to do it again.

Lights
For Younger Kids:
- View Master
- Flashlights of different colors
- Glow-in-the-dark Magna Doodle

For Older Kids:
- Glow-in-the-dark marble run
- Shadow puppets on the wall
- Lite Brite

Sounds
For Younger Kids:
- Rain sticks (make your own by putting rice in a wrapping paper tube with duct tape on both ends, or buy one)
- Party blow toys
- Bells, shakers, drums, etc.
- Hide a toy that makes music and find it together
- Turn up the music and then turn it down
- Sing favorite songs then throw in an unexpected pause and see what happens.

For Older Kids:
- Dance around and then stop the music suddenly and wait for your child to indicate you should turn it back on
- Take turns "rapping" and adding silly lyrics
- Play "what's that noise?" by hiding an object that makes noise under a towel, behind your back, etc. Make the sound, and then wait expectantly
- Furby toy—take turns guessing what he is saying

Whole Body Sensory Experiences

For these physical, active games, the important thing to keep in mind is to do an action and then pause expectantly at the most exciting part to encourage your child to look to you and include you. You want to create that reciprocity over a number of turns.

For Younger and Older Kids:

- Swings at the park—get face to face and pull the swing to you and wait expectantly for your child to indicate that he wants to "go."
- Wait at the bottom of the slide to catch your child and say "gotcha!"
- Swish your child around in the pool on a noodle and then stop and wait for him to want you to continue.

For Older Kids:

- Pillow fight
- Make your child into a hotdog or burrito by wrapping him up tightly in a blanket and then putting "toppings" on him. Of course, attack and "eat."

SUMMARY OF RUNG #1:
JOINT ATTENTION

If you suspect that your child:

- does not attend to nonverbal cues such as facial expressions…
- prefers to interact with objects rather than people…
- is struggling to interact with other children…
- prefers to pursue his own interests in a solitary way or only on his terms…

Then, joint attention with a familiar adult is where to begin. Once he can share an experience with a familiar adult over a number of turns, try to move toward similar activities with a well-matched peer.

It's important to be aware that your child may have a lot of other skills. He may be able to speak at an advanced level or be the first on his street to ride a two-wheeler, but he might have a very real gap in his social development. If so, he needs to fill this gap to develop healthy interactions with friends.

Joint Attention "Cheat Sheet"

- Find a toy or activity to "hook him."

- Get his attention.

- Keep him interested and get him to include you by using a toy or activity that he needs your help with.

- Include yourself by bringing the desired item up to your face.

- Include yourself by waiting expectantly for him to initiate a request.

- Wait for him to include you by requesting that you do it again.

- Do it again and again.

RUNG 2

Do You Feel Like I Do?
Identifying Emotions

A nother skill that has its developmental roots in infancy is our innate desire to attend to faces and respond to facial expressions of different emotions. Babies are hardwired to actively seek out faces even as newborns. This was clearly demonstrated in the Still Face experiment designed by Dr. Edward Tronick in 1978.

In this study, a mother engages an infant with smiles and sweet words and then stops. Her baby clearly enjoys the smiling part and actively looks and imitates the facial expressions and sounds the mother makes. When the mother stops smiling and talking but continues to look, the baby starts off trying to smile, make sounds, and reengage the mother to continue to do the happy part of the interaction. When the mother continues to simply look at the baby without other feedback, the baby tries to reengage her by smiling. When that doesn't work, the baby tries pointing, then shouting and reaching, then grows visibly agitated, cries, and looks away. After watching infants respond so strongly to this experiment, it becomes obvious that even young infants have "already formed clear expectations of social interactions, and find even short temporary violations of these expectations upsetting"(Mesman et al., 2009).

At the earliest age that they are able to develop nonverbal understanding of emotions, infants learn to attend to feelings by paying attention to three crucial things: facial expressions including eye gaze, changes in tone of voice, and body language. You can see that this learning is happening when infants react by showing distress if a caregiver turns away, sounds angry, or when babies giggle if a parent shows obvious delight in being with them. Babies rapidly develop awareness of their own feelings of pleasure and satisfaction the more they interact with their caregivers.

From early on, children develop an ability to recognize the big three emotions (happy, mad, sad) beginning with others and then in themselves (Harris, 2008). A child's understanding that the word "happy" equals "smiling face" comes months and months later with more exposure to smiles, facial expression, tone of voice, and language. With more interaction experience, toddlers and preschoolers then fine-tune that ability to understand basic emotions. They learn to appreciate that more subtle feelings sometimes come into play and that different people may experience different emotions during the same activity. Two things that most help very young children learn to identify feelings are exposure to and interactions with people, and conversations with important adults.

As children get even older, it's obvious that they can experience and do perceive a wider range of feelings than simply sad, mad, and happy. Anyone who has brought a new baby home to a preschooler knows that young kids can experience murderous jealousy.

Not all feelings are created equal in terms of identification and understanding. When you really take time to think about it, some of these later-understood feelings such as jealousy, surprise, and frustration are harder to learn about because they require the child to have ongoing relationships with others and a true understanding that what she feels is not necessarily the same as what her friend feels about the same situation.

Here's an example: For your preschooler to be able to recognize that her friend Tom is jealous because Tom wanted a coveted Transformer and got a Spiderman instead, your child would need to be able to:

- know and recognize that Tom thinks the Transformer is better even if she doesn't agree;
- recognize that Tom is sad because he thinks that he has a lesser toy;
- recognize Tom's facial expression and body language;
- recognize that just because she is satisfied and happy with what she has, doesn't mean that Tom is happy too.

Identifying how other people are feeling can take some pretty sophisticated skills. Just to make this subject more interesting, consider that recognizing emotions in others requires being able to follow their facial expressions and body language, which are dynamic. Our facial expressions and body language are always moving and changing, which can make them difficult to decipher, especially if you're not someone who is focused on looking. Learning to interpret body language requires a great deal of noticing and watching. It's no accident that we refer to perceptive people as being able to "read" another person. Being able to interpret nonverbal communication is like having to decode a forever-changing story full of plot twists. With all of these elements to juggle, it is a miracle we are able to figure this all out at all.

Difficulty Reading Other People's Cues

Most kids who struggle socially tend to have little difficulty understanding when *they* are mad, sad, or happy. The breakdown usually occurs in attending to the nonverbal information that a peer or adult is providing and then interpreting these clues as to what the other person may be thinking or feeling.

That was the case with Andrea.

An easygoing four-year-old who loved school, Andrea even played teacher when she was at home, and had elaborate, daily education sessions for her huge stuffed animal collection in her room. The youngest of four children, Andrea yearned to be a "big girl too." When she was three, she asked for a backpack that she could leave by the front door every morning just like her siblings.

So, her parents were quite surprised to hear that only one month into kindergarten, Andrea was spending much of free play time in tears. The teacher was also at a loss to explain. She described Andrea as a lovely, academically inclined, engaged little girl who was keen to play with the other children.

It was decided by the school that a speech-language pathologist would observe Andrea in the classroom a few times over the coming weeks to better understand what might be happening socially with her.

During circle time, Andrea ran to sit beside another little girl she clearly liked. As the teacher progressed through the calendar, Andrea was not-so-subtly moving closer and closer to her classmate. The classmate kept moving away and sending irritated looks until by the end of fifteen minutes, the kids sitting on their mats looked like a train going off the rails. Andrea appeared oblivious to the other little girl's annoyed expression and heavy sighing. No words were exchanged. Clearly, both little girls took the "no talking during calendar" rule very seriously.

During free play, Andrea sought out her "circle partner" and ran to the house center. There she copied her friend making dinner. She was animated and provided a run-on narrative of exactly what she was doing. When she didn't get a response from her circle buddy, she leaned in very close (eyeballs practically touching) and repeated what she was saying. When that didn't work, Andrea's only strategy was to say the same thing over and over again, not picking up her peer's growing frustration.

"I'm having spaghetti. Want spaghetti?" (Annoyed glance with head-shake "no" from circle buddy.) "This is my spaghetti. Mmm…good spaghetti. Want some of my spaghetti?" Andrea asked. The circle buddy said, "I'm washing dishes right now." Andrea persisted, "I'm having more spaghetti because it's my favorite. Here's your spaghetti." It went on.

Her circle buddy was getting rapidly more annoyed, but Andrea seemed to ignore her annoyance until finally the other little girl moved on, saying "I want to play with Stella now." Andrea was devastated and started to cry.

This scenario played itself out in a variety of ways throughout the week. It became clear that Andrea was experiencing challenges with understanding personal space boundaries, recognizing others' body language cues, and dominating conversations.

But Andrea had things in her corner: ability to share an experience/joint attention, a willingness to interact, and an ability to be flexible and copy how other children were playing. She just needed some support around paying attention to and interpreting other people's nonverbal cues.

When It's Information Overload

Sometimes children have difficulty with understanding other peoples' emotions because they can't process all of the nonverbal and verbal information that is coming at them all at once.

Matthew was a first grader who had trouble in this area. He was a gorgeous little guy with huge brown eyes, an easygoing manner, and impossible-to-tame brown hair. He was a participant in a group designed to help kindergarten kids develop interaction skills and to help parents learn how to facilitate schoolyard friendships.

Matthew's mom was an inspiration. She was raising him and his two brothers on her own. She had some health problems that made it difficult to work long hours on her feet, but her limited education meant she was only offered jobs that required long hours standing up. Somehow she managed to suffer through and worked days as a cashier at a department store. One of the other things she managed with grace was to get Matthew to a social skills group by taking three buses.

Matthew had some language comprehension issues, and his sentences were a bit shorter than those of other four-and-a-half-year-olds. His mom found that he understood what she was saying to him better when she broke instructions down into shorter chunks, repeated them, and used simpler language.

Her big concern was his school. He had been frequently suspended for noncompliance. His teachers spoke of continual frustration with Matthew because he lacked empathy for other kids and just didn't "seem to care" about his teachers' frustration.

Nothing the teachers did—putting him in time out, offering explanations, sticker charts, sending him to the office—worked. Sometimes when another kid was crying, he would just laugh. His mom was so worried that he would grow up to be some sort of super-villain. What kind of kid laughs when another kid is crying?

His mom's concerns about him being a psychopath just didn't seem to jive with the sweet little boy who had been coming to group over the previous month until one spring day when he and some other children were outside playing with a balloon. The big yellow balloon was a real hit with the enthusiastic little boys. They were all running around the climber chasing Kyle-the-balloon-holder, when he misstepped and tragically let go of it.

Matthew, wanting to join in, grabbed the balloon and started tossing it high into the air, laughing. Kyle asked Matthew for it back a couple of times, but Matthew kept playing happily. It was as if, as Kyle astutely observed later, "he didn't hear me." In complete frustration, Kyle sat down in the sand with his head in his hands, biting back tears.

When the therapist walked over to ask Matthew what was going on, the boy had a puzzling interpretation. "He fell down," he explained. Since she had seen the event transpire, that answer seemed like a bit of a head scratcher.

The therapist probed a bit and said, "Look at Kyle. How do you think he feels?"

Matthew responded by saying he thought Kyle was sad. When asked what could be done to help Kyle feel better, Matthew's solution was to offer up a Band Aid.

It would have been a great solution if Kyle had actually *fallen* down and not simply sat in the sand out of frustration.

When the speech pathologist clarified the real reason Kyle was sitting in the sand looking more and more upset, Matthew was surprised. His face conveyed a "Well, why didn't you just say so?" expression. He happily handed the balloon to a confused Kyle and ran off saying, "C'mon!"

So what exactly happened here? Matthew didn't interpret the situation accurately because he either didn't understand or attend to what Kyle was *telling* him about the balloon, so it *looked like* Matthew didn't care. Put another way, Matthew clearly was unable to process the words that Kyle was saying to him quickly and so appeared to lack empathy. What he really lacked were strong auditory processing/language comprehension skills and an ability to integrate the words he heard with the actions and body language. He was confused, not unsympathetic.

If Matthew was going to survive recess, he needed to use his eyes even more to notice what was happening around him to compensate for his auditory processing challenges. And he needed to do so more quickly. Michelle Garcia-Winner, the speech therapist who wrote *Social Thinking,* encourages children to, "listen with their eyes and engage in whole body listening" to help children better interpret the complexities of verbal and nonverbal communication.

Many children like Matthew have trouble understanding the words that quickly fly around their heads. In Matthew's case, he became distracted by his new toy and trying to figure out what Kyle was saying and doing at the same time. He couldn't, so he compensated by trying to guess based on what he could *see* (Kyle sitting in the sand). He was certainly on the right track using this compensatory strategy; he just needed a speech therapist to work with him to strengthen his listening skills and his understanding of language. He could also benefit from learning to self-monitor and compensate for his weaker comprehension and ask others for clarification. For example, he could check in and ask something like "What happened?" or "What's wrong?" or "What's so funny?" That way he could get more information to more accurately interpret social situations. Requests for clarification can go a long way in avoiding misunderstandings.

So, in summary, if a child has trouble with understanding words or with paying attention to words or others' actions, it can be hard for her to learn why other people are reacting the way that they are.

When People Don't Say What They Feel

To make things even trickier, as your child's world expands and social perspective taking becomes even more sophisticated, she will grow to realize that sometimes there is mismatch between the nonverbal and spoken information being provided. What that means is that sometimes we say one thing but feel another. How many spouses can attest to that? "No, really, it's fine" certainly does not always mean that something's fine. Sometimes it might mean "If you dare go on that fishing trip with the boys and leave me to take care of two children with the stomach flu and a broken washing machine, you will pay...." How many spouses have forcibly participated in the "reading your partner's nonverbal cues program" and grew to quickly realize that no trip with the boys is worth what comes next?

Put simply, sometimes we don't really say what we feel a lot of the time.

That means that someone might be saying something with her mouth but showing something different with her body or face. It's hard enough for kids to identify emotions in someone else without adding that maybe what the person is saying is not really what he or she is feeling. That is one reason why many people who have trouble reading social situations find lying, hinting, and sarcasm so difficult to understand. You only have to spend ten minutes with a five-year-old with a favorite knock-knock joke to know that she is not always sensitive to more subtle nonverbal cues.

Saying "I didn't do it" when your child has chocolate all over her fingers is pretty typical for a five-year-old. This combination of bad lying, joke telling, and teasing is all part of your child learning to participate in a social world that often says one thing but means another.

It doesn't seem fair that after children put in such hard work to figure out how to socialize with peers, they find out later that those rules are not always followed. Come to think of it, it really is incredible how complicated this business of making and keeping friends can be. There is so much that can be done to support children who find this challenging. First and foremost, children need to be accurate in their reading of true emotional verbal and nonverbal information.

Loving adults should point out reactions to situations as they are happening. For example, when your child sees you laughing, tell her, "I feel happy! That's why I'm laughing. I am happy that you got ready for bed." Or, "I feel happy watching you do that dance."

You can and should talk about how others feel. Examples: "Oh no, baby Kathy's crying…She is so tired." Or, "The dog's tail is wagging—that means he's happy." Or, "Dad's sneezing and blowing his nose. I bet he's feeling sick." Also, take time out to label what emotions *your child* might be feeling in different situations.

Using books that illustrate emotions in main characters can also help teach vocabulary and understanding that others have similar feelings. Here are some books that are recommended for young children:

- *I Was So Mad* by Mercer Mayer (mad)
- *I'm Not Scared* by Jonathan Allen (scared)
- *Kyle's Snowsuit* by Robert Munsch (frustration)
- *There's a Nightmare in My Closet* by Mercer Mayer (fear, sympathy)
- *Good News, Bad News* by Jeff Mack (happy, mad, sad)

Be sure that you don't just rely on helping your child learn to identify emotions from books or flashcards. Remember that facial expressions work in conjunction with always-changing body language. So, pointing out emotions as they are happening, in the moment, is very important. Also consider watching videos of people obviously experiencing emotion and pausing the scene to point out emotions: "Oh look! Ellen is happy...See, she is smiling and dancing."

Some excellent programs have been developed to help children better identify and monitor their own feelings:

- Leah Kuyper's *Zones of Regulation* (2011) provides a color-coding system for children to learn to evaluate how they are feeling in a given moment (e.g., blue = sleepy, low arousal; green = alert, ready to learn; red = explosive, etc.). Once a child has a clearer understanding of her emotional state, she is in a better position to accommodate her own needs and move toward optimal color state (e.g., "I'm feeling like I'm moving into RED....I could take some deep belly breaths or jump on the trampoline.")

- The Incredible 5-Point Scale (Dunn Buron & Curtis, 2003) was developed to help children with autism (but is of benefit to all children, really) better understand their own responses to situations. It is essentially a rating scale that helps kids identify behaviors and feelings by visually breaking down what a specific feeling may physically look like, describe what it feels like, and understand what to do about the feelings. For example, a red 5:
    - ➤ looks like: screaming, crying, fighting;
    - ➤ feels like: "I want to smash things" and "I am going to blow up";
    - ➤ I can try to: tell my mom that I need to go on the trampoline.

  The 5-point scale can also be used to clarify socially expected behaviors such as voice volume and anxiety related behaviors.

- A feelings thermometer is a simple, visual, color-coded picture of a thermometer that shows the range of feelings from calm to outraged with the more intense feelings at higher "temperatures."

- The book *How Full is Your Bucket?*, by Tom Rath, can also help children understand the impact of situations, others' words, and actions on emotions through a visual story format. Giving your child her own "bucket" and carrying one around for yourself after reading the book can be a visually memorable and fun way to clearly show your child the effect of words and actions on her own and others' feelings (e.g., You gave me a beautiful dandelion....that's two blocks in my bucket. You hit me and screamed, "I hate broccoli"....that took a block out of my bucket).

Whether you use the Zones of Regulation Program, "feelings thermometers," *How Full Is Your Bucket?*, or the Incredible 5-Point Scale, you will be helping your child identify and learn to respond to her own, and then to others' inner states. This emotional self-awareness will help to provide insight into how others may be feeling and what their needs may be as well. Strong emotional self-insight is essential in supporting children to develop perspective taking, respond to situations in an emotional way that makes sense for the situation, and learning to put themselves in others' shoes.

SUMMARY OF RUNG #2: EMOTIONS

Your child is at risk of being stuck on this rung if she:
- does not attend to nonverbal cues such as facial expressions
- has reduced eye contact
- is often "in her own world"
- is highly distracted
- is highly active
- often has her own agenda or is "too independent"
- has trouble understanding words

This goal of recognizing emotions is very closely tied with making sure your child is paying attention to another person, which means you can work on identifying emotions while continuing to develop joint attention. For Andrea, her challenges with attending to and interpreting her peers' nonverbal communication had to do with underlying inattention issues. For Matthew, his challenges with identifying and interpreting emotions in others had to do with being overwhelmed with more verbal and nonverbal information than he could handle.

Remember, your child may have many other skills that mask this challenge. Maybe she sounds like a college professor when she's talking about different kinds of bridges, or maybe she's four and already reading or can climb up to the top of a ridiculously high rock wall. However, if she has barriers in paying attention to other people's body language and facial expressions, chances are that she will need extra help identifying her own and others' feelings.

RUNG 3

Can You Do What I Can Do?
Imitation

Some kids just don't notice what is happening around them. Teachers and parents may describe them as "dreamy" or "distracted" or perhaps even as having ADD (attention deficit disorder). Of course, it makes sense that if your child is "dreamy," he may have problems with listening at school. You may also have to play "broken record" with your child every time you try to get him ready to go out.

But what about friendships? How can that distracted quality affect the ability to make and sustain friendships and to engage in and sustain play with others? These concerns lead us to the topic of imitation.

According to psychologists Harriet Over and Malinda Carpenter (2012), "Children's imitation is a profoundly social process. Imitation is a way to learn from others, it is also tied to children needing to belong to a group and affiliate with those around them." In other words, imitating friends helps kids fit in.

Tuned in or Tuned Out?

Kids can struggle with imitation for a variety of reasons. As Olivia's story illustrates, a prime reason can be simply not consistently paying attention to what the other kids are up to.

At her kindergarten, Olivia bounced to the beat of her own drum. She was happy to play by herself, but she liked other kids too. She didn't have trouble joining in play. She could play pop-up pirate or animal emergency or be the princess from the movie *Frozen,* among other things. But often, she would lose focus, not notice that the game had moved in a new direction, or would not respond to a playmate's comments.

This resulted in frustration for Olivia's friends and bewilderment for Olivia, who was unsure what was going on. Her parents frequently said that she just didn't listen, while her teachers said that she just didn't pay attention. Her friends said that she kept bossing them around.

Bossing?

When Olivia was at play, she was often out of step with the play that was happening around her, like a radio station coming in and out of range. When the other kids were playing Batman crashing the bad guys, she was still hiding out in the Batcave and was not sure what was happening when she resumed paying attention.

So she compensated by just doing her own creative thing, which worked sometimes because she is an interesting and original thinker. But often the other kids would leave her in the dust, get mad at her for changing the subject, so to speak, or generally respond as if she had been disrespectful because she wasn't doing what she was *supposed* to be doing.

What exactly does that mean?

Well, imagine you are at your work party and spouses are invited. You start talking to a colleague and her partner. The wine is flowing, your heels aren't pinching, and you've even lined up a sitter. All is well. You and your colleague talk about how nice the venue is, and the spouse you've just met agrees. You and your colleague then go on to talk about Motown, and the spouse says something insightful about the music.

You are warming to both of them.

You "put yourself out there" and disclose that you are simply thrilled to be out with your husband because you two haven't gotten a sitter to go out since your last child was born (eight months ago). Your colleague responds in kind, saying she is just as thrilled to actually be wearing a stain-free skirt for a change. Her spouse says, "I really hope that they use this DJ again next year."

That husband was still in the Batcave and didn't even know it. He'd missed that the ladies had moved on from talking about music to discussing how nice it was to finally, though temporarily, be free of the shackles of child rearing for an evening.

Consider the same conversation: You, thrilled, out, husband, sitter, eight months…Colleague, thrilled, stain-free…Husband tunes back in, hears "stain-free," and says, trying to be a sport and fit in, "I try to frequent stain-free parties." Now that might be funny if you're a wacky comedian on a bender, but it's hard to have a conversation when one side is only catching parts of it. While that husband realized everyone was out of the Batcave, he missed all of the conversational turns and simply took his best guess at what they were talking about.

Kids who struggle to keep up with all the twists and turns conversation takes during play can be as out of it as the husband in the first scenario or might just seem really funny to their friends with their wacky, off-topic suggestions. But the reality is, for these kids, their contributions are not something that they can help without extra learning and support.

When kids struggle to keep attuned, we can help most by really trying to get them to notice with their eyes first what is going on around them. Second, we can get them to notice with their ears what is being said. And third, we can get them to imitate what is happening. Imitation in play is crucial for being allowed to enter in and be allowed to stay. Now, that doesn't mean that there isn't room for kids to honestly share ideas and differences of opinion, but to be able to stay, you need to be on the same page.

For some kids, it is simply enough to alert them to notice more what is happening around them. For other kids—whose inattention may or may not turn out to have a neurological basis (e.g., ADD)—the teaching and compensatory strategies may need to be made more obvious and may take more time to put into practice.

Not Imitating Can Lead to Taking Over

Kids who seem to dominate play too much can also have poor imitation skills.

Kyle, for example, was a firecracker. Fast talker, fast runner, and all around funny little guy. When he had an idea, he acted. When he wanted to play with someone he did—ready or not. This was a recipe that didn't always work and often left him fighting, crying, or getting in trouble.

Kids got fed up with him quickly because he would just enter into play in progress and try to take over. It didn't help that he was quick to scream, cry, and hit when kids didn't go along with the changes he was trying to implement. Kyle's brain was bursting with ideas and his body was already moving to make his ideas happen before he thought about whether they would be well received.

Sometimes this approach worked really well for him, like when he burst out of his preschool with a soccer ball in hand and kicked it to a buddy, calling out, "Akashi, here!" with his winning smile.

More often, though, Kyle's quick action and lack of social scanning caused him problems.

When Mr. and Mrs. Burns, Kyle's soft-spoken, well-educated parents, came into the clinic for help and were asked about their concerns, his dad began by explaining that Kyle was a really smart little boy. He then described Kyle's history of challenges with expressing himself as a preschooler and speech sound challenges, which seemed to have resolved following speech and language therapy.

Kyle's parents indicated that he could play really well with his big brother, but he couldn't seem to get along with the kids at school. Kyle's mom shifted uncomfortably in her chair with her head down. When she looked up after a long pause, she said, tears spilling and voice trembling, "Nobody likes Kyle: the kids, the school. I just want my child to be wanted."

She said that whenever the phone rang at home, her first thought was that it was the school asking her to come and get him because he had done something else wrong. Things like hitting other kids, dropping an F* bomb at the teacher, or pushing someone into a puddle.

She described feeling assaulted by the school's complaints, frustrated with her son's behavior, and unsure of what to do about it. Time-outs didn't work. Mrs. Burns sounded like she was at her wit's end, and it was only junior kindergarten.

Mr. Burns felt that the school was unsure how to control his son and didn't have enough patience or resources with all the other kids and their needs in the classroom.

When asked whether Kyle could follow instructions at home, both parents felt unsure that he understood the words, but agreed that it was probably more that he didn't want to do as he was asked. Kyle's father went on to say, "Yeah, we have to say it a hundred times before he gets his teeth brushed, and it can be a battle, but he gets things done eventually. " Both were wondering if his challenges had something to do with being frustrated with not being understood by his classmates, perhaps having trouble putting his ideas together, or maybe being unable to keep up and understand the complex language that was being used at school.

Sometimes kids do act out in the classroom because they can't seem to express themselves or have difficulty with understanding language. Sitting and being expected to complete worksheets and listen to long explanations can be torturous for kids who struggle with speech and language. Also, Kyle hadn't really had a lot of experience navigating complex social situations, other than those involving his brother or cousins. With that in mind, the first step was to look at how well a kid like Kyle could follow all the words flying around his classroom.

The speech pathologist administered a variety of tests examining his ability to do the following:

- understand important concept words
- follow complicated instructions with just words (no pointing or contextual cues)
- remember and be able to repeat sentences that were said to him
- understand and use grammar
- understand and use vocabulary
- identify and explain how ideas relate to each other
- put his ideas into words completely and in an organized manner
- retell stories and things that had happened to him completely and cohesively
- produce clear speech sounds in words and in conversation

Kyle scored average to above average on all testing items. What was significant, however, was how often he needed body breaks that allowed him to get up, run to get things down the hall, play a quick game of "find the sticker," etc. to complete the subtests. Kyle could only be redirected to stay on task with reinforcers to snap his attention back into place when it wandered. That looked something like telling him, "Okay, Kyle, do three pages, and then you can look in the surprise bag where there are wind-ups, interesting little light-up toys, puzzles, etc., or you could spend some time on the iPad."

A week later, when she was reviewing results with Kyle's parents, the therapist explained that Kyle was able to understand spoken instructions, that he was able to remember complicated instructions that were said just once, and that he had a rich vocabulary, an ability to construct complex sentences, and could retell a story in an organized, cohesive manner.

She and Kyle's parents talked more about what was required to get Kyle through testing. Essentially, Kyle needed something "new" all the time to keep his interest or he would lose focus and act impulsively. Both parents leaned forward and appeared to be both relieved and distressed by this information. If Kyle's problems didn't come from an inability to understand or use language, then what was it? His mom anxiously said, "So does that mean he has ADHD? I don't want to put him on medication."

Since sitting still and focusing seemed to be a significant challenge for Kyle, the therapist encouraged his parents to contact either their pediatrician or a child psychologist with specialty in attention difficulties.

Waiting for a possible diagnosis and being stuck in the unknown can be the most stressful and frustrating part of helping children in need. In the meantime, Kyle's parents were encouraged to let the teachers know how he was kept engaged during testing and to spend time researching parent information and support groups for children with ADD/ADHD. (See appendix.)

Testing Kyle's language development alone was clearly not enough. Many children have age-appropriate speech and language skills but can't *use* language functionally. No matter what the underlying *cause* of a child's struggle with social use of language, all children need to develop skills in the same areas. It's a question of where a child is stuck in his development and what social skills need to be supported. With that in mind, Kyle and the clinician sat on the floor to play for a few minutes. Again, he cycled through activities until the room looked like a garage sale gone wrong.

Kyle kept coming up with new things to do and didn't really even notice what the therapist was doing with the toys. His parents were encouraged to pay attention to exactly how many times (if any) Kyle looked at what the therapist was doing with the toys and copied her. The answer was zero times in fifteen minutes.

Kyle's parents were assigned the task of watching Kyle play with his brother, cousins, and other kids in the schoolyard after school over the next week. These were the key elements they were to watch for:

- How long did Kyle stay with one activity? If longer than five minutes, what was he doing?
- How many times did he play something that was initiated by someone else?
- Did he stay with the activity without changing it?
- Did he ever copy what someone else was doing in play?
- Finally, did it ever go well? Why?

A week later, the parents came in without Kyle to discuss their findings and to set objectives for the weeks to come. As soon as everyone sat down, his father indicated that they had made a special effort to have Kyle play with his cousin and a little boy who lived in the neighborhood. Both parents appeared stressed and agitated. When encouraged to describe what happened, Mr. Burns said, "Kyle always had to be in charge of what they were doing. He mostly wanted to play this chasing game with Rescue Ranger characters."

"He did play a game for a full fifteen minutes, though," his mom added.

The therapist probed a little more and asked if both kids were having fun and if the interaction was balanced. Both parents appeared a bit confused. "Balanced?"

In balanced interactions, both play partners participate during the same activity. Ideally, one child wouldn't be doing all of the directing; there would be some reciprocity in the exchange of ideas and comments.

Mrs. Burns said, "Well, they played really nicely until the other boy wanted to be the green ranger or Captain America or something and Kyle started to cry." When asked to describe what happened next, his mom said that the boys got stuck. His friend insisted that he was Captain America and Kyle insisted that wasn't the game. "Kyle was just about ready to *really* lose it."

Kyle's dad said he had to change the activity quickly and started throwing both boys onto the couch, pretending he was a bad guy to avoid a conflict.

Both parents agreed that play did go really well as long as the other child did what Kyle wanted and he was in charge of the decisions.

Hmmm.

When Mr. and Mrs. Burns were asked why they thought that was the case, his mom responded, "Honestly? I think he is bossy and has to have all of the control of a game."

The therapist and parents agreed that Kyle was a leader, and that he might make an excellent CEO of a big company some day. There was disagreement as to whether Kyle had a choice in how he was interacting. Is it really bossy when you lack the skills to behave cooperatively?

The therapist encouraged Kyle's parents to reflect on whether Kyle seemed to care that his friend was upset. They both described Kyle as becoming increasingly agitated as the conflict escalated and seemed upset that his friend was unhappy as well as being upset that his friend wasn't cooperating with Kyle's agenda.

They were then asked to think back about whether Kyle was excited to have his friend come over to play. Both emphatically agreed and chuckled because Kyle could barely fall asleep the night before because he was so excited. Then his dad said, "Yeah, he was over-the-moon happy to play with his buddy until his friend had an opinion."

The therapist nodded and said, "Yes, until his friend had an opinion that was *different* than Kyle's." It would seem that Kyle was taking personally the fact that his friend wanted to do something different than he did. Kyle was actually a very thoughtful little guy who was always surprising family members with treats—a flower for mom, picture for dad, unwanted broccoli for the dog.

Nor was he unusually selfish. But his behavior needed to change and fast because other people might be misinterpreting his reactions as "selfish" or "bossy" when really he seemed to be missing a couple of rungs on his social skills ladder.

There is a growing body of research looking into something neuroscientist Giacomo Rizolatti discovered in the early 1990s called **mirror neurons**. He observed that there was a part of the brain that was activated when people observed others doing an action. Put another way, the other person's action was mirrored in the watcher's brain.

Mirror neurons, some theorize, explain why we yawn when we watch someone else yawn, or why at staff meetings, if one person crosses his arms, a few minutes later, many others have crossed their arms. Researchers have expanded on the function of mirror neurons to say that this imitation is a fundamental precursor to mind reading or perspective taking and that activation of our mirror neurons/imitation takes us one step closer to being able to put ourselves in someone else's place (Williams et al., 2001).

It makes sense, then, that if a child has difficulty sustaining interactions, he might miss cues from others and be delayed in his development of imitation. We needed Kyle to slow down enough to give his mirror neurons a chance to engage.

By developing imitation skills, Kyle would also be able to notice more what other people did, thought, and said. This would then hopefully highlight for him that there are differences in other's perspectives and opinions about things that are separate from his own.

Once he became aware that his friends liked different things than he did, and therefore wanted different things, he wouldn't personalize their differences of opinion so much. He wouldn't see those differences as a personal attack or act of aggression.

However, even with stronger perspective-taking ability, Kyle's heightened activity and passionate responses would likely still remain. He might need to further develop a space between his reactivity and response, but he could certainly begin to work on recognizing what his friends might be doing differently. He could also be encouraged to try other people's games (imitation). Then he could begin to work on seeing that differences in opinions are not always attacks on him by first noticing differences between people that don't really matter to him (e.g., Dad only reads business magazines; I like comic books).

Both parents seemed to be mulling these ideas over. Kyle's mom said, "So we shouldn't be so quick to judge Kyle as being stubborn or selfish? You're saying he feels personally attacked when another kid doesn't play the way that he wants to?"

The therapist nodded and said, "Add in a natural inclination perhaps toward being 'passionate' and quick to react, and you can see how things can break down pretty quickly."

Figuring Out What Social Skills Kyle Was Missing

The therapist asked Kyle's parents to review the social skills ladder together to determine where Kyle might be stuck and need some support:

Rung #1: Joint Attention

Kyle's parents were asked to reflect on whether Kyle frequently checked to see if others around him were noticing the same thing he was. Both agreed that he was very interested in social interaction and actively sought out others to share in joyful experiences.

When he played with a cool truck or saw something really interesting, he would often look at his parents to make sure that they saw it too. The therapist asked his parents if they heard Kyle use alerting words like "Mom, Dad, look!" to get their attention and share an experience. Both parents looked at each other and laughed saying, "He might have that skill a little too much, actually."

Based on Kyle's active social engagement, it appeared that he was not challenged in the area of joint attention.

Rung #2: Understanding and Identifying Emotions

Kyle's parents were asked to reflect on whether he looked at them when they were interacting and whether he seemed to be able to recognize their feelings. In other words, was he able to attend to verbal and nonverbal cues in other people?

His mom responded excitedly, "Actually, he is very perceptive when someone is unhappy or angry, and he will frequently ask, 'Are you mad at me?' if I'm having a bad day, or ask me if something happened at work or whatever." Kyle appeared to have developed understanding at the second rung of the social development ladder.

Rung #3: Imitation

The therapist then asked Mr. and Mrs. Burns to remember back to the last visit when Kyle and the clinician were playing with Hot Wheels and a track on the floor. Kyle was happily zooming cars down the track, as was the therapist until she started zooming marbles instead. She asked Kyle's parents to recall if he tried to do what she was doing. Did he try to zoom marbles instead of Hot Wheels as well?

Both parents shook their heads no.

Mrs. Burns said, "Actually, he did look up for that big glass one and say "cool" and tried it once, but then he went back to the Hot Wheels."

It was agreed that Kyle did not easily copy or imitate what other people were doing. In fact, he sometimes became so engrossed in activities he didn't look around to see what others were doing at all. At worst, he would get upset when he did come out of his seemingly hyper-focused state and notice that his friends were doing something different. At other times, he seemed to really struggle with being able to stay with one activity long enough to even begin to include his friend in play. No imitation was happening then because Kyle was not attending to one toy or activity long enough to notice.

Herein lay the fundamental problem, which was most probably a result of Kyle's impulsivity, short attention span, and heightened activity level.

Kyle's lack of attention to what other kids were doing or saying was preventing him from realizing that others might have new and even better ideas of what to do than he did. Of course, he wasn't imitating yet. Furthermore, he wouldn't have a chance to expand his understanding of play in ways that he hadn't thought of, and he would be prevented from having balanced, fair interactions with friends. His parents agreed that Kyle was stuck on the social skills ladder at the level of paying attention to other people's actions and imitating others.

The plan was to get Kyle engaged and attending to a friend during a high-interest activity and to encourage him to try imitating some of his friends' ideas—all so he could move toward building his perspective-taking skills.

"Sounds great," said his dad, "but how in the heck do we do that?"

How the Heck Do We Teach Imitation Skills? Rung 3, Continued

The single, best way to teach kids imitation is to imitate them.

Say what? Seriously, we grown-ups tend to relate to and talk to our kids like they are little grown-ups, and it just doesn't work.

Grown-Up Way: When Meeting a New Colleague at Work

Adult 1: "So where are you from?"

Adult 2: "Just moved here from Philadelphia."

Adult 1: "Wow...I've never been, but I hear that it's beautiful. What brings you to Ottawa?"

Adult 2: "I have family here. How long have you lived here?"

Adult 1: "About fifteen years. It's a great place to raise a family. Do you have kids?" etc.

What do you notice about this interaction? A lot of questions, right? It's what works when you are trying to get to know an adult and express an interest.

Grown-Up Way: When Trying to Play with a Child

Now let's take these two people and remove thirty-five years from one of them and have them both on the floor playing with a plastic farm set.

> **Adult 1:** (behaving as adults do trying to have a conversation):
> "Where's the cow?"
> **Kid:** "Dere" (pointing).
> **Adult 1:** "What's he doing?"
> **Kid:** "Eating."
> **Adult 1:** "What's that?" (pointing to the pig)
> **Kid:** "Pig." (with a "duh" look on his face)

Would you be able to tell from this interaction that the child was capable of producing eight-word-long sentences?

How Imitation Works

The thing is, kids talk more, initiate more, and have more balanced conversations when adults stop asking so many questions and use comments instead (Pepper & Weitzman, 2004). Not trying to be ironic here, but if you are like most parents, you probably have a question brewing right about now. Something like, "What do we comment about?" This is where the imitation comes in.

Let's go back to the farm set scenario:

> **Kid** (note: this conversation started with the **kid** leading): "The cow's going in the barn."
> **Adult:** "OK. My cow is in the barn too."(You just gorgeously modeled imitation.)
> **Kid:** "Now he is going to sleep."
> **Adult** (putting his cow in too) (epic snore sound effect): "He is going to sleep...Night night cows. See you tomorrow."

By imitating your child and using comments much more often than questions, you are following his lead in play. By following his lead, you will be doing and talking about what *he* is interested in doing, and he will want to continue the interaction with you longer. If he stays and plays with you longer, you have more chances to model language for him to learn and to build trust and enjoyment in your interactions.

Once a good rapport and trust in play has developed, then you have a chance to gently add new elements into the play. And, because you have done such an excellent job showing your child how to imitate through your example over time, perhaps he will try to imitate *you*.

New, improved farm scenario with your child given an opportunity to imitate you:

> **Kid 1** *(*note: started with the kid leading again):* "The cow's going in the barn."
>
> **Adult:** "OK. My cow is in the barn too."(You just gorgeously modeled imitation again.)
>
> **Kid:** "Now he is going to sleep. "
>
> **Adult** *(putting his cow in too; epic snore sound effect):* "Night night cows. See you tomorrow."
>
> **Kid:** "Wake up."
>
> **You:** "Wake up, cows. It's time for breakfast." (You then model your cow eating hay. And then hand some hay to your child.)
>
> *Cue trumpets:* Your child *imitates* you by feeding his cow hay.

This is the beginning of your child learning to attend to his play partner, accept changes in the play routine, and then imitate those changes.

To start, you will most certainly have to imitate your child most of the time, but once your child begins to accept your gentle additions and imitates them, you can gradually add more and more until it is a more balanced interaction.

If imitation works with the farm (a favorite activity), then you might try building this skill with trucks, then Legos, and then just generally expanding into all kinds of play.

Taking Turns

Once your child is more flexible and balanced in play with you, then you move toward helping him generalize this skill with peers. You will probably want to begin with leaving toys out that your child is pretty skilled with playing.

But what if letting your child lead in play and copying what he is doing isn't enough because he just quickly cycles from one activity to the next without giving you both a chance to really develop an activity? Remember back to the scene with Kyle and the therapist and the toys in the room strewn about like a garage sale gone wrong?

To imitate, you have to play long enough to have an interaction that is back and forth. We do that by modeling TURN TAKING.

Sometimes, children who are struggling to play with friends are not imitating friends because they don't sustain an activity long enough to engage and notice what is happening. This is especially common with younger children. We can keep these kids interacting and playing longer by using high-interest activities and toys and being sure to incorporate turn taking.

If you've ever seen a speech-language pathologist with a young child, you have almost certainly heard him or her use the term *turn taking*. It is rather unfortunate that we refer to this skill as *turn taking* because people often equate this fundamental interaction/communication requirement with good manners. Like, "Look at how nicely Katie is taking turns. Share your toys, Katie. What a good girl, Katie." So sweet, but not really what we are trying to get at here.

While it is important to teach good manners, we professionals are more concerned with helping kids develop their ability to focus on one activity long enough to learn new information and develop their *social noticing* skills. If your child learns to notice other kids and learns that they like to play too and that it's no fun if you don't get a chance to play, then he or she will become empathetically motivated to "share" and "take turns."

To keep your child engaged and playing for longer with the same activity with a friend, it is important to have age-appropriate expectations around turn taking as well.

For really young children, playing beside, rather than with, a friend using the same materials is part of typical development. You can help foster turn taking (which leads to cooperative play, by the way) by first practicing using high-interest toys or activities such as throwing a ball, kicking a ball into a net, jumping on a mini-trampoline, and pushing a truck back and forth to each other.

When your child is ready to move from more physically based games to playing on the floor with a toy, try having both of you take turns with the same fun toy. This back and forth encourages turn taking, which leads to your child paying increased attention to a play partner. This leads to staying and playing for a longer time, which leads to more cooperative play, and then *TA DA*...imitation!

Put another way, if you facilitate turn taking, it will help your child notice what the other child is doing because he will be very motivated to pick up on cues that indicate it is now his turn. This positive behavior gets reinforced repeatedly by other kids wanting to play with him, which gives him more practice using language and social skills, and so on.

Your child will develop a bank of turn-taking memories to learn from, including how awesome it was when he and Colton pushed Thomas the train up the hill and how sad he was when Colton grabbed Kyle's train and didn't let him try. You can round out your child's learning by discussing turn taking gone wrong. For example, you can point out how he is feeling when another child is not letting him have a turn and talk about what would make it better (offer Colton another train to exchange, ask Colton for a turn, etc.).

You can, and should, frequently point out to your child turn taking gone right.

"Look, now it's your turn. Colton is letting you push the train. I love how you are being patient and waiting for your turn." Or, "It's so hard to wait when you want a turn right away. Look at how happy Colton is when you give him a chance with the ramp. Colton will want to play longer when you take turns and play fairly."

Here are some practical examples of simple, fun, turn-taking activities that you might want to try:

- Prop a piece of plywood up to make a ramp and take turns zooming cars down.
- Take turns: you imitate your child fixing something like a toy stove. Each of you has a tool and takes turns fixing.
- Take turns putting puzzle pieces into a puzzle.
- Take turns stacking blocks.
- Take turns putting an item of clothing on a doll.
- Take turns putting Band-Aids on sick dolls or animals.
- Take turns putting furniture in a toy house.

SUMMARY OF RUNG 3: IMITATION

In summary, you'll know that you need to work on imitation skills if your child does/has most of the following:

- has some joint attention;
- can recognize some feelings in himself and others;
- plays beside other kids or may not stick around long to play with friends;
- often dominates play and interactions when trying to play cooperatively;
- has a lot of disagreements when playing with others; often because other kids are not playing the way your child wants them to.

RUNG 4

Why You Need Seniors, Babies, and Pets:
Early Perspective Taking

It's been four months since superhero-loving, CEO-aspiring Kyle, the little boy from the previous chapter, and his parents had their consultation appointment. They came into the speech-language clinic with a recent video of him playing with a friend so that the progress of his social skills could be assessed.

On the video, he and a buddy were lying on the floor, deeply engrossed in watching a Hexbot negotiate its way through a plastic obstacle course and around a ramp. Kyle's parents had cleverly provided just one Hexbot so that the boys would have to include each other and share rather than do their own thing. The unpredictable nature of the moving bug robot kept both boys interested for more than ten minutes. That was significant for Kyle, as he tended to cycle through activities very quickly.

As the video played, something especially exciting emerged. Anthony, Kyle's little friend with the very unfortunate low-rise pants (what's up with that fashion statement anyway?), had taken the Hexbot and moved it to a racecar ramp that was normally used for Hot Wheels. Kyle followed, and both boys laughed like crazy when the bug robot awkwardly went around the track.

Now here's the kicker: Kyle then got the Hexbot and did the same thing as Anthony had. When Anthony later added a self-moving Hot Wheels car to chase the bug robot, Kyle did it too, clearly appreciating Anthony's genius. That meant that Kyle had noticed what a friend had done and was sending the message to his buddy that he liked it. Anthony liked being noticed and imitated, and both boys were really enjoying each other. So they kept playing, which meant that Kyle's social skills had the opportunity to develop further.

Now that Kyle had gained the ability to imitate some ideas, the stage was set for him to graduate to perspective taking. In general, *perspective taking* means being able to recognize other people's feelings, thoughts, and perceptions about an experience as similar to or different from your own. Perspective taking is written into the fabric of human connection. Hence the many slang terms that summarize perspective taking including walking in someone else's shoes, seeing things through another's eyes, stepping outside yourself, looking at it from another point of view, etc. The development of perspective taking marks a real leap away from being "me centered" to "we centered" and is a critical component to being able to relate socially in a balanced and well-received way.

Appreciating Other People's Points of View

Of course, just because Kyle was willing to imitate some ideas, it did not necessarily mean that he always appreciated it when other kids wanted to do something different than he did—especially when he perceived his idea as being better than his friend's. Kyle sometimes continued to have trouble with taking different views or perspectives personally, and that could cause kids to avoid interactions with him. When he felt confronted, he would explode too often and for too long.

When kids personalize differences of opinion, it often means that part of the problem is that they need more work in perspective taking. Adults can and should build children's skills up to avoid clashes and stop relying on platitudes that don't really get to the heart of the challenge. Instructions like "use your words" and "you need to share" are only moderately helpful when a child doesn't yet understand the concept of other points of view.

Realistically, most four-year-olds don't always want to graciously accept a friend coming in and changing the plot of their pretend play scene. To be fair, many adults also don't appreciate others amending what they think is an excellent plan. It's like when your spouse suggests a stop at Home Depot to choose a fan for the bathroom when you just want to stay home, drink coffee, and read the paper.

Kyle simply showed his disdain for others' input more dramatically than his classmates did. His more dramatic and frequent outbursts and protests made him stand out.

This is not the sort of attention we want our children to attract. Many studies have been done about who bullies and is bullied, and research points to the kids who "stand out" as the most likely culprits and victims (Vail, 1999).

Keep in mind that children like Kyle at this stage of development truly believe that their play partners inherently like and want to do the same thing as they do. Lack of perspective taking can explain why some kids feel so betrayed and perceive their friends as being "mean" when they have different ideas or preferences. It really would seem vindictive if you thought a friend deliberately set out to make your life difficult simply to be unkind. No wonder kids with this worldview can often become angry and oppositional very quickly.

Here's an illustration. Imagine a four-year-old who is very particular and likes things to be "just so." He has invited a friend over to play Legos and has planned out exactly which Lego pieces will be used, where they will play, and exactly who will build what. Now picture what you think happened when his friend arrived, saw construction trucks, and wanted to play with them instead.

The hurt on the face of the Lego child was real. He had some anxiety when faced with hosting a playdate because he was rapidly realizing that while he wanted friends, he couldn't control what they would do when they came over. That unpredictability was stressful for him, as he genuinely could not understand why they would want to do something different than him. Making matters worse, he didn't yet have the skills to know how to explain or respond to his feelings and confusion.

It's not easy to relax and enjoy yourself when you feel you must maintain hypervigilance to prepare for your friend to repeatedly let you down, seemingly without reason.

It is important to emphasize that these kids are not selfish. Instead, they are not yet capable of seeing an alternate, considerate way and choosing it. They appear self-absorbed only because they have not yet fully developed the understanding that different people think differently.

This difficulty with perspective taking is *not* the same thing as lacking empathy either. It is instead a symptom of a child's inability to understand that others don't necessarily have the same opinions or wants. Kyle was actually an unusually compassionate little boy. When spiders were found in the house, Kyle was the first one to capture them and take them outside. Even at four, Kyle noticed that with snow outside the spiders might die. That brought him to tears, which led to the creation of a spider condo in the family garage.

Kyle's parents continued to work diligently, organizing playdates so that he could practice taking turns, and using high-interest toys as a strategy to keep him playing longer. They also gently added an important new element: the introduction of slightly differing ideas while playing, which Kyle accepted more and more often. His parents were encouraged to think of introducing their new ideas with Kyle as desensitizing him to other peoples' input during play.

Significant progress was being made now that Kyle was noticing when his friends were playing differently, and he was able to accept those different ideas without taking them personally. He wasn't feeling "attacked" when playing with friends who wanted to try something different.

He had now truly moved from self-directed play to true cooperative play. To broaden his ability to take others' perspectives, he needed to build his catalogue of experiences involving change.

Essentially, he needed to better understand that different people

- like different things;
- act on what they like and don't like;
- want different things and act based on that;
- might feel differently than their friend about something in the same situation;
- know different things and act based on what they know (Bartsch & Wellman,1995; Sussman, 2006).

We are talking about flexibility of thought. Some children really struggle with flexible thinking, and it can be the biggest barrier to understanding and accepting other points of view.

Learning to Think More Flexibly

Ariana was a blonde, little, four-and-a-half-year-old princess who was brought into our speech and language clinic to have her social use of language evaluated. She confidently entered the room in head-to-toe pink and purple with a two-foot-wide poufy princess skirt. She had a toy ring on every finger, and even her light-up sneakers were sparkly making her impossible to miss. She had an encyclopedic knowledge of Disney princesses and wasn't afraid to share it.

Her parents, Mr. and Mrs. Mendez, were lovely, caring, and concerned. We asked them to describe how often Ariana played with friends at home and what those playdates looked like. They both tried to regularly invite a classmate or two over, but children often wanted to leave after only half an hour or so. Playdates usually started out with the girls playing with plastic princesses but ended up with everyone in tears. Ariana's parents were growing increasingly concerned that their daughter seemed obsessive and would only play princesses.

The more they met other four-year-olds, the more Ariana's parents began to realize how unusual it was that the only books she would read were princess books, that she would only watch princess movies, and that she would refuse to play anything else when she was with other kids.

"She's really bossy and tells the other kids what to wear and what to say almost like a script, and she is the director. It's getting harder and harder for kids to come over, and she isn't being invited to any of the other kids' houses," Ariana's mom said with concern in her eyes.

When asked about school, Mrs. Mendez continued. "It's only half a day and the kids get on the bus right away after school, so they don't really spend time playing outside of the classroom. There is no recess or outdoor play yet."

The classroom teacher had recently called Ariana's parents because she wasn't happy with how Ariana would barge into play already in progress, try to take over, and leave the other kids upset. When she wasn't getting rejected, she was off in the corner by herself whispering elaborate memorized chunks of Disney movies with her princess dolls. The teacher was at a loss because Ariana's behaviors were not changing, although the teacher had talked to her using a variety of approaches.

To get a more complete understanding of the history of Ariana's challenges, the therapist asked her parents to think back to how well she interacted with peers in preschool.

"We didn't really think that there were problems at the time," her mother reflected, "but we've been talking and have come to realize that she really relied on her teacher. I mean, she loved her teacher and followed her around a lot—especially outside in the yard. Ariana didn't seem upset or lonely, so we didn't worry about it too much. We just figured she was happy and she wanted to be with her."

Mr. and Mrs. Mendez recalled that there was one little girl in their daughter's preschool group with whom she played. This other girl was extremely easygoing and didn't really challenge Ariana's plans or ideas. She pretty much did what Ariana told her to do, so the problems weren't yet exposed. Now that she was in kindergarten, Ariana's concerns appeared to be around her uncertainty about how to enter into play with friends and how to handle the unpredictability of peers without simply leaving or relying on an adult to escape.

More information was needed to better understand Ariana's pretend play, and specifically, the inflexibility of her play, even with herself. Her parents began describing a pattern of Ariana becoming very focused on one subject or another: animals, then dinosaurs, then cats, and finally, princesses. "I can't believe how much we now know about cats," her dad said.

Mrs. Mendez recounted how her daughter used to "script" her during her cat obsession phase. Ariana would say, "You are the rescue worker, and you say, 'Oh my gosh! Was that a stray cat?' Then Ariana would come out of the playroom looking absolutely adorable in her kitty ears, pretending to limp.

"She would then tell me, 'Now you say, she is so beautiful! Is she hurt?' Ariana would then limp more dramatically, and I would have to say what she told me to and add, 'Stop the car! We have to help her!' Then we would have to fuss about her injury, pet her, and take her home and keep her."

While this type of highly directed and scripted scene may seem adorable or cute, it also raises a yellow flag. Whenever parents use descriptions such as, "now you say" or "we would *have* to say," or "we would have to…" they are describing children who have challenges with flexibility. Children who compensate for challenges in processing the unpredictability of life and social interactions often present as "scripting" themselves and others in dramatic play. That "scripting" requires the players to maintain sameness, which may serve to reduce the child's anxiety.

When asked if they ever tried to deviate from Ariana's play scripts and what might happen if they did, her parents indicated that Ariana would sometimes accept slight variations, but that she really stuck to the same routine in her dramatic play. If either parent deviated too far or often, they said, Ariana would lose it. "Her tantrums were loud enough that we had to close the windows in the summer or the neighbors would think we were torturing her," her dad said.

Mr. and Mrs. Mendez described an active, curious, and intense little girl even in infancy. She was always someone who thrived on consistency, and when her routine was off, everyone around her suffered. We then asked her parents to give more information on eating and sleeping and basic daily living aspects of Ariana's life to better gauge how pervasive her challenges with flexibility were.

They described a little girl who stressed about the introduction of new foods, strongly preferred safe, bland things to eat such as bread, crackers, and pasta, and seemed to suspect that mixed foods were the result of evil parental plots. Sleep was also a challenging area. Ariana woke up a lot during the first three years. "For a while, she would just thumb through her dinosaur encyclopedias from two to four in the morning," said her mom. By the age of three, Ariana had memorized the names of most of the dinosaurs in a 300-page encyclopedia.

Clearly, this little girl's challenges with flexibility had extended to all areas of her life and fell outside of typical developmental parameters. Her parents indicated that they often felt "judged" by family, acquaintances, and strangers in the mall. They often received ill-timed and misplaced advice: e.g., "You're spoiling her and that's why she thinks it has to be her way all the time," or "Don't worry about it…she's just little."

It is important to understand that Ariana was not a "prima donna," nor were her parents in any way responsible for the way she needed to try to control her environment to reduce her anxiety. When Ariana would dig her heels in and insist something needed to be a certain way, it came out of genuine anxiety and discomfort about change and uncertainty.

Her need for control in play stemmed not from being "spoiled," but rather from her lack of understanding of how to interact socially with peers. Instead, she would "memorize" ways of playing and repeat them to feel comfortable.

Mr. and Mrs. Mendez went to see a psychologist who specialized in assessing young children. They reported feeling relieved at the psychologist's suspicion that Ariana might have nonverbal learning disability, which could better explain her strong need for things to be the same and her challenges with navigating social cues in the classroom.

Her parents brought a video to the clinic of Ariana playing with an active little girl from her kindergarten class. Before her friend had much chance to even take her shoes off, Ariana had led her to her bedroom. "Come upstairs…We're having a ball…I'm Cinderella, and you are the fairy Godmother. Here's your wand."

The little girl appeared excited and agreeable. Ariana continued, "I get the blue dress, and wait…I need the black headband for my hair. Where's the black headband?" Ariana was getting visibly agitated at not being able to find the exact headband that she needed to complete her outfit. The rest of the ten-minute tape went pretty much the same way. Ariana was in control, in her domain, with her classmate going along for the ride. Luckily, her classmate was agreeable and had similar interests.

Ariana needed to learn flexibility and perspective taking skills quickly, or the gap between her and her peers would quickly grow.

When Inflexibility Masquerades as Stubbornness

Brittany, a quiet five-year-old, was doing just fine in school, according to her parents. They described her as being a bit of an independent spirit who could be "stubborn."

When asked to elaborate on how Brittany displayed her stubborn streak, her mom described a little girl who had to have her way in everything, especially when they played together. "She has always been very particular about where her Pretty Ponies go. Minty had to be beside Princess Pony, for example," her mom said. If Minty decided to expand her social horizons and hang with Rainbow Pony, then Brittany would get "huffy" and would promptly "uninvite" her parents.

"Literally told to leave...uninvited from playing," her mother said.

Mr. and Mrs. Lewis were being "uninvited" from playing with Brittany most days, and if they confronted her, she would simply gather up her toys and leave.

School was apparently going very well for Brittany. Academically, she was ahead of her classmates. Her parents knew that she was capable and clever, but they had bigger concerns. "We're finding it hard to connect with her," her mother said.

Classmates did not call, nor did Brittany want to invite anyone over. There were no birthday party invitations, either.

In the classroom, a different, yet not-so-different picture of Brittany emerged. Brittany could be best described as Jade's shadow. Brittany copied everything that alpha girl Jade did. If Jade was the mommy in the house center and brushed her bangs out of her eyes while sighing dramatically, Brittany was right beside her doing the same.

When Jade decided to paint, Brittany wanted to paint too.

Bathroom break. Check.

Strawberry fruit roll-ups at snack. For two.

When Jade was absent from school, Brittany was totally lost. At those times, she stayed close to the classroom teacher and simply watched the other children. She didn't even attempt to initiate play with other kids. Even when the teacher tried to set her up with a play partner, Brittany would often get up and leave.

Again, she had no trouble following the classroom routine, finished all of her seatwork, and liked to quietly look at books.

It was as if Brittany was cleverly using Jade as a kindergarten social scene translator. She was using imitation to help her understand how to play like everyone else.

Simply having the desire to observe peers, notice how classmates play differently, and sometimes imitate those different approaches is a great starting place for developing perspective taking.

But it's just a start.

There is a lot more that parents can do to help their child interpret the actions of their classmates. As parents, if you recognize aspects of your child on this rung of the ladder, then a good first step is to teach your child that everyone arrives in social situations with different thoughts, feelings, ideas, knowledge, and wants. You also will have to be diligent in gently easing flexibility into your child's life. For these regimented little people, habits can quickly become engrained and become obstacles to being accepted by friends.

You'll know that your child is on this rung of the social skills ladder if he or she:

- Needs to be in control of play with friends most of the time, even when she can see that it is not working for either party.
- Gets very frustrated when others around her won't "cooperate" and play the way she thinks that they should.
- Might not know what others like/dislike and assumes they like/dislike the same things she does.
- May assume that you want or don't want the same things that she does.
- Doesn't seem to use or understand more complicated thinking words like *know, idea, think, remember.*
- May not have a lot of good strategies for entering into play that has already started and has trouble trying to join in.
- Has difficulty solving conflicts or feels that she has no other option than to hit, yell, leave, or "uninvite" others from play.
- Has a limited repertoire of pretend play or relies too much on building (e.g., Lego), cause and effect (e.g., cars), physical chasing games, or video games.
- Is capable of only very rigid dramatic play that is repeatedly done the same way.

Helping Your Child with Perspective Taking

There are so many ways to incorporate perspective taking and flexible thinking into your child's life. Here are some suggestions:

- Expand pretend play scripts to include your ideas too. For the cat rescue scenario described earlier, perhaps consider that there is also an injured bird or change the nature of the injury. Or add a new perspective—maybe the driver who hit the cat feels terrible and is crying.

- When your child is hosting a playdate, have her call and ask the friend which toys he or she likes to play with and whether he or she likes your snack options.

- Read books with different perspectives and talk through which characters feel what and why. When choosing stories for bedtime, of course pick out three of your child's favorites but gently insist on reading even just a page or two of something that is a little different than what your child would want.

■ Use mealtime as a great, natural way to demonstrate different preferences. For example:

> ➤ Talk about different preferences in the family. At the grocery store, remind your child who likes bananas in their lunch and who prefers an apple. At the dinner table, have your child pay attention to who needs a fork, who can't drink milk because of an allergy, etc.
>
> ➤ When serving a meal, have your child offer a couple of choices to different family members with you setting it up so that one of the offerings is something that your child likes but that the other person doesn't.
>
> ➤ Have family members ask your child for more of a food item that your child finds disgusting.

■ When you go shopping, be sure to have your child get some Brussels sprouts (or similar food disliked by your child) for your spouse because he or she loves them even though your child finds them disgusting.

■ When coloring together, talk about your favorite colors. Help your child learn different perspectives by saying things like, "I love pink and purple, but orange is my favorite. Can you please draw me a princess with an orange dress?"

■ When buying gifts for people, talk about different interests and have your child help guess which gift would be most appreciated. Gift shopping with kids is terrific for identifying others' likes and dislikes. Be sure to let your child hear all the thoughts and consideration for others when choosing what to buy.

■ Watch YouTube videos of funny situations and hit the pause button frequently to have your child identify feelings and thoughts and predict what might happen next.

■ Try to expand play whenever and however you can. You can use favorite subjects as a springboard to a variety of ways to look at them. If princesses are the hot topic, then introduce knights, princes, different kinds of castles, different princesses in other countries, princess fashion through the ages, princesses throughout history, and princess roles today.

■ Expose your child to people with different worldviews such as seniors or other adults. Figure out what music Grandma would like to hear when she comes over. Maybe she would prefer quieter music than the super loud rap songs that your children like to bounce around to most days. Or a family friend who is from a country with a warm climate and experiencing their first cold winter might like to learn to build a snowman.

■ Use pets. Point out that your dog looks sad because his tail is droopy and his eyes are down. Why might he be sad? Does he have water? Has he eaten? Is he sick? Has he had his walk? Point out how happy he looks now that your child said "Walk." His tail is wagging and he is now waiting expectantly at the door.

■ Use babies. Why might the baby be crying? What could we do to help her feel better? If you don't have a baby and can't borrow one, then people-watch at a playground with lots of babies and toddlers around. By the time your ice cream is finished, it is probable that your child will witness a number of crying scenarios to figure out.

■ Visit sick, elderly, or lonely people in your neighborhood, and bring them soup, some cookies, or a nice child-drawn picture. Talk about why you are doing this. You can then reflect and point out for your child how the seniors, babies, and dogs responded to your gestures and how that might have made them feel.

SUMMARY OF RUNG 4:
Early Perspective Taking

Your child many need support with early perspective taking if she:

- Can share focus on the same activity over multiple turns (sustain joint attention)
- Can recognize and identify different emotions
- Notices peers playing and shows interest in what they are doing
- Can and does imitate actions and words in play
- May not yet engage in dramatic play
- If she does engage in dramatic play, prefers that actions be performed the same way each time
- May assume that if she likes/wants something, everyone else must feel the same way
- When trying to play cooperatively, can dominate play and interactions to keep things the same
- May have a lot of disagreements or easily abandon play with others
- Seems to expect others to just "know" what she wants and seems hurt or angry when others don't respond appropriately

RUNG 5

Why Kids Are Lousy at Hide & Seek:
Theory of Mind and Dramatic Play

Before delving into what additional skills kids need to be able to truly put themselves in someone else's shoes, let's pause and address those readers who may be shaking their heads and thinking that all this ladder stuff is a bit over the top. If you're in this group, perhaps you're thinking something like this: "Kids just need to work it out themselves. Classmates will straighten them out fast." Sometimes that's true.

But consider this: Is that how you would want to be treated if you felt frustrated most of the time and didn't have the ability to do much more than scream? Or were so anxious that you needed everything to be exactly the same, or you felt like you would fall apart? Or that you were so lost socially, that you were willing to do anything your classmate did to be accepted because you couldn't perceive any other options?

These kids stand out because they tend to freak out more, cry more, fight more, and linger when uninvited more. If we accept that no child or adult would choose to behave in a way that leaves them ostracized, then it makes sense that steps should be taken to figure out the problem and solution.

Some of these kids just need a little extra guidance and teaching to help them climb up the rungs of their social skills ladder. Others need a lot of extra learning, practice, and guidance, and still it won't come naturally. But, if we meet these kids where they are and gradually build their skills, we at least provide them with the ability to interact. Then they will truly be able to choose for themselves whether they want to or not.

Everyone, including (and maybe especially) children, wants to feel like they belong, and that they are valued, important members of their social culture. And everyone wants the security of knowing that they know what to do in order to feel successful.

All of the kids described in the previous chapters are inflexible in their social thinking because they really don't understand why people act the way they do, and so they struggle for control of what they can.

So, let's break the steps down to help them learn. And help them better understand what the heck is happening around them so they can gain control over their world and other people's places in it.

Problems with More Advanced Perspective Taking

Kyle, Brittany, and Ariana, who were introduced in the previous chapter, have made significant progress in their social perspective taking, but there is no quick fix in this area. For different reasons, they have been slower to climb the social skills ladder, and have now gotten stuck at later perspective taking.

Kyle has made excellent progress in making friends. He now regularly has two or three kids over, and he is able to play cooperatively with a wide variety of toys and activities. He knows which friend likes Legos and which prefers shooting a tennis ball at the hockey net, and now knows to bring those things out when these particular friends come over. With some accommodations in the classroom for his extra energy, Kyle hasn't had to warm the thinking chair seat in over a month.

So why is he sitting in the hallway during afternoon recess today?

Apparently, while playing over the lunch hour, Kyle, with some prompting from his teacher, asked a new student, Omar, to play with him and his buddies. The game that the boys had been playing for the previous two weeks was zombie-ninja apocalypse. For those who have never played in a zombie-ninja apocalypse league, the basic rules to the game are pretty obvious. Some of the boys are zombies (bad guys), and some are ninjas (good guys). The zombies are determined to take over the world, and the ninjas must save the day.

Omar, being astute, picked up on this classic schoolyard scenario pretty quickly. And, because Kyle was improving significantly in his perspective taking, he thought to explain the good guy/bad guy basics to Omar and invited him to be a ninja with him. What Omar didn't know is that he couldn't go after zombies if they were on the play structure, nor could he go after the zombies if a zombie touched him first unless he was "rescued" by a fellow ninja by being given a pretend throwing star.

Omar unknowingly, enthusiastically, went after a zombie on the play structure. Kyle, who takes these games pretty seriously and was immersed in his role, was outraged. He ran after Omar and shouted, "YOU CAN'T TAG THE ZOMBIES ON THE STRUCTURE! NOW YOU HAVE TO BE OUT!" Omar, being new, of course had no sweet clue that this was a rule and yelled back that he didn't have to sit out. Kyle, with his heightened sense of justice, kept saying that was the rule and that Omar was cheating. Things continued to escalate until the two boys were separated by the teacher. Because Omar was new, Kyle was given a punishment for not playing nicely with the new boy.

When Kyle's parents asked why he had to sit in the hall for second recess, Kyle really didn't understand. He was frustrated because he had invited Omar to join him and thought he had explained the rules, but he was punished for what he perceived as Omar cheating. He really hadn't grasped completely that Kyle hadn't thought to explain everything and Omar did not know all the rules.

When kids are just beginning to understand more complex perspective taking, they may make more assumptions in their interpretations of others' behavior based on what they themselves know or think.

Theory of Mind

To be able to imagine what someone else might be thinking, you first have to be aware that *you* think and what your thoughts are. Then kids begin to develop their understanding that different people have different thoughts, which leads us to a concept called *theory of mind*. First coined in the late 1990s by Simon Baron-Cohen in his book called *Mind Blindness,* the term is based on something psychologists call a "false belief" task. An example of a false belief task would go something like this:

Picture two four-year-olds sitting at a kiddie table. There is a big box of chocolates on the table. You come in, lift the lid, and show the kids the chocolates. Child number one is asked to go into another room and get a couple of napkins because the chocolates are messy. While he's gone, you dump out the chocolates, put cotton balls inside instead, and put the lid back on. Child number one comes back in from the kitchen.

To test child number two's understanding of theory of mind or false belief tasks, you would ask, "What does child number one think is in that box?" If the child has developed theory of mind or the understanding that different people know and think different things, he will answer "chocolates." If he doesn't, he will answer—you guessed it—cotton balls. Why? Because *he* knows that there are cotton balls in the box.

Here's another example. Have you ever played hide-and-seek with a young child? Young kids often choose hiding spots that are less than stellar. Sometimes, these kids are so new to the game that they think if they cover their eyes and can't see you, then you can't see them either. These kids have not yet developed the notion that different people have different knowledge and thoughts than they do.

So how do you get kid number two to understand that people know and think different things?

As was mentioned in chapter 4, the best place to start is to help your child recognize that different people like/dislike different things and act based on those preferences. To remember this, just think about Repacholi and Gopnik's 1997 "broccoli study," in which fourteen-month-olds were shown a woman being provided a choice between Goldfish crackers and broccoli. When she bit into the fishy crackers, she made a face like she found them completely revolting. When she bit into the broccoli, she made a face like—"mmmmmmm delicious!"

Then the kids were given broccoli and a plate of fishy crackers and instructed to give the woman one. At age fourteen months, the kids gave her fishy crackers because that's what *they* would prefer. At eighteen months, many of the kids gave her broccoli. What happened during that critical four-month period? In that short time, kids made the leap that others might want different things than they would.

We all know that this willingness and ability to think of what another person wants is on a continuum. That's why we appreciate some gift givers more than others. For example, there is a certain husband who shall remain nameless who gave his wife a fishing rod for her birthday that he "borrowed" first for a trip with the guys. I am happy to tell you that after more than twenty years together, my husband gives great gifts that are very thoughtful and now knows that used fishing rods and wooden decoys won't be well received.

This learning about different people begins in infancy and develops over a lifetime of interactions. There is no one "score" that means you've achieved good-enough perspective taking. Rather, success is measured by the social/ emotional well-being of every individual in relationship with others.

Once your child is able to identify likes and dislikes in others that differ from his own, then the next step will be to realize that you might know something that he doesn't. This may be reassuring to the parents who feel like since they've had children, their name has been changed to "Mom/Dad… Do you know where the _____ is?" As in, "Mom, do you know where the…keys, milk, towels, stuffed elephant, etc., is?" Every time that situation is played out in front of your child, you are modeling for him that people know different things and act on that knowledge.

Once you are aware that your child understands that you have different knowledge than he does, you can begin to model for him the fact that *he* might know something that you don't. Perhaps you can make a big show of not knowing where your boots or the Thomas trains are, or perhaps he can teach you how to make a macaroni necklace.

So how do you know if your child is struggling with higher-level theory-of-mind-type perspective taking?

Kyle, for example, often got frustrated when playing with kids who weren't following the rules at recess. He made assumptions that other kids knew how to play, even when it was quite obvious that they had no experience with playing zombie-ninja apocalypse or some other game du jour.

Ariana often reported that her friends "hated her." Like Kyle, she has also made significant positive gains in her ability to make and keep friends. She now regularly spends time with three or four little girls in her home or at theirs. While they all like to play princesses and do begin most play times with a ball and dress-up, Ariana has become much more flexible in her play with friends. She is now drawing with sidewalk chalk, playing more physical, rule-based games, and listens and includes others' ideas in dramatic play. Her parents knew that she had come a long way when she, albeit reluctantly, agreed to be the little boy when playing "family" with two friends.

So why did she regularly come home to report that one of her regular playmates from school "hated her?" Whenever a friend was angry about something or wasn't nice to her, Ariana appeared to personalize the experience and assume it was because the friend didn't like *her*. But Ariana didn't know what she didn't know. She was unaware that others don't always tell why they feel a certain way. Perhaps her friend was in a bad mood because her dog just died, or her friend was grouchy because her parents were fighting that morning as she was dropped off.

Ariana was also quick to be disappointed with friends because she assumed that her friends should just magically "know" how *she* was feeling about something. When her friends didn't know, for example, that Ariana was scared of dogs and one friend offered her a stuffed dog for her pretend pet, Ariana assumed that the friend made that choice because "she hated her." Ariana didn't understand that her friend didn't know or had forgotten that she is afraid of dogs.

This mind-reading expectation is not something that people necessarily outgrow, either. Think back to your first more serious relationships, when you were internally seething about something, and your partner, sensing something amiss asked, "What's wrong?" To which you of course answered, "Nothing." Internally, in those sorts of moments, we assume that our partner *knows* (theory of mind expectation) or at least should know why we would be upset. We shouldn't have to tell him or her, and we may erroneously attach meaning to how deep that person's feelings are about us based on whether or not he or she can guess.

For Ariana in first grade, this expectation that her friends should just "know" what she knew, and her deep disappointment in others when they didn't, represented a lack of development of theory of mind and perspective taking. When these skills were highlighted, supported, and taught, Ariana learned not to personalize others' lack of knowledge in a negative way and to stop feeling that friends "hated" her when they are sad and don't tell her why, or when they couldn't guess what she knew or felt.

If you walked into Brittany's first grade class and saw her playing on the floor with the other children, you would not believe that she was the same girl who followed Jade like a shadow. She was now able to initiate a variety of games with a wide variety of people, and was able to pick up on others' different feelings about the same games. She was not stuck at the theory-of-mind rung of social skills development, as evidenced when she ran over to give Jada hug during a class role-play. Jade came in late, saw everyone yelling at each other, and started to cry. The teacher was engaged in a dramatic exercise with the class and had her back to the door when Jade entered. The enactment was a role play around conflict, but Jade had no way of knowing that, and Brittany in those few seconds read Jade's mind and ran to comfort her and to offer an explanation.

Activities for Encouraging Theory of Mind

Your child may need to work on social perspective taking in higher thinking areas such as theory of mind under the following circumstances:

- You suspect your child has difficulties with making assumptions about other people's knowledge of things.
- You see your child personalizing others' emotions.
- Your child makes assumptions that others don't care about him when they don't know what he knows.

You can begin to focus on this area if your child is now recognizing that different people sometimes like/don't like or want/don't want different things.

We also want to help your child understand a bit more about thinking and further develop skills leading toward stronger theory of mind.

Games Appropriate for All Kids

What these activities have in common is the need to get into the head of the other player to be successful:

- Hide and seek
- Charades
- Headbandz, a game in which each player wears a head band with a picture of an object stuck to it. The idea is that the wearer cannot see the picture and has to guess what it is based on the answers he gets when he asks other players questions to help him guess. Teaches kids that not everyone knows the same thing that they do.
- Guess Who, a two-player game in which each player knows the other person's answer and can't tell. The idea is for each player to ask questions, and, based on the answer, rule out pictures of people until one player narrows it down to the correct picture. Excellent game to help children recognize that other people do not necessarily know what they do.
- Guess Where is a game that operates the same way as Guess Who, except the player has to guess what room characters are in. Teaches children that not everyone knows the same things.
- Memory, a game in which pairs of matching pictures are turned picture–side down and players take turns finding the matching pairs based on what they can remember seeing. Teaches children memory skills, taking turns, and the understanding that different players may remember different things, which leads to the concept that different people may know and think differently.
- Fibber, a game in which players might be telling the truth about what cards they have or might be fibbing. The idea is to try and catch your opponents when they are fibbing. Teaches children that what people say is not always what is really happening.
- Hide the _____, a variant of the game hide and seek. One person hides something (e.g., a teddy bear, a toy car). The other player has to guess where the item is or follow clues or guidance based on getting closer or "hotter" or farther away or "colder." Teaches children that different people have different knowledge.
- Can you guess what I'm thinking about?, a guessing game with clues. For example, "I'm thinking of an animal....Can you guess what it is?" Child: "Is it a pet?" Adult: "No, it's a wild animal." Child: "Does it eat plants?" etc. Helps children

learn that different people know and think about different things and that you can ask to better understand what other people are thinking.

- Who is it?, a game where you knock on the door and pretend to be somebody from a movie and the other person has to guess who it is. You can also have your child call family members and have them try to guess who is calling.

You can also work on theory of mind in the context of daily life. For example, you and your child can surprise a family member together with something that he or she enjoys. (e.g., "Let's surprise your brother with something nice when he gets home from school. We could make his favorite snack and bring out the Nerf guns for a big Nerf battle.") This activity can help your child learn to think about other people's preferences, even when they differ from his own. He can also learn that a surprise can mean he knows that something good is coming when the other person doesn't.

Using Pretend Play to Work on Theory of Mind

It's no accident that theory of mind begins developing in earnest at about four years of age, just around the time when a child's elaborate, dramatic pretend play usually takes off. For typically developing kids, early pretend play can begin as early as two years of age (e.g., the child pretends a block is a car). As the child gets older, steps are added to pretend play, moving from familiar situations (e.g., pretending to feed a baby) to situations only observed (e.g., pretending to go to the dentist), with more and more elements gradually added.

Here is how a typical play scenario might progress at different ages:

- At age two to two and a half, Lily might get a block, pretend it's a bottle, and give the baby a drink.
- At two and a half to three, Lily would still pretend to give the baby a bottle, but now she also puts baby to bed, tells everyone around "ssshhh," and turns out the lights.
- At three to three and a half, Lily might do all of the above plus give the baby a bath, act out bedtime and wake-up routines, and pretend to make dinner.
- By three and a half to four years old, she might give the baby a bottle, burp baby, change his diaper, walk around rocking fussy baby, act out how baby is all better, sing baby a song, and finally put baby to bed.

- From four to four and a half years old, Lilly might do all of the above, plus read baby a story, put baby to bed, welcome the pretend sitter, pretend to go grocery shopping, talk on the phone while waiting in a pretend line, and include pretend siblings.
- From age four and a half to five, Lilly might follow the same routine, but maybe now the mommy includes a dad who reads the book to baby. Mommy tells Daddy (who just came in) that baby has been "fussy," so be careful with baby when he puts him to bed. Then she may have to go to "book club" with the girls and pretend to get her purse, etc.

Notice the arrival of theory of mind in pretend play. The little girl knows that the new boy arriving on the scene to be the "daddy" doesn't know what has been going on up until then, so she tells him, "The baby's been fussy."

Dramatic, cooperative play provides the perfect backdrop for entering into others' minds. Pretending to be someone or something you are not forces you to be flexible in your thinking, and to think like the other person. You'll notice that even voices can change when a little boy or girl becomes "Batman."

You can be sure that if complex, dramatic play with multiple players is happening with your child, then he is participating in an excellent social skills environment for young children. Dramatic play is rich with perspective-taking opportunities and helps children move from self-orientation toward true cooperative play. Put another way, "high-quality pretend play is an important facilitator of perspective taking and later abstract thought" (Bergen, 2002).

When your child is exposed to, and participates in, a variety of dramatic play scenarios with a range of children, he may be a grandma, a unicorn, a dentist, a baby, a career woman, and an astronaut—all in one day of kindergarten! Dramatic play provides so many different perspectives to explore and to expand thinking.

It will probably be easiest for your child to first stretch his social skills with you before trying them with peers or siblings. That means it's time to break out that tiara, sparkly shoes, and spacesuit!

What if your child doesn't do dramatic play? What if your child is a needs-to-be-outside-running kid or a Lego-head, and he just cannot or will not pretend, or strongly leans toward moving or building to the exclusion of pretend? The rest of the chapter is for you.

Kids Who Move/Boys' Boys

The following section contains material that some readers may find sexist. While there will of course be exceptions, during the early years at school, it is not an overgeneralization to say that most boys tend to be more physical in play.

Of course, there are girls who love trucks, Lego, and chase n' tackle, and there are boys out there who groove on playing house and think My Pretty Ponies is pretty awesome. Actually, there is a college-male-dominated Pretty Ponies (Bronies) fan club that is pretty popular (but that's for a different book).

Many well-intentioned parents, perhaps veterans of gender studies classes, have provided their sons with a toy baby doll and their daughters with trucks. But many report that as soon as their son can push something along and watch it go, he does. And as soon as their daughter can nurture something, she does. One mother reported that her daughter insisted that she make a Kleenex wedding dress for the big day with T-Rex.

Let's look at how some boys, especially those who are on the tail end of the continuum of typical boy play, may miss out on the perspective taking and flexible thinking that are learned through dramatic play.

Boys' Boy Quinn

Quinn was in kindergarten. He had a jacket that was usually undone and pants that didn't seem able to keep up with his growing legs. He was also the loudest in his class and the most enthusiastic presenter of various designed-to-gross-out show-and-tells, and he loved to laugh.

When a parent would ask their child in his class, "Who did something funny today?" the answer was almost always Quinn. When asked, "Who got sent to the thinking chair?" the answer again was often Quinn. He kept the seat warm for the other rowdy little people in his class.

After school, about half of the kids from the class would play around in the yard most days. At that age, the girls went off and did their thing and most of the boys did theirs—a natural separation.

While they waited for their kids to finish playing, parents stood around, usually talking about the weather, wishing for coffee, and talking about their kids. Quinn's mom clearly had had it with the teacher. "I'm sick of getting the phone calls telling me, 'Quinn is being disruptive, Quinn is too silly, Quinn broke someone else's macaroni house.' I feel like I brought my sweet son and handed him over to get stomped on. I know he's no angel. I'm not a deluded parent, but he's not a bad boy."

She volunteered a couple of times in the classroom to cut pumpkins out of construction paper to get a more behind-the-scenes perspective of the classroom dynamics. Quinn seemed to find sitting through the hello song, calendar, weather, letter of the week, who has news, story, and then show-and-tell too long. He wanted something to *do,* not something to listen to. When that wasn't presented for him, he would *find* something to do, like making a rude sound and pretend it was Kevin or grab his mat on each side and rock back and forth, simulating a rowboat in a storm.

When it was free play, it looked like the room wasn't big enough for him, and that he needed all play to lead to something big happening. It would seem ridiculous to Quinn to build a tower or to make a castle without crashing something into it. Likewise, it seemed pointless to him to play in the house center and not have a monster come in and eat all of the food.

The teacher's response to Quinn's destructive acts was to give him repeated warnings, try to talk to him, and inevitably put him in the thinking chair. But that seemed to only make him think, "I can't sit here a second longer."

When the teacher would ask, "Who did _____" or whatever negative thing had occurred in the classroom, the other kids were quick to jump to the conclusion that it was probably Quinn. Not a good path.

When Quinn burst through the school doors at the end of the day, he played variants of tag for the most part. There were often physical confrontations with kids complaining that "Quinn punched me" or "Quinn called me the 'sh' word." Quinn would then get in the 'sh' word with his mom. She could be seen taking him by the arm and dragging him toward home crying.

It was obvious to all who knew Quinn that he wanted to do well but couldn't seem to let his talents shine in the classroom. It was also clear that he understood completely what the teacher wanted from him. No one could recite the classroom rules faster than he could: "hands on your own mat, sit still, listening ears, no talking, no touching other people's work," etc. Small wonder; he was reminded of them more than anyone else was. So why was he spending so much time having the other kids yell at him, his teacher disappointed in him, and his mom pulling him out of the playground?

Teachers and other adults hinted that Quinn might have an underlying issue such as ADHD. While this was a possibility, his parents were not willing to explore the issue. As his mom stated, "There is no way that I am putting him on medication at five years old so that Mrs. Buford can get through her weather chart. He is not the only kid in that class who can't wait to get out of there at the end of the day, and he is definitely not the only boy who doesn't listen. He's just the one that gets caught. Now he has the reputation of the bad kid and it's almost like she expects him to be bad."

There may be some truth to the mother's assertion. Research has shown that the more a teacher shows frustration and publically criticizes a child for being off-task or disruptive, the more that child develops a reputation and the likelihood of being rejected by peers increases (McAuliffe et al., 2009).

But what if Quinn's mother was wrong, and the teacher was not chronically criticizing Quinn in class? According to research (Mikami, 2014), a teacher can help draw positive attention to socially vulnerable children and help that child be accepted by peers by going out of their way to point out to the class a child's genuine strengths that are not related to his behavior such as his athletic ability or acting skills. Perhaps Mrs. Buford unabashedly praised Quinn in front of his peers and made daily attempts to raise him up and draw peers' and his own attention to the many positive aspects he brings to the classroom. Let's hope for all involved that Quinn's mom was a bit hard on Quinn's teacher. Let's suppose that the teacher had been doing her own reading outside of class time, and was actively behind-the-scenes trying to engage extra school support for Quinn.

With the insights of the school speech-language pathologist and a behavioral consultant, Mrs. Buford held a meeting with Quinn's parents. She gently brought up the idea that perhaps Quinn would have more success playing at school if he were paired with some of the more easygoing classmates for playdates at home to practice how to play more cooperatively. She felt that the sheer number of kids playing with him outside might be overwhelming for him. Mrs. Buford suggested that inviting a classmate or two over on the weekends might be a good way to build his social skills.

The parents' responses were interesting, "Oh no. I'm sorry; we can't. Our weekends are crazy with swimming and gymnastics. My husband coaches and we have out-of-town tournaments almost every other weekend." Playdates were not possible during the week after school either.

When Quinn's parents considered this option, it became clear that between Tae Kwon Do, swimming lessons, Kumon reading program homework, and dinner, the only thing left to have time for was bed. "I know it's crazy, but our schedule should slow down when swimming season is over. Do any of the boys in the class do competitive swimming?" asked his mom.

If you looked at Quinn's schedule, you would see that his parents had lovingly committed to supporting his physical needs and abilities. They attended the swimming, Tae Kwon Do, hockey, etc. as a family and cheered him on while he was doing what he knew he was good at. What's wrong with that?

Nothing—except that this lifestyle didn't allow enough time to help busy, physical Quinn learn to stop, look, and think about how his actions affected his peers and teacher. In other words, how could his parents slow Quinn down enough to help him with social perspective taking?

There are so many boys (and girls for that matter) who may or may not have an underlying neurological disposition toward being very active who spend most of their time moving and looking for cause-and-effect action. Actions like chasing, crashing, and playing ball games certainly teach children many skills. But the question is, at younger ages, do kids miss out on learning to think about other people's perspectives because they don't pretend and role play?

One of the great things about team sports or organized physical games in the school yard is that for children to really participate and even "win," they have to be watching to see what the other kids are doing. Team sports and group play require joint attention, turn taking, imitation, and even theory of mind if the game requires hiding or tricking another person.

It's no accident that when three- or four-year-old kids are playing soccer, for example, it looks just like a pack of wolves all chasing the ball in one group with one goal, "I wanna get the ball and kick it in the net." They haven't yet learned to think about what each player on the team can and should do. They may still, for example, need to better understand that the whole is more important than each part and that if I pass the ball to Jimmy over there, he has a better chance than me to get it to the net and score one for our *team*.

That's normal. As children have repeated exposure to playing as a team, they benefit socially from learning to think and do things cooperatively. With sensitive coaches, children also understand that while they may be faster than Cooper, for example, Cooper gets to play because it sucks to be on the bench all the time and that sometimes compassion is more important than winning.

But, do these preschool and kindergarten kids miss out on a chance to develop their social perspective taking because they aren't engaged in dramatic play? Quite possibly.

It can be challenging trying to get little people who do not seem naturally predisposed to engage with peers in this way to slow down long enough to participate in dramatic play. You can bridge these two worlds by bringing pretend into active games that your child is already playing.

Consider the classic "chase, run, and tag." You could play variations of this game with your child that include dramatic play elements. Add good guys and bad guys. Reverse loyalties and talk about how it's no fun to have to be the bad guy all the time doing the chasing. Pretend a crime has taken place:

- What was it? Who was the victim? Why is he upset?
- What would be a fair penalty if the criminal gets caught?
- How's he going to feel about it?
- Do you think after you put him in "jail" that he will do it again?

Those are all examples of the kinds of thinking that happen with dramatic play.

Maybe a volcano has just erupted. You know the only safe place, but you have to catch the people who are running away and tell them. Once you tell them, they will try to catch the other people too.

Use books, movies, and superheroes as springboards to expand into physical, dramatic play. Really, the options and variations are only limited by imagination.

And when things go sideways, as they often do, you can also support perspective taking by pulling the kids aside and talking through where it went wrong, how each person feels, and what they think they should do to make play go better.

Important phases of development are there for a reason. If anything gets in the way of exploring that stage, there are ramifications for the child. If a child is so physically driven that he misses out on dramatic play, there could potentially be consequences for fully developing social perspective taking.

Kids Who Build

This portion is devoted to the Lego-heads here. The future engineers. The world needs them, of course, but if you talk to the spouses of many engineers, they will tell you that the Christmas parties aren't the most fun.

Of course, this is said tongue-in-cheek, but there is a point to be made, and that is this: Dramatic play helps develop perspective taking at three to five years old. So if your child is exclusively building with Duplos, Thomas tracks, marble works, Gears, or Links, then he may have no trouble with joint attention, turn taking, and imitation, but might not have the same depth and frequency of exposure to flexible social thinking. This may sound familiar if you're a mathematical, engineering, linear-thinking type. Lack of exposure to flexible thinking can later develop into trouble with telling and understanding jokes, taking things literally, and misinterpreting idioms, sarcasm, and lying.

Flexible thinking leads to strengthened social perspectives and leads children into considering the following types of questions: What might that other person *think* about this? How might another person *feel* in this situation? If I am a baby going to the dentist for the first time, what might I say and do? This example was a real scenario acted out in a preschool among very concerned four-year-olds.

We humans like to do what we are good at, and so it follows that if playing with building toys is what makes your child shine and keeps his attention for long periods of time, then we should not prevent him from doing what he loves. But parents should be aware that too much of anything is not a good thing, and, at these ages, your child may be missing out on a critical stage in his social skill development. The question becomes how we should incorporate these dramatic, pretend elements into the kind of play he naturally gravitates toward.

It's also important to consider pairing your child with a friend who has similar interests but may encourage him to try different ways to play. Maybe his friend will build with Legos for a bit, and then encourage your child to come out and play "Olympics" on the trampoline, videotape each other being silly, or play superheroes.

If your child is building, and you want to incorporate flexibility, you could try the following:

- With your child's permission, add your own touches and flourishes to structures your child has made or suggest a small addition if including your idea is a big challenge for him at first. This will help encourage flexibility and acceptance of others' different ideas. You could encourage your child to consider adding a garden to his block tower or an amusement park or some toy people to live in it.
- Try adding a dramatic scene. Your son builds a Lego racecar, you get toy figures to be the audience, and it is the Indy 500. Talk about where the racers are from, who you think is going to win, and so on.
- Add characters to the situation. Your son has been working with gears, and along come little toy animals to play on the new, awesome "play structure" that someone built.
- Add new elements to blow his mind. Your son has often built excellent marble runs, but instead of sending marbles down the structure, try water, sand, little figures, or whatever your imagination can come up with to encourage flexibility.

The principal idea here is to expand your child's experience of play to create new ways of looking at what he usually does. You will, of course, keep including yourself in play by taking turns and participating. But by adding something you like and expanding play to include dramatic elements, you are stretching your child in new, flexible directions.

There are some interesting and evidence-based social skills programs that are centered around cooperative building with Lego blocks. Lego therapy is based on the idea of taking a child's natural interests and collaboratively encouraging peers to work on a single project (Owens et al., 2008). In this way, there are many opportunities for taking turns, noticing each other, compromising, complimenting, and empathizing when things don't work.

Flexibility can be further worked in when your child is not simply following a pre-ordained builder's "cookbook," but there is some room to try out things that your child has created.

Kids Who Prefer Screens to Toys

The Canadian Pediatric Association recently came out with the statement that "Too much screen time negatively impacts aspects of cognitive and psychosocial development and may adversely affect body composition." (Tremblay, et al., 2012). The association therefore recommends these guidelines: "Exposure to screen-based activities in children younger than two years should be discouraged. Toddlers two to four years old should be limited to educational programming of less than one hour/day. Families need to encourage movement in young children by reducing passive transportation (commutes by car or stroller) or time spent simply sitting or 'resting' during waking hours."(Lipnowski & LeBlanc, 2012).

Let's face it, in this modern world of video everything, it is not that easy to take this stance with children. The world of play and interaction for children has changed substantially in the last fifteen years since the first Baby Einstein videos came out. Now "educational" video games are available implanted into bouncy chairs via Newborn-to-Toddler Apptivity™ Seat for iPad® devices. What's next? Avatars for frustrated toddlers struggling with walking or toilet training?

Experts are saying that to be able to learn anything from the educational television shows and games, cognitively the child needs to be older than two years and to be able to draw on their experiences of direct social interactions (Richert, Robb & Smith, 2011). Further, there is no evidence that DVD viewing enhances cognitive ability of children under the age of two. Even Disney is now willing to refund parents who do not feel that their Baby Einstein DVDs fulfilled the educational claims that their advertising promised (*New York Times*, October 23, 2009).

While it's hard to envision what technology will look like for the next generation, it is clear that many experts are concerned about the negative consequences of screen time during the sensitive, critical period of development for young children under five and particularly among those under two.

There is much debate among experts about whether different types of screen experiences (DVDs, educational games, TV for entertainment, etc.), for different durations at different ages help or hurt young kids. Currently, it would seem that we really don't know for sure and are still learning. Dr. Michael Cheng, pediatric psychiatrist at the Children's Hospital of Eastern

Ontario, described the effects of technology on young children as a "great social experiment," since we have never before had access to or lived in a society where technology usage, both social and otherwise, was so pervasive, and we therefore do not know what the outcomes might be.

The genie is apparently out of the bottle, and screen time is now embedded in our culture. In this time of change and learning, it is wise to be knowledgeable about some of the potential negative ramifications of too much screen time on young kids, which are summarized here:

- early screen exposure associated with attention problems at seven years of age
- adverse affects on reading at age six among kids who viewed TV under three years of age
- decreased vocabulary
- negative impact on executive function development
- tendency toward decreased physical activity
- increased risk of being overweight or obese
- fewer opportunities for direct interaction with caregivers
- fewer opportunities for uninterrupted, focused play with toys
- fewer opportunities for direct play with others
- more potential for language delay
- increased risk of overall delays
- increased risk of behavioral issues
- increased risk of bullying
- increased risk of social challenges

    (Parkes et al., 2011, Christakis et al., 2004, Zimmerman et al., 2007, Katoaka, 2002, Schmidt et al., 2008, Strasburger, 2008).

Apparently, you don't even need to be watching the screen for it to have an impact on your family. Studies have found that approximately 30 percent of all American households have the TV on in the background all of the time. Just having a television on as background can lead to an average of 500 to 1000 fewer adult words spoken per hour (the average adult speaks 941 words per hour) and has been linked to significantly reduced parent/child communication (Zimmerman, Christakis et al., 2007; Vandewater et al., 2007). Exposure to words at home in the early years and subsequent vocabulary size has been described as a reliable predictor of academic success (Hart and Risley, 1995).

Ironically enough, many parents believe that one of the motivations for having the TV on or providing educational video games is to help children develop their language skills or school readiness abilities (e.g., letters, colors, numbers).

The Impact of Screen Time on Social Skills

Clearly, social skills are being developed between two eight-year-old boys sharing an iPad and playing Minecraft while waiting for their dentist's appointment. They are taking turns, using joint attention, negotiating who gets to go again, and learning how to give and receive advice, and they have an opportunity to complement each other or not support each other. These are all good social skills.

A game like Minecraft is constantly changing and fast-paced, and it requires a great deal of concentration on the *object*—but not the other player. Interestingly, these two young boys have not looked at each other once in the past ten minutes, though they are clearly enjoying each other and sharing the experience.

There are inherent problems with engaging infants, toddlers, or preschoolers in fast-paced, object-focused, all-engrossing, stimulation with virtually no need for eye contact. Those minutes—let's be honest, hours—spent absorbed in activities like this is time that is crucially not used actively interacting with the environment and with other people.

The compromise for parents here might be to first ensure their child acquires face-to-face social interactive skills during the critical first five years to ensure that he has an adequate social base. *Then* it is probably okay to expose their child to video games/screen time on a more regular basis.

Video games, apps and the like are powerful and engaging tools—and they're not going away. With older children, many social skills are supported, including teamwork, negotiation, and collective problem solving. However, younger children have different needs when it comes to communication, attachment, and social development. We want our children more attached to us parents than their iPads. As an illustration, let's look at Abdul, four, who came into the speech and language clinic with his mother because she was concerned that no one could understand what he was saying.

Abdul's mother and the therapist watched as he banged toys together, dumped toys out of containers, put things in containers, and climbed up onto the chairs and tables. He came across as a little boy who was very much on the move and self-directed in his play.

He talked almost constantly, but not to anyone in particular, and in a kind of run-on monologue. It was really hard to make out what exactly he was saying, and it was clear quickly that something was seriously amiss with this little guy. Things were complicated by the fact that he had been exposed to approximately 60 percent English and 40 percent Arabic, so some of the words were not in English.

As the therapist listened in closer and tried to engage and play with Abdul, it became apparent that the cadence or intonation of the sentences mimicked cartoon characters' voices. Mixed in were some memorized lines from TV...phrases like "No swiper, no swiping" (*Dora the Explorer*) and a strange mash-up of dialogue about saving the day from superhero movies such as *Iron Man*. But the words were smushed together without real meaningful content or effective communicative use.

With a growing sense of alarm, the therapist began the assessment and quickly realized that the reason this child was difficult to understand wasn't because he couldn't pronounce sounds. When asked to describe a typical day in the life of Abdul, his mom responded with, "Well, he gets up at around 8:00, we eat breakfast, he watches cartoons or maybe a movie, then we have lunch and he has a nap for two or three hours, we go and run an errand or two, and then he watches his show while I make supper, then dinner, bath, and bed."

When asked to clarify how many hours a day Abdul spent in front of the television, his mother replied, "Maybe four or five—all educational shows and some superheroes because he loves superheroes."

So, how many hours of prime education real estate does Abdul actually have in a day to play and interact with *real* people—not the plugged in kind? Here's the breakdown:

8:00 to 9:00: eat, get dressed, putter around

9:00 to 12:00: screen time (iPad, phone, computer, or TV)

12:00 to 1:00: lunch, TV on, books

1:00 to 3:30: nap

3:30 to 4:00: snack, TV on

4:00 to 5:30: out (grocery shopping, errands), in the stroller, not moving, not really interacting or exploring (sometimes playing games on ipad or Phone)

5:30 to 6:00: Screen time, while mom makes dinner

6:00 to 6:30: dinner usually (sometimes with TV on, especially if he is tired, cranky, or won't stay at the table otherwise)

6:30 to 7:30: bath, playtime, bed

Maybe an hour or two?

This little boy has had his physical needs met for sure, and his mom is a sweetheart who is insecure about her English, which, though accented, is excellent. She strongly wants her son to learn English, so she, with the best of intentions, uses TV as a teacher. This is a story that is played out every day in many households, and it is a big deal. In extreme cases such as the one outlined above, a child becomes fluent in "cartoonese" with little understanding of the words he or she is speaking and what words are even used for. The very big problem here is that TV is passive, not interactive. That means there is no back-and-forth communication, no exchange of ideas, and no exploration during a critical time in a child's communication development. Abdul has unintentionally been held back in his development, with the outcome being atypical language and severely delayed social interaction skills.

Babies, toddlers, and preschoolers especially need to interact with physical objects and real people to experience trial and error in their learning. They need to move their bodies and communicate with others to learn the names of things and to better understand *why* we communicate in the first place.

Specifically, we learn words as a means to an end. Without people to figure out what to do with the words you hear, you simply parrot words without function. In the early years of language development, children learn to communicate dynamically to protest and request, and then move on to commenting, and then to asking questions, answering questions, and so on. Abdul did make minimal requests during snack by pointing, but was so self-directed that he would climb onto counters to help himself to what he wanted.

So, as a result of the lack of face-to-face interaction, Abdul had developed into a little boy who didn't use the words he had functionally, was extremely independent, and was about three years behind in play. While he may have been a bit behind anyway because there was a family history of speech and language delay, his delays were now in the severe range. His atypical communication and severe delays may have been avoided if he had spent his early years parked in front of his parents, engaged in play with others, and had a chance to get out of the stroller, explore, and share experiences with his mom as tour guide.

The good news for Abdul and his mom is that with some stimulation, he learned and purposefully used two new words during just an hour of demonstration therapy. His mother was shown and encouraged to get on the floor with him in a face-to-face way, hold something that was of high interest (in this case, bubbles), blow them, and then wait expectantly while giving him a model to communicate that he wanted more—either with a wiggle, a sound, a point, or the word. Abdul's mom was delighted because he was delighted. His whole face lit up, and the two of them really had a chance to enjoy each other.

Mrs. Ali was learning how to do what her son wanted to do in play and engage in back-and-forth communication. Abdul was learning that playing with his mom is fun and that when he uses words, he not only gets what he wants (requesting), but he can alert his mom to what he thinks is interesting (commenting). He was beginning to see the value in sharing an experience with someone else as more rewarding than experiencing it by himself.

Mrs. Ali was also beginning to realize that *she* was the best teacher that her son could ever hope for. She was better than any educational television show, because she loves Abdul, she loves seeing him happy, and she can read his communication (verbal and nonverbal) better than anyone else because she is invested in her son more than anyone else is. The more time that she spent tuning in to him and learning what he liked to do, the better her teaching and his learning became. Abdul and his mom strengthened their connection, which is about so much more than just learning words.

Attachment and relationship building creates the perfect classroom for learning language. In the past, Abdul's mother had him watch his shows while she made dinner and did housework since those things were much harder to do with him around. Fair enough. Remember, however, that young kids learn so much by imitating us. They feel so good when they are included and can emulate us.

While it is harder to get things done efficiently with kids around, including our children in our chores and jobs is a great way to connect, and it is fun for them to learn from us. Making sure that both boys and girls learn how to do household chores also makes for better marriages when they grow up! Here are some ideas for including young children in household chores:

- When vacuuming, have your child "dust" with a Swiffer or wipe off furniture. Or give him a spray bottle of water and a rag. Talk about what you are doing while you are doing it.
- When tidying up, take turns picking up toys and sort them into bins. If it won't cause damage or be too loud, make cleanup fun by trying to gently "toss" items into the bins without missing.
- When making dinner, have your child "help" by washing vegetables.
- Give him some plastic containers and spoons to play drums with.
- Bring out some pots, pans, and pretend food to give him a chance to copy you.
- Have your child set the table; let him pour ingredients in the bowl—just get him involved in your day.

When Abdul came back after a couple of months of parent training and language stimulation, he was no longer "scripting" superhero/Dora jargon. His television watching had been reduced to half an hour a day. Abdul and his mom were also attending community-based play groups a couple of times per week to give him a chance to see how other kids his age played and to give his mom a chance to meet other parents. Abdul and his mom were now truly playing together, and he was learning so much more language.

Mrs. Ali had stopped selling herself short. She was better equipped to help him than she knew, and the two of them were really engaged in each other in a healthy, attached way. Abdul still needed some language intervention, but his skills in *communication* and *use of language* were much more appropriate. He was now making eye contact, seeking his mom out to show her things that he thought were interesting, and was really listening to her when she was talking because they were doing things that interested him. His play skills had moved from an infancy level (banging, dumping, throwing, and crashing) to imitating the kinds of everyday activities he was seeing at home. (He related toy food to a pot, for example, and pretended to stir and serve "soup" in bowls.)

Dr. Gordon Neufeld, author of *Hold On to Your Kids: Why Parents Need to Matter More Than Peers*, stresses the importance of parents being mindful of the amount of time that they let their children interact with "screens," be they educational iPad games, computers, phones, or TV, instead of actively interacting with their real environment and others. Preliminary findings in this area strongly suggest that for good social and mental health, our children need to be in environments where the dominant force is attachment to parents and not over-attachment to technology.

Put simply, we adults should be paying attention to this societal shift and be concerned about this digitization of childhood, particularly in the early years. When screens replace real interactions and attached, face-to-face relationships, where does that leave us, our kids, and our relationships? Who wants to live in a Brave New World where futuristic preschoolers are encouraged to play alone and communicate by muttering memorized scripts from Dora?

If you have concerns about screen time, you may want to do the following:

■ Pay attention to your own use first. Are you chronically distracted, always saying "Just a minute" to your kids as you check your smart phone? Consider putting your phone, laptop, or whatever away until the children are fully engaged elsewhere (e.g., in bed sleeping).

■ Make limiting screen time part of a "family initiative." For instance, say, "As a family, we are going to try not to use our devices from after dinner until bedtime."

■ Map out your child's day, keep track of how stealthily and steadily the minutes can creep into hours.

■ Consider only having wi-fi on for certain time periods in the day.

■ Engage your children to fully participate in daily activities—including the boring ones like unloading the dishwasher.

- Sit with your child and watch shows together. Use the pause button and ask him what he thinks might happen next.

- Use toys and props and reenact what you and your child watched together.

- If you find yourself using screens as a babysitter more than you would like, consider getting a live babysitter so that you can take a break or be more efficient in your daily life while your child has an opportunity to interact with someone.

- Remember that it's not just about how long children are tuned into screens, it's also *what* they are tuning in to. Not all televisions shows are created equal for kids. If and when your child watches TV, be sure to choose shows that are not too fast-paced, have good role models, have a simple story line that makes sense, are designed for your child's age, use good language models, and have good parenting/family models.

- Avoid shows that include violence or characters who are bullying or that are geared toward adults.

- Try to minimize background media noise, which may reduce the language your child is exposed to and overall learning.

SUMMARY OF RUNG 5:
Later Perspective Taking/Theory of Mind

In summary, you'll know that you need to continue to work on later perspective taking if your child has most of the following abilities/behaviors:

- Can share focus on the same activity over multiple turns (sustained joint attention)
- Can recognize and identify different emotions
- Notices peers playing and shows interest in what they are doing
- Can and does imitate actions and words in play
- Can participate cooperatively in dramatic play
- Can participate in a variety of dramatic play scenarios and may continue to have a preference for sameness but can include others' ideas
- May make assumptions that others just "know" what your child is feeling
- May make assumptions that others have the same knowledge about rules of games
- Seems to expect others to just "know" what your child wants and seems hurt or angry when others don't respond appropriately
- May have a lot of conflicts due to personalizing differences in perspectives (e.g., Harris is a "jerk" because he doesn't want to go outside too)

RUNG 6

Auntie Lou Won't Stop Talking:
Narratives

Can you picture this? It's lunchtime, you're famished, and the phone rings. It's a dear friend, but one who, shall we say, has never met a thought not deemed worthy of speech. Turns out she's feeling particularly verbally encouraged this day, and she starts telling you about something that happened at work. After about five to ten minutes of her talking at you, you just can't butt in to say you have to get some lunch. So you think...do I dare? You put the phone down, make yourself a sandwich, get a glass of milk, and come back. Only to find, as you had suspected would happen, that she didn't even know you'd gone!

Or, to flip that coin, how about this conversation with the "yup, mmmhmm" person?

> *You:* "How was the party last night?"
> *Yup guy:* "Fine."
> *You:* "Who was there?"
> *Yup guy:* "The usual."
> *You:* "Was so-and-so there?"
> *Yup guy:* "Yup."
> *You:* "Well, how did he manage to get released from jail?" *(Not really—just written for impact.)*
> *Yup guy:* "Mmmm hmmm."

Then there are the Auntie Lous. Everyone has experience with an Auntie Lou. Auntie Lou is a lovely lady who has the warmest face and most welcoming demeanor, but can't tell a story to save her life—or yours. Stories usually go like this, "Well now, that was the year that we took the bus to Colchester, or was it Westminster?" [Long pause.] "Yes, I know it was Westminster because of that big windmill…and it was so cold that we had to go in there, but we couldn't because it was closed…so then we…Well, maybe it was Colchester after all because Sasha was there." We've all been cornered by Auntie Lou at some point in our lives while we shoot lasers at whomever we came to the event with to be rescued.

And finally, there are the story masters. The ones who weave tales with words that take us right there with them. They know what to say, how to say it, and who to say it to with uncanny perception. They're like maestros—hitting all of the right notes with perfect timing. People with a gift for story telling have no troubles with social perspective taking. They know what the listener needs to hear, how to deliver the story in an organized, cohesive way, and how to pay attention to nonverbal cues to determine how much more they should or should not say.

Storytelling skills are a crucial part of social skill development, and narratives are simply stories: stories of our day, stories about something good or bad that happened, stories of things that happened to us or to other people. Narratives are important because they bind us to others; provide depth and intimacy in relationships. One might even say that if experiences are the bricks in a friendship's structure, the stories we share with each other are the mortar.

To be able to present narratives, children need a number of advanced language and social communication skills, including the ability to do the following:

- put together an organized memory of events,
- use complex language,
- take the listener's previous knowledge of the characters and events into consideration, and
- pay attention to the listener's nonverbal cues about his or her level of interest and the need for more or less detail.

Many children who can make friends initially but have challenges *keeping* them have difficulties with expressing their ideas in an organized, cohesive way. Retelling events and explaining ideas to friends requires the following:

- organizing thoughts into a beginning, middle, and end,
- adequately explaining what and who the main characters are, and
- being able to guess the information that others need to follow your train of thought.

Narratives also help kids develop stronger thinking skills so they are able to hold multiple ideas in their heads and organize and plan what to say. Those skills are also essential to be able to verbally reason through conflicts with friends. Retelling something that happened in the past also helps a child develop hindsight and the ability to review and reflect upon past experiences.

Developing Narrative Skills

Kids typically start telling stories in the preschool years. These stories tend to be pretty basic and require a lot of support from others. You might have experienced something like this: Your child runs up to you at the park and is crying.

> *You:* "What happened?"
> *Child:* "Hurt my (shows you) leg."
> *You:* "What happened?"
> *Child:* "Fall down."
> *You:* "Where did you fall down?"
> *Child:* "Falled off the slide."

As your child moves toward four years old, she may now be able to tell you a simple sequence of events that is about four steps long. Here's an example of how a four-year-old might describe making chocolate milk: First you get a glass of milk, then you pour in chocolate sauce, then you stir it all up, and the last thing you do is drink it.

When you begin to notice that your kindergarten-aged child participates in cooperative, dramatic play and is now using more complicated language and combining sentences, you'll see an increase in frequency and complexity of oral narratives.

Around the time kids are in kindergarten, their stories begin to have some cohesion and actually start to make sense on their own without you having to fill in all of the blanks. Stories about who got a time-out at school, who threw up in class, how they got the scrape on their knee.

Kids will also tell *on* you. Maybe that's why kindergarten teachers have show and tell. "Mommy said she was getting aspirin because she had a wine headache again"....Or, "Mommy was embarrassed because she put her skirt in her tights and went to work like that."

That's why parents should never go to kindergarten parent-teacher interviews. Who knows what your child has told about you!

Just as we grownups like people who can tell a good story with appropriate inclusion of detail, a problem, and a resolution, so too kids gravitate more toward other kids who are able to express themselves in a thoughtful manner that incorporates just what the listener needs to know.

Imagine you are in a kindergarten class at circle time and everyone is sitting on the floor. Each child is meant to tell about something that made her sad but then it got better. This is a classic oral narrative framework. Here is what a good story would include:

- Who was affected/who was the main character?
- Some details that set the scene
- What was the problem?
- A few details about the problem and why it was so bad
- The solution?
- The big wrap up

Here is an example of a kindergarten narrative done well:

- "Well, I was just a little kid—maybe one or two—and it was really hot." [intro to character]
- "My dad bought me a big, double-scoop ice cream and we sat down to eat it." [setting the scene]
- "My dog was sitting beside me, and then someone beeped their horn. It scared me and I turned around [makes the gesture] and my ice cream went to the side, and then my dog ate it!" [problem]
- "I wanted that ice cream so bad and waited all day for it. I started crying, and then my dad said, 'That's okay, I'll get you another one.'" [resolution]

Here are some examples of ways that young kids can struggle with spoken narratives and the ramifications for keeping friends.

The ice cream story told by that overly verbal phone friend at five years old:

"I was a little kid, maybe two or three, and it was summer and it was so hot! I had to wear shorts and no shirt because it was so hot! So I said, 'Dad, can I have an ice cream?' And he said, 'Did you finish your vegetables at lunch time?' And I said, 'Yes I did. I had carrots, some beans, and two cucumber slices.' Then my dad wanted to know if my mom said it was okay, and I said, 'Yes, she said that I could. '

"But then I was like, 'What kind of ice cream do I want?' I love bubble gum, but maybe I wanted cotton candy, or chocolate chip mint or strawberry cheesecake. I picked bubble gum and had a sample of peanut butter chocolate, but I hated it…etc., etc., etc."

This child certainly had an excellent memory and language skills, but her story-telling had two things that would prove alienating to her peers: too much inclusion of unnecessary detail and dominating the conversational floor for too long.

Ice cream story by "yup guy" friend at five years old:

"I got an ice cream. It fell off and the dog ate it. Then I got another ice cream."

Clear, well-organized, and to the point, but it doesn't generate much interest from the child's friends. In this version of the story, there is not enough inclusion of detail and no consideration of what might add some color to keep friends listening.

Ice cream story by off-on-a-tangent "Auntie Lou" at five years old:

"So then I had ice cream and then we were there—you know that place where they sell ice cream and I got some...I went there before with my friend Anne when we got gum but she didn't have enough money. I don't know what's next...No wait...then the dog ate ice cream and then Dad said I'll get more and it fell or maybe I dropped it or maybe...I don't know. I think it was in Florida."

The story is difficult to follow because it is not following a logical sequence of events and doesn't include enough appropriate detail. The storyteller has trouble staying focused on the main story and gets sidetracked by the bubble gum part.

Kids who are nonspecific may not be organized in expressing themselves, or may have challenges with staying on topic. They may also find that their peers don't wait around long enough to piece together what the message actually is, may simply override their story with their own, or may ignore the child and talk about what they are doing instead.

Some children simply don't have the expressive vocabulary to provide specifics when telling an oral narrative. Their stories might look something like this:

"So, then I went there and got that, that ice cream. And it was so good and it went there, and Dad said, 'Don't worry, I'll get another one.'"

Kids with challenges with vocabulary may use a lot of words like *that, there, here, it.* These stories can be hard to follow because there are not enough details to piece together the main idea. Again, when kids have these challenges, they are at risk of having peers ignore them, override them, or move on without understanding what the child was trying to convey.

Activities for Encouraging Narrative Skills

If you suspect that your child may have challenges with oral narratives, here are some different ways young children use them and some ideas on how to help them develop further:

Retelling something significant:

You can support your child's narrative development by helping her learn to talk about things that have happened or to describe things that she enjoys.

1. Try repeating back what your child has said to show you are listening and give her more time to think about what she is trying to say. For example, your child says, "Abe fell off the slide." You: "Your brother fell off of the slide and then he bumped his head."
2. Then expand on her ideas to help her understand that you have a different perspective to add. For example your child says, "He was running and crying." You: "Oh no. Poor guy. He was running and crying because it hurt, and I bet he was surprised that he fell. He goes on that slide everyday and has not fallen off before."
3. Also help keep her thinking organized and on track by asking leading questions before she has a chance to let her thoughts go astray. Your child: "He slides super fast and zooms like this (hand gesture), and I went on the climbing wall and then…. You: "He does slide super fast and so do you. I hope next time he will slow down a bit so he doesn't fall. What happened when he was running and crying?" Your child: "I gave him a hug." You: "Thank you for giving him a hug. I bet that helped him feel better. You are a very caring sister. Now tell me about the climbing wall…"

Retelling a favorite story from memory using the pictures in a book:

Your child doesn't have to be a strong reader to be able to look at pictures of a much-loved book and tell someone else the story. Your child can practice story retelling by telling familiar stories to younger siblings or to you.

Explaining a movie or favorite part of a show:

A very natural way to help your child to verbally summarize and organize an event is to watch a familiar, favorite video with her and run upstairs to quickly "do something." When you come down, pause the video and ask, "What happened while I was gone?" If your child has difficulty explaining, ask leading questions to help organize her thinking. For example, "When I left, Jack was just planting the magic beans. Now there he is up in the clouds. What happened after he put the magic beans in the ground?"

Telling/explaining steps/how to do something:

Teaching family members the steps for making things like toast or cereal or for brushing teeth offers an excellent opportunity for young children to feel knowledgeable, organize their thoughts, and include appropriate details.

What's great about these types of activities is that children need to be specific enough and include all of the steps or their instructions won't work. Adults being taught are encouraged to follow the steps exactly as the child tells you to do them. If your child is nonspecific and says "pour milk" but doesn't say "in the cup," you may pour milk on the counter instead. You will only have to do this once for your child to learn that what and how she communicates matters and that not including an important element can change the meaning. This kind of natural consequence in learning is the most effective method of reinforcing. Don't be afraid of a bit of mess. The best learning happens when things get messy!

Young children are so often told what to do and how to do it. It must feel so good for them when they have a chance to know more than other people do and be the boss sometimes.

Another good activity to encourage telling a sequence of actions is to have your child call or Skype relatives and teach Grandma, for example, how to do something. Grandma can begin and help organize your child by first making sure that she has everything that she will need to carry out the plan.

Let's take making chocolate milk as an example:

> **Grandma:** "Okay, Kailey. What do I need to get?"
>
> **Kailey:** "You need milk, chocolate, and a glass."
>
> *Grandma gets those things.* "Okay. Got it. Now what do I do *first*?"
>
> **Kailey:** "First you get the milk."
>
> **Grandma:** *(repeats back)* "Okay, first I get the milk. *Then* what do I do?"
>
> **Kailey:** "Pour it."
>
> **Grandma:** *(requests clarification)* "Pour what?"
>
> **Kailey:** "The milk, silly."
>
> **Grandma:** "Okay, then I pour the milk into the cup."
>
> **Kailey:** "Now the chocolate."
>
> **Grandma:** "Now the chocolate in the cup?" *(repeats and adds a detail)*
>
> **Kailey:** "Yup! Now it's chocolate milk!"
>
> **Grandma:** (clarifying) "Oh, that looks so good, but the chocolate is all at the bottom. What should I do?"
>
> **Kailey:** "You gotta stir it."

> *Grandma:* "Oh. Okay, stir it with a spoon. Let me get a spoon. Can I drink it now?"
> *Kailey:* "Oh yeah, now drink it."
> *Grandma:* "That's delicious! Thanks so much for telling me how to make this delicious chocolate milk, Kailey."

You can best help children become better storytellers by really listening to what they say, repeating back and adding elements, and not-too-intrusively asking requests for clarification.

Here's an example:

> *Child:* "Then Jack put the booby trap there…"
> *You:* "Wait! That is so cool! Jack had a booby trap?"
> *Child:* "Yeah, and he put it over there."
> *You:* "Over where?"

Using Books to Encourage Narrative Skills

There are also some excellent books that lend themselves to helping children develop the shape and form of oral narratives. Here are some recommendations of books you may want to use:

■ *Once Upon a Time,* by Nick Sharrat

This book and others like it create the shape of a narrative by introducing the character, setting, problem, and resolution. The child chooses from an array of pictures to change the story elements to keep it changing and interesting.

■ *Carl's Sleepy Afternoon,* by Alexandra Day

Really, any Carl the dog books are excellent for story retelling. These stories have very clear characters, settings, problems, and resolutions—all without words. The child can figure out what is happening from looking at the pictures.

■ *The Mitten,* by Jan Brett

All of Jan Brett's books follow a similar format of character, setting, problem, and resolution. What makes them particularly excellent for oral narrative development is that there is often a little cameo picture in the corner that helps the child predict what will happen on the next page.

When looking for picture books that will help your child develop the understanding of the basic framework of oral stories, look for books that clearly show character, setting, problem, characters' feelings about the problem, solution, feelings about the solution, and a clear ending.

Real-Life Applications

Narrative skills are also so important for children to verbally solve problems and be able to explain more complex ideas. It's clear that to be able to "use your words" to resolve conflicts, your child will need to be able to, for example, retell the teacher why Amy has a blue-painted handprint on the back of her pretty dress in a way that makes sense and gets to the point while offering up a good reason.

Just as kids need to practice their passing and shooting to improve their athletic abilities, they need to practice telling narratives so it becomes more automatic. Narratives become your child's internal mental voice, and when strengthened, they will dramatically increase your child's ability to think through social situations and sort through social conflicts.

SUMMARY OF RUNG 6:
Narratives

You'll know that you need to work on narratives if you child has the following abilities/behaviors:

- Can share focus on the same activity over multiple turns (sustained joint attention)
- Can recognize and identify different emotions
- Notices peers playing and shows interest in what they are doing
- Can and does imitate actions and words in play
- Can participate cooperatively in dramatic play
- Can participate in a variety of dramatic play scenarios and may continue to have a preference for sameness but can include others' ideas
- May continue to, but not as often, make assumptions that others just "know" what your child is feeling
- May continue to, but not as often, make assumptions that others have the same knowledge about rules of games
- May continue to, but not as often, expect others to just "know" what she wants and seems hurt or angry when others don't respond appropriately
- May continue to have a lot of conflicts due to personalizing differences in perspectives (e.g., Harris is a "jerk" because he doesn't want to go outside too)
- May leave out important details that you need to follow her retelling of an event
- May need the listener to work hard to draw information out of her
- May give too many details for you to *want* to follow her retelling of an event or explanation of something
- May change subjects abruptly without completing her thoughts
- May use vague vocabulary (e.g., "Then it went there to give that his thing")

RUNG 7

"Use Your Words" to Stop Bossy Ruby:
Conflict Resolution and Executive Function

It's a scene that is oh-too-familiar for parents. It's Saturday, and after a leisurely breakfast with your beautiful young family, it's time to get this day going. You have gone upstairs to brush your teeth, when you hear your four-year-old little girl's window- shattering scream, followed by your six-year-old son's indignant and hostile, "GIVE IT!" More screams. You wait, ears scanning. An unholy silence, and then SMASH. Now screaming times two. The dog is running upstairs looking for shelter, and you run downstairs to witness what can best be described as an eruption of Legos, hair pulling, and tears.

This sort of scene plays itself out in households everywhere, everyday. What might vary is how often and to what degree these explosive episodes take place. Learning to resolve conflicts, whether it be over toys, rules of a game, or being invited to play or not, develops over many years.

To be able to work through problems with a friend, a child has to coordinate the foundational social skills already described such as joint attention, identifying emotions in self and others, imitation, and perspective taking and then pull them all together using language that makes sense. Boiled down, a child has to coordinate his emotions, thinking, and behavior.

That, in its simplest form, is what *executive functioning* does. Like the executive of a company, your executive functions manage resources and activities—in this case your brain—so that you can achieve goals through your behaviors and actions.

When you coordinate emotions, thinking, and behavior, and apply them to other people, you have now created the most fertile ground for social skills to blossom.

Put another way, thinking impairments related to executive functions do not just affect an individual's ability to manage himself. They also directly affect his ability to interact with others.

Many, many children's challenges with making and keeping friends can be attributed to delays in, or disorders of, executive functioning. Sometimes kids are simply behind and need extra focused practice to catch up to peers. But sometimes underlying learning challenges are obstacles to being able to access and develop executive functioning fully and easily.

So, for example, a child who has difficulties with executive functioning might have trouble inhibiting himself and therefore act impulsively. He may jump up out of his seat during silent reading and do something silly to a friend that embarrasses him. Or he may drum on his desk without realizing he's annoying a classmate because he is not paying attention to her reaction or can't see things from her perspective. Or, he may have trouble changing gears and get stuck thinking about something the same way—like insisting that the group project has to be done a certain way even if the other students have come up with a different idea they want to try.

Because coordinating emotions, thinking, and behavior apply to so many skills and have far-reaching ramifications for how a person lives and behaves in this life, there is a lot of confusion about what executive functions are exactly. Experts have described executive functions as the "conductor of the orchestra," "the air traffic controller" of the brain, or the grand poobah (right, maybe not the grand poobah, but it's such a great term) of all of these skills. Dr. Joyce Cooper-Kahn, psychologist and coauthor of *Late, Lost, and Unprepared,* describes executive functioning as more like coordination of pathways in the brain working together—like riding a bicycle. She goes on to say, "When it works, the CEO has a master vision, reacts to changes, reallocates resources, steps back, and evaluates."

What Does Executive Functioning Have to Do with Erupting Legos and Hair Pulling?

In the opening story, strong executive functioning in both kids would have prevented the hair-pulling Lego fight from happening in the first place. And if a conflict did occur, the kids' mature executive functioning would have enabled them to problem-solve a mutually satisfying way out.

Let's imagine the same scenario, but this time Dad is able to magically freeze both children, press a magical button on each of their foreheads around their frontal/prefrontal cortexes, and activate mature executive functioning pathways.

Now he unfreezes his children and watches dumbfounded as darling daughter says, "Would you mind if I had a turn putting the wheels on the Lego truck? I loved how you did it last time and would like a chance to try it." Sagely, son says, "Thanks. That's really nice, but if you do it now, the structure might collapse because it's not yet reinforced. Would you mind waiting a minute while I attach a couple of other bricks?" Darling daughter responds, "Of course not. Why don't I just gather up the pieces for the next step while you finish? Then I can have a turn."

By now, you are probably thinking, "Tell me more about this executive functioning thing, and where do I get that button or freezing ability?"

According to Dr. Adele Diamond, research chair and professor of Developmental Cognitive Neuroscience at the University of British Columbia, executive functioning includes the following key components:

- *Inhibitory Control:* the ability to resist what you want to do because you should do something else (e.g., have a salad instead of the cheesecake or pay attention to the voice mail message even though the doorbell is ringing).
- *Working Memory:* the ability to hold information in your mind and work with it, despite being distracted or while doing something else (e.g., remembering the address while you punch it into the GPS).
- *Cognitive Flexibility:* being able to change your thinking and look at other perspectives (e.g., "Maybe he was right; maybe I should pay more attention to putting the sink stopper back properly").

Executive functioning has also been linked to emotional regulation—your ability to control your emotions. This means that thinking and feeling are closely related. What you think about a situation can determine whether you become overwhelmed emotionally and overreact. For example, if you burst into tears when another car cuts in front of you and nabs that parking spot at Wal-Mart, you may not be accessing your most appropriate executive pathways to complete the goal you have set for yourself (getting a parking space). In the same situation on a better day, you might think to yourself, "Perhaps that person didn't see me there—it is pretty busy today," and you are able to tame the emotional tiger that threatened to roar.

Executive functions contribute to the coordination of thinking before reacting and regulate our emotional responses to situations. As Leah Kuypers, author of *Zones of Regulation,* describes it, "Emotional regulation allows us to monitor, evaluate, and modify the intensity of one's emotional response" (Kuypers, 2014).

At its fullest, matured potential, executive functioning coordinates our thinking, feeling, and actions, leading to the sort of "magic" conflict resolution described above.

How Executive Functioning Develops

We are not born with fully developed executive functioning, but its development has its roots in infancy. Even infants who are between eight to twelve months old can resist the impulse to grab a toy that they can see through a clear barrier and problem solve a way to reach around the barrier and get it. And bilingual toddlers are flexible enough in their thinking to know which parent to speak what language to (Diamond, 2006). That being said, no two-year-old would ever pause and think to himself, "I'd better not grab this piece of cake now; it might spoil my supper." That inability to defer gratification and project the consequence of an action is what spurs a two-year-old to bite a playmate who won't give him the ball. Essentially, a two-year-old's executive is functioning in a sandbox and still wearing a diaper.

However, as children's language develops and as they gain experience interacting with others and with solving problems as they play with toys and people, they strengthen and develop their executive pathways. By the time that two-year-old is firmly into adulthood at around twenty-five to thirty years old, his functioning executive is now a business-suited CEO sitting right behind his forehead, managing the complex, myriad pathways that lead to emotional self-control and planned responses to social and nonsocial situations.

The good news is that we are always learning and adapting. From infancy we develop this higher-thinking system over many years, as we experience more of the world and as we problem solve with different people in different circumstances. As our language grows more complex, so too does the inner voice of our executive functions as we reflect on past experiences and plan next steps in social situations. Put another way, language development becomes the mental self-talk that guides our choices and behavior.

Here's another good thing. While working with your child on the rungs of the social skills ladder, you are also helping your child develop his executive functioning.

For social interaction to be "social," children's brains have to begin to employ executive functions. If children are not able to focus or to shift their focus from an object to another person, then that experience is not being shared or social in nature. Your gentle guidance in establishing joint attention (rung #1) during an activity helps your child attend to what is important, change focus to you, and ignore or inhibit outside distractions. Your guidance and modeling during this stage is what helps your child build the executive functions of inhibition of outside distractions and flexibility of thought by attending to you.

Developing a vocabulary related to emotions and learning to self-monitor them (rung #2) also helps your child with mapping emotional regulation to thinking and behavior.

Imitation (rung #3) helps your child mirror what another person is doing, which requires *focus* on someone else. While focused, your child needs to hold in his memory the sequence of actions or words that his play partner modeled (working memory). That too is an executive function.

At higher rungs that require perspective taking, your child needs more and more coordination of the executive pathways to allow him to think flexibly, remember sequences, inhibit his own interests, manage distractions and emotions, and interpret others' emotions as different than his own (rungs #4–7).

Here's a real-world example of the role that executive function plays in social conflict resolution:

During pretend play, children copy sequences of actions that they have seen in daily life, and, with more experiences in the world, these sequences get more and more elaborate. For example, your child pretends to get into the car (which is actually a chair), pretends to fasten the seatbelt, pretends to put the key in, pretends to find a station on the radio, and then "drives." Your child has just completed a five-step, organized, and *planned-out sequence*. That organizing and planning is related to executive functioning.

Besides using his executive functions to drive the chair/car, your child, a.k.a. "Daddy," is enacting a complex social drama in which the pretend baby (his sister) is going to daycare, Daddy is driving, and the baby doesn't want to go. Dramatic play demands *flexibility* of thought and *perspective taking*, which are also higher-thinking skills.

Let's say that your child (Daddy) and his sister (Baby) get into a disagreement because Daddy tells Baby she has to go to daycare, but Baby doesn't want to do that game anymore. Baby now wants to be the teacher and wants Daddy to be the baby at daycare. Daddy is pretty annoyed, but *inhibits his emotional response* (executive skill). Instead, he mentally identifies what he wants and what his playmate wants (flexibility of thought/perspective taking, also higher-level thinking), replays in his mind a previous, similar scenario, including recollecting what he said (inner narrative, also executive function), and comes up with a very flexible compromise that works.

Wow! Maybe "Use your words" isn't such a simple task. Who knew so much was happening to help your children learn to regulate, think things through, and apply their verbal skills to help them "use their words" to resolve conflicts?

Using More Than Just Words: Honing Conflict Resolution Skills

As children grow and socialize more and more with different people, the complexity of their language goes from two-word phrases (around two years of age; e.g., "No car") to sentences that hold more complex ideas at four years old, and even more, of course, when they're older. (e.g., "I don't want to go in the car because I want to play soccer.") By this age, their language ability and understanding of concepts have developed enough to support more complex attempts at conflict resolution with peers.

Children will now understand the concept of "why? because _____,"which is needed to help them think through their own and others' reactions. (e.g.,"Why is my brother crying? Because I won't let him touch my Pokémon cards.")

Your child does not necessarily understand these why/because concepts when he goes through the "why" phase, by the way. For example:

> *You:* "You can't go play until you drink your milk."
> *Child:* "Why?"
> *You:* "Because milk is good for you."
> *Child:* "Why?"
> *You:* "Because it has calcium and vitamin D and those are good for your bones."
> *Child:* "Why?"

More likely, your child is trying to figure out a thought process that is pretty complicated and is testing a hypothesis. Isn't that reassuring for all the parents out there who want to jump up and down yelling, "I don't know why! Just drink your milk, okay? Because, because, because!"

To which the child responds with "Why?"

You can now rest easy knowing that your child is developing higher-order thinking.

Children also need to build their organizational, planning, and delaying gratification skills to be able to resolve conflicts using their words effectively. One way children at these ages develop this is through understanding and using verbal sequence concepts. Sequences of actions refer to step-by-step processes that typically include important concepts of *first, then,* and *last,* or time concepts like *before* and *after.*

It is no accident that around this time of sequencing and being able to create verbal narratives, children are beginning to be able to answer "how" questions. An example of an everyday sequence might go something like this: "**First,** I brush my teeth, **then** I put my pajamas on, and the **last** thing I get to do is cuddle and read a story. " Or, "**Before** I tell Tony that he can sleep over, I have to finish my worksheet."

The more steps that a child can hold and understand in his head, the more he can begin to organize his thinking sequentially. Compare this to a game of chess. Verbal conflict resolution requires a sequence of events, a strategy, and a desired outcome.

Developing executive functions in young kids is kind of like that book by Laura Numeroff called *If You Give a Mouse a Cookie.* It is a picture book that clearly shows how one thing happens that leads to another thing, then another thing, and so on.

Executive functioning pathways begin in infancy and build upon each in kind, and one aspect leads to another and so on. Reframed in this context, the story might go like this:

- If my child can organize sequentially,
- then he can plan out his thoughts in a more organized way.
- And if he can plan out his thoughts in a more organized way,
- then he will be waiting a bit longer for what he wants to happen while he is planning.
- And if he is waiting longer for what he wants to happen, he is not acting as impulsively.
- And if he is not acting impulsively, he is inhibiting his impulses and delaying gratification.
- And if he is delaying gratification, he might not be so quick to overreact.
- If he is not overreacting, then he has the thinking space to organize and plan out a more "thoughtful" response to the conflict at hand.
- And if he is planning a thoughtful response to social situations,
- he will be thinking more flexibly.

- And if he can think more flexibly, then he might see his friend's perspective too.
- And if he can see his friend's perspective,
- he might be able to come up with a compromise of ideas that works.
- And if he can come up with a compromise that works,
- he is on his way to **Getting from Me to We**…
- and making and keeping friends.

When Saying "Use Your Words" Falls Short

As parents and our kid's first teachers, we begin to help children develop a vocabulary around feelings, conflict, and resolution almost as soon as they can talk. Think about how many times you have seen the following sort of scenario in your home, at friends' homes, at playgroups, or out in the community: Two lovely little two-year-olds are playing happily with trucks until Tyson comes over with a *garbage truck*. And suddenly Markus must have it. He must have it *now*. Markus grabs the garbage truck roughly from Tyson, and, well, you can guess how things go down from there.

Enter Markus's dad, who says, "Markus! Look at Tyson. He's crying and looks so sad. He was playing with the garbage truck first! Let him have a turn and then it will be your turn."

Or, "Markus… if you want the garbage truck, why don't you *ask* Tyson instead of grabbing it? Use your words."

Or, "Markus, you want the garbage truck and Tyson wants the garbage truck. Maybe you could trade Tyson your digger and he will give you a turn with the garbage truck."

Or, "Markus! Get off of Tyson's back and let go of his hair. The cops are coming."

In early years, parents teach their children about fairness, taking turns, sharing, offering trades, and vocabulary for expressing emotions. Especially when dealing with little people, it can seem as if you are playing a broken record with little effect. Yet you are modeling for your child how to develop higher thinking skills such as not overreacting, staying calm, sorting through the issue, thinking of alternatives, and mentally talking through next steps toward resolution.

As your child leaves the preschool years and moves into early school ages, presumably his language skills will allow for more complexity of thought to build on all of those previous years of figuring out what's fair with the garbage truck in the sandbox. Here's an example:

Sassy, confident Ruby, age five, bursts into the house center in her kindergarten class and says, "Okay, guys...We have just *got* to give David a haircut. His hair is a *mess* and we have to go to that party. Let me get my purse and we'll go."

Enter Hannah, with her executive functions on lunch break. Hannah says, "I want the purple purse and I want to be the mommy!" Here's what makes things even worse. Ruby *always* gets to be the mommy and she *always* gets to use the purple purse.

Ruby says, in character, "We can't always get what we want. It's time to go."

But Hannah has been waiting since circle time to get her hands on that purse and is now furious. Face getting hot and fists clenched, Hannah says, "Gimme that purse."

Ruby says, "NO! I had it first" and yanks it back.

Now the girls are engaged in a tug of war until the purse strap breaks and the teacher walks over, irritated.

When a child's executive functions are delayed, it is pointless for adults to intervene and advise the child to "Use your words" if he or she has escalated into fight or flight instinctive mode. Carefully guided reflection during a calmer period makes the most sense in those circumstances.

What if instead, Hannah's teacher and parents had spent a great deal of time supporting her executive function skills and working through issues in a socially accepted manner by using visual supports (see next chapter), books that highlight skills necessary, and on-the-ground learning. What was required of her mentally and emotionally to be able to figure her way out of the Bossy Ruby situation?

Hannah needed her higher thinking skills to be poised and ready if she was going to think through and verbalize a real solution, meaning either a compromise or an alternative. To be able to think through the conflict and come up with possible solutions, she first needed to be able to inhibit her anger and be willing to not get what she wanted right away. To suppress her initial, overly emotional reaction, she had to actually stop her thinking in its tracks and wait. Then, she needed to think things through.

Next, she needed to be flexible and redirect her thinking to what the source of the conflict was for her, and why the other person wasn't cooperating with her vision. Then, she needed to think back and visualize past experiences that were similar to the one she was in and what the end result was. Then, she needed to plan out an alternative, including visualizing and hearing in her mind what she would say and do and imagining how the other person would receive her idea. Then, Hannah needed to do it.

Small wonder so many young children bite and hit as a shortcut to the end result.

For the instruction "Use your words" to work as a conflict-solving strategy, it needs to lead to your child either providing a compromise or an alternative solution. And for that to happen, the following executive functions from your child are required:

1. Inhibiting/suppressing an emotional response (e.g., "I want to kick her in the pants and grab that purse, but I won't"). This requires children to stop what they are thinking and find emotional space to pause before acting on their impulses. Practice during role plays and non-stressful times, showing your child by saying out loud that you are going to stop, take deep breaths, and calm down when you are upset and practicing with a visual reminder (maybe a picture of a stop sign) can help with this.

2. Processing the problem inside of himself and trying to imagine what the other child wants. This requires your child to stop merely reacting to the situation and realize he needs to find alternatives. Is he able and willing to stop, change, and be flexible? Dramatic play, incorporating flexibility of thought into play, perspective-taking building, video/book review, and collaborative problem solving, can help here.

3. Visualizing in his mind's eye similar past experiences. Visual strategies can help with this (see the next chapter).

4. Planning out an alternative or a compromise. Practice using visual strategies, narrative development, collaborative problem solving, books and videos to teach, and active listening can help children with this skill.

5. Predicting what the proposed solution will look like. Visualize and formulate in your child's internal voice what the words will be and what the effect will be. Narrative development and visual strategies help with this.

6. Doing it! (Requires courage and motivation.)

Let's imagine that Hannah's executive functioning is charged up and ready to go.

Hannah says, "Hey! I'm the mommy and I get the purple purse!"

Ruby, with her hands on her hips, says, "Listen, Missy, I'm the mommy and I need the purse or you can't play!"

Hannah, irritated, stops and inhibits her initial Hulk-like response. She identifies her problem: she wants the purse. And she identifies Ruby's problem: she also wants the purse and to be the mommy. Hannah then remembers and visualizes in her mind's eye the last time she was in the house center—the time when she and Ruby got into a fight over the purse and broke the strap.

The teacher told them both to go read a book instead, and she wasn't invited to play with Ruby and her friends at recess.

Hannah decides on another approach and mentally talks through and visualizes telling Ruby her plan and Ruby agreeing. Then Hannah puts her idea into action and says, "Why don't you be the mommy going to the haircut, but then I get to be the mommy who makes dinner when you get home?" Hannah can see that being the mommy is important to Ruby, and she came up with a compromise to ensure fairness to both. Yay, Hannah! She did nab that purple purse when Ruby got "home" from the haircut, by the way.

Use Your Words to Help Young Children Learn to Use Their Words in Conflicts

The best way to work with your kids on verbal negotiation, problem solving, and predicting outcomes of behavior is in the course of daily life. That means you deal with problems on the ground, in the moment. Most kids, but especially children with social challenges need your guidance and modeling to sort through conflicts with their friends. It is simply too overwhelming to figure their way out of highly charged situations on their own. That is not to suggest that we adults step in and solve the situation for them, but rather, help systematically work through what happened, the impact on each person and options to resolve the situation.

Sometimes, when kids look stuck or you think things may soon escalate to a dangerous level, you have the opportunity to step into conflict between kids and catch the disagreement at the "tipping point." When that happens, a consistent cue such as "STOP!"…"THINK"…"WHAT'S THE PROBLEM?" can help a child halt a too-strong reaction in its tracks. Then you can help the child reengage his thinking ability to construct a more appropriate interpretation of the social situation and response.

In highly charged situations, instinctive fight-or-flight rage may cloud your child's ability to *receive* your wisdom. In these situations, it may be a better plan to help your child work on problem solving after the incident is over. That is, you can help him reflect on what happened, talk through what happened and possible reasons why it happened, and come up with possible solutions for the next time. Clearly, to be able to work through problems this way, a child needs strong verbal narrative abilities, as described in the previous chapter.

Narrative practice will allow your child to develop that inner voice that he will use to mentally talk out problems and potential solutions. Approaches such as Collaborative and Proactive Solutions, outlined in Ross

Greene's book *The Explosive Child,* provide a framework of adult verbal support that encourages children to learn and develop better thinking paths through explosive situations.

Books to Help with Conflict Resolution & Perspective Taking

Reading books that show characters working through conflict and provide examples of different perspectives is a great way to help your child learn and reflect on the skills necessary to socially problem solve. Try to look for books that highlight a misunderstanding or that have a subtext that your child will need to pick out to understand what is happening.

Here is a book list in developmental order from youngest (three and a half years) to oldest (seven years) that highlights skills that may help with facilitating social perspective taking, identifying and resolving conflicts, and exploring more complex emotions:

- *It's Mine,* by Leo Lionni
A simple picture book about not wanting to share, conflict resolution, and feelings.

- *No David,* by David Shannon
David gets in all kinds of trouble in this book that addresses problem solving, conflict resolution, feelings, and perspective taking.

- *Olivia,* by Ian Falconer
Not surprisingly, strong-minded Olivia's perspectives about what should be done are not always the same as her mother's. Explores different perspectives, thoughts, and conflict resolution.

- *Grumpy Bird,* by Jeremy Tankard
Grumpy Bird is, quite frankly, grumpy, and his friends show remarkable commitment to problem solving and finding a resolution. A surprise ending encourages perspective taking and flexibility.

- *I Was So Mad,* by Mercer Meyer
The main character's parents just don't understand in this cartoon-illustrated book focusing on conflict, resolution, and exploration of feelings.

■ *There's a Nightmare in My Closet,* by Mercer Mayer

A conflict between a little boy and his "nightmare" results in surprise perspective, exploration of feelings, and a resolution.

■ *Good News, Bad News,* by Jeff Mack

Conflicts abound between an optimistic bunny and his more negative friend. Lots of opportunities to explore different perspectives and resolutions.

■ *The Day the Crayons Quit,* by Drew Daywalt

The crayons are all fighting and have different ideas about how to get along.

■ *Goldilocks and the Three Bears*

Issues covered include conflict, perspective taking, taking/using things that don't belong to you, and theory of mind—what do the bears know?

■ *The Little Red Hen*

Hen didn't give Pig, Dog, or Duck any bread. Is it fair that the hen did all the work of making the bread and her friends wanted to eat the bread without helping?

■ *How Do Dinosaurs Go to Bed?* by Jane Yolan and Mark Teague

Parent/dino-child conflicts, resolutions, and opportunities for perspective taking and conversation.

■ *The Three Little Pigs*

There are actually a number of versions of this classic story from a variety of perspectives, including one where the wolf is actually the nice guy and the pigs vicious. Of course, the conflict and resolution are quite gruesome (cooking the wolf!), but flexible thinking is always available. What other solutions could help the pigs and that hungry wolf? Maybe the pigs teach him about vegetarianism? Maybe the wolf gets a free ticket to an island far, far, away? This book can also provide a springboard for conversations with your child around fairness, motivations, etc.

■ *Little Red Riding Hood*

The conflict in this well-known story is that the wolf would like to eat Little Red Riding Hood. The resolution is maybe not the best, but it's still an excellent story about perspective taking (helping grandma because she's sick, wolf is hungry) and theory of mind (the wolf tries to trick the little girl; what does the little girl know?). Story can also be used to promote flexible thinking and problem solving: What could Little Red Riding Hood offer the wolf to eat instead as a compromise?

■ *Alexander and the Terrible, Horrible, No-Good, Very Bad Day,* by Judith Viorst and Ray Cruz

A funny, realistic story that is good for exploring typical family conflicts, resolutions, feelings, and perspective taking.

Executive Functioning: The Good News and the Bad News…

When you examine how complicated resolving social conflicts is for kids, it's no surprise that this is an area that many vulnerable children can get stuck in for years.

The good news about these executive functioning delays is that development is ongoing. Many children have the potential to catch up in the executive functioning department. The bad news is that some children's development may not be happening at the same time as it is for their peers, so delays may contribute to their challenges in keeping up and standing out socially (Cooper-Kahn, 2015).

Another big issue for children who have social skills challenges related to executive function delays is how their difficulties are perceived. All too often, adults do not see their difference as being brain-based, but rather behaviorally based, and therefore within a child's control. As a result, adults often have unreasonably high expectations for managing emotions, thinking, and behavior based on their expectations for classmates who don't have executive functioning delays.

On the outside, a socially challenged child may walk, talk, and look like a six-year-old, but his executive functioning skills may be 40 percent behind and still at the preschool level (Barkley, 2014). These huge disparities in children's EF skills are most apparent among peers in classrooms during typical brain-based, "developmental surges" that occur around kindergarten, fourth grade, and in the later years of high school (Cooper-Kahn, 2015).

Russell Barkley, an expert in ADHD and executive functioning, says that all children, regardless of diagnosis, who experience executive functioning delays and subsequent social skills challenges, should be given continual support to help them compensate for their delays. He states, "The key is to design prosthetic environments around the individual to compensate for their executive functioning deficits." That is, just as students wear glasses or contacts if they have trouble reading the board at a distance, so should classrooms be designed to support kids with delayed executive functioning. The idea behind using external supports is to create as even a playing field as possible for children with executive functioning issues in the classroom to allow the same opportunities for successful interaction and learning. As children learn and change, the supports need to be adapted, reduced, or enhanced as demands change.

There are many ways input and environment can be modified to support children with social skills difficulties due to executive functioning delays. The most common is the use of visual strategies. The next chapter illustrates how adults can use visual strategies to support kids who stay stuck too long in navigating social conflicts, whether due to problems with executive functioning or issues covered in earlier chapters.

SUMMARY OF RUNG 7:
Conflict Resolution

You'll know that your child is getting ready to be able to use his words effectively during conflicts with peers when he:

- Notices peers playing and shows interest in what they are doing
- Can share focus on the same activity over multiple turns (sustained joint attention)
- Can recognize and identify different emotions in himself and others
- Can identify why he might feel a certain way in certain circumstances. (e.g., I'm disappointed because I can't play outside after dinner)
- Can identify a reasonable theory about why someone else might feel a certain way—even if it differs from his own reaction (e.g., a classmate is crying because he is afraid of thunder, and your child loves thunderstorms)
- Can and does imitate actions and words in play
- Can participate cooperatively in dramatic play
- Can participate in a variety of dramatic play scenarios and may continue to prefer sameness but can include others' ideas—even if he doesn't like them or particularly want to do them.
- Can verbally relate a short sequence of events (e.g., first I _____, then he_____, and last he_____)
- Can verbally retell an event with a beginning, middle, and end and the right amount of detail

- Can verbally explain with the right amount of detail a problem and what might happen if he tries a possible solution
- Can identify that someone else may want, think, and feel differently than he does and come up with possible reasons why
- May continue to, but not as often, make assumptions that others just "know" what he is feeling
- May continue to, but not as often, make assumptions that others have the same knowledge about rules of games
- May continue to, but not as often, expect others to just "know" what he wants and seem hurt or angry when others don't respond appropriately
- May continue to have conflicts due to personalizing differences in perspectives (e.g., Harris is a "jerk" because he doesn't want to go outside too)
- May continue to respond to differences using "black and white" thinking (e.g., Anna didn't want to come over to my house after school and went to Natalie's instead—"I hate her! Or "She isn't my friend anymore." Or "She hates me now and is Natalie's best friend now.)"

CHAPTER 8

How to Create a More Even Playing Field:
Using Visual Strategies to Support Executive Functioning and Social Skills

Visual strategies will help your child to develop her mind's eye, to increase her ability to mentally visualize past experiences, to problem solve, and to reduce anxiety about expectations in new environments.

Instructional and compensatory use of visual strategies was pioneered by Linda Hodgdon, a speech therapist (usevisualstrategies.com), in her work with children with autism. She was one of the first professionals to notice that children with autism often learned best when words were paired with pictures. Her work has inspired teachers and specialists all around the world to use picture schedules in classrooms, visual timers to let children see how much longer something will go on, charts, visual lists, and so on.

Although visual strategies are often associated with teaching kids with autism, they actually benefit all children—especially those who struggle socially in a busy classroom. Use of visual strategies can support children who:

- have trouble with organizing and planning,
- may need things to be "just so,"
- have language challenges,
- have behavior challenges,
- are English as a Second Language learners,
- have recurrent ear infections/hearing loss,
- are inattentive

- are physically active, or
- in general are demonstrating delayed executive functioning

They can also help adults, and pretty much everyone.

What Are Visual Supports?

Essentially, visual supports involve using pictures, real objects, and written words to *show* kids what we want them to know, rather than just telling them. Visuals help children to better organize sequences of actions, which draws on the executive functions of organizing, planning, and predicting. For example, using pictures, photos, or words to create a "things to be done list" helps young kids develop organizing and planning skills. Children can actually see what is coming next, have the satisfaction of taking off or crossing off the item that is finished, and know when they have completed the task without a grownup nagging them to do things over and over again.

When visual schedules are used at home for daily routine tasks, parents encourage independence in their children and reduce nagging fatigue.

Most commonly, teachers create visual schedules of things that will be happening in the course of a day. For example, a line drawing schedule in a first grader's cubby might list the following activities:

- backpack up
- put agenda book in the bin
- go to the mat and read a book
- circle
- language arts
- snack
- recess
- science bins
- lunch
- and so on

Visuals give children who have trouble listening or understanding language an extra tool to help develop their understanding.

Using visual supports can teach kids who have trouble waiting to learn to delay gratification a bit longer because they can see how much longer until the task is done and what will happen next. Using visual timers on the microwave, specialized timers that show in red how much time is left to wait, or timer apps helps children see that they are capable of holding off on what they want. Here are some specific examples of visual strategies that will help your child see and better understand waiting, planning, and delaying gratification:

FIRST...THEN Visual Schedules

Using First...Then visual schedules helps to clearly outline for children what they need to finish before they can have a reward. For young nonreaders you can tape real objects to paper or use photos. For older readers, you can simply write the words down.

As an example, you might write the word **FIRST** in bold, black marker on a brightly colored piece of construction paper and tape a toothbrush to the paper (for a very young, nonreader). Then, beside the **FIRST** paper, you place a piece of construction paper in a different bright color with the word **THEN** written on it and a Hot Wheels car duct-taped to it. You can then help to organize your child and teach her to defer gratification by modeling and showing, "First you brush your teeth...then you can play Hot Wheels."

Timers

Phrases like "One more minute" or "Five more minutes, honey, and then we're leaving" are pretty much meaningless to young children who have very little sense of time. It's even more challenging for children to understand if you are like most people and use the "one more minute" cue loosely depending on how much fun you are having talking to your friend, finishing checking your e-mails, etc.

Using low tech timers such as the clock on the microwave or a kitchen timer can help physically show your child how much time is left. If you want a timer that gives even more visual information, you might consider ordering a Time Timer or Time Tracker.

The **Time Timer** visually shows in red how much time is left before something happens, the activity changes, etc. The red area gradually decreases in size until it vanishes, and time is up. The Time Timer can be ordered at Timetimer.com. There are also apps for iPhone, iPad, and Android devices with the Time Timer feature.

Time Tracker is also an excellent timer option, as it shows in a color-coded way how much time a child has left: green meaning plenty of time, yellow meaning a bit more time, and red meaning the activity is going to stop very quickly. The colors mimic a traffic light, and there are sound options and, perhaps most important for parents, a pause button. A Magnetic Time Tracker is also available. Both versions can be ordered from the manufacturer at www.learningresources.com.

By using visual timers, children better develop their own concept of how much time one minute means (no, you actually won't have time to go swimming before leaving for school…) and reduce the bad kind of surprise that happens when Mom or Dad suddenly looms large in front of the child's face and insists enthusiastically that it is time to go NOW!

Let's face it, many young children with social skills issues struggle with flexibility and may find changing activities and time judgment particularly difficult.

Using timers, and even better, encouraging young children to set their own timers to help them measure time and change activities can lay down an excellent foundation for time management, deferring gratification, and planning skills as they get older.

Remember that waiting skills can be strengthened so that children are less reactive and demanding in social situations with peers. "Me now!" responses can be stretched into more socially acceptable responses such as "Me…but a little later. " Many people who have highly reactive young children have used timers successfully to time the length of turn a child gets before it is a sibling's or friend's turn.

Video

Beyond timers, you can use visual supports to teach social conflict resolution when your child has had time to cool down and is no longer in "Hulk Smash" reactive mode.

Video and the pause button are a powerful combination in helping children learn to interpret social conflict and brainstorm solutions during calm moments. For example, to build thinking skills that can carry over into the schoolyard, watch YouTube clips with your child of children in conflict. Some good examples include the following:

- "Double Trouble," by Simon's Cat
- "My 2 Year-Old Fighting with his 2 Year-Old Cousin"
- "Toddler Car Jacking," by Adrienne Wallace
- "You Poked My Heart," by Tara Willmott
- "It's Too Heavy: An Oscar-Worthy Toddler," by Cr8zy family
- "The Olive Branch: COLD," by Pablo Smith
- "Classic Sesame Street - Ernie Counts Fruit," by sawing14s
- "Sesame Street: Robin Williams: Conflict," by Sesame Street
- "Snoopy in a Bad Mood"
- "Social Skills Training: Resolving Disagreements," by TDSocial Skills (for older children)
- "Social Skills Training: Taking Turns Speaking," by TDSocial-Skills (for older children)

When watching video with your child, you will want to hit the pause button to ask questions such as these:

- Why is he angry?
- What does he want?
- What do you think that he should do?
- What do you think will happen next?

You could try videotaping a couple of five-minute clips of your child once in a while during playdates (with parental permission of course), at recess, or while playing with siblings. Try to catch the kids playing well together for review and discussion later. You will want to notice turn taking gone right (or wrong) and the positive or negative effects on play partners.

You will also want to point out facial expressions and talk about what happened right before that led to that facial expression (e.g., if one child is laughing suddenly, you could ask your child what was funny, or if one child looks angry, ask what happened that caused that). It is totally okay if your child is unsure why her friend was angry. This provides an opportunity to speculate and talk about the kinds of things that rightly or wrongly may create that response in a friend and what the plan would be if it happened again next time.

Video clips act as a springboard for discussion about what works when playing with a friend, what doesn't, and what to do about it.

Sometimes parents direct kids to role-play conflicts and film it. Catching a conflict on video and reviewing it later can also be a powerful tool.

There are a number of reasons why video can work well in helping children:

- Kids love to see themselves, so there's an instant "hook."
- Getting kids to role-play gives them a chance to experiment and figure things out in a safe environment.
- If reviewing a conflict, you can give kids a chance to try out the same situation differently with a plan (after things have had a chance to calm down) to allow them to experience success.
- Highlighting an opportunity to catch kids in good social interaction, when they are being particularly kind or empathetic, is so important in reinforcing the behaviors you are looking to develop.
- If you think that your child might have trouble reading nonverbal cues or body language (e.g., interpreting what crossed arms or a frowning face means), you can ask questions like, "Do you think _____ liked that? Let's look at her body and face and see if there are clues that show us that she was unhappy."

Using Stories as Visual Supports

Using photos, pictures, and written words can be powerful in helping children understand the actual rules of the game and the social expectations in playing the game with a friend as well. For example here is a story template that young children could follow:

Playing Pop-Up Pirate
By _____

- First you put all of the swords in the holes. [page 1]
- Who will take a sword out first? [page 2]
- Now it is _____'s turn to take out a sword. [page 3]
- Now it is _____'s turn to take out a sword. [page 4]
- Be careful when you take out a sword. You don't want the pirate to come out. [page5]
- The game is finished when the pirate pops out. [page 6]
- Tell your friend that was fun. Then you can ask, "Do you want to play again?" [page 7]

You can also use simple stories to help figure out how to handle conflicts before they happen. Here's an example of a story that explains and helps a child to plan out what she should/could do if both she and her friend want to be first.

Who Goes First When We Play Pop-Up Pirate?

- I like to be first when I play Pop-Up Pirate. [page 1]
- Kyle likes to be first when we play Pop-Up Pirate too. [page 2]
- We can't both be first. [page 3]
- Sometimes I feel mad when I am not first. [page 4]
- When we both want to be first, we could play "eenie meanie, miney, moe" to decide. [page 5]
- That is fair even if I don't get a turn to go first. [page 6]
- If we play two games, then I will go first the next time. [page 7]
- I can wait patiently if I have to. [page 8]
- I love Pop-Up Pirate and can wait. [page 9]

Each page would have either a photo that represents the words or a drawn picture made by both you and your child. The beauty of reviewing this story during calm moments is that you can come up with possible solutions and a plan in advance with your child. You may choose to review the book right before a playdate. That way, if the issue raises its ugly head during Pop-Up Pirate, your child can be reminded of the plan already in place and not have to come up with it in the heat of the moment. In the example above, it was decided that "eenie meanie" or "choose a hand" would be fair.

Here is an example of a very simple picture story for a three-and-a-half-year-old who hits his brother when his brother takes his toys.

No Hitting
By Brady

- I like to play trucks. [photo of Brady playing trucks happily] [page 1]
- Noah likes my trucks. [photo of Noah loving Brady's trucks] [page 2]
- Sometimes Noah takes my truck when I'm playing. [page 3]
- I might feel angry. [page 4]
- Sometimes I even want to hit Noah. [page 5]
- No hitting. [page 6]
- I can trade. [Photo] [page 7]
- Noah likes my truck. Noah is a baby. [page 8]
- I can give Noah a different truck. [page 9]
- Then Noah is happy and I am happy too. [page 10]
- The End. [page 11]

Realistically, even if Mary Poppins faithfully reviewed stories like this with Brady, there would still be fights with his brother over trucks. You can use stories and pictures to help explain and reflect back on highly charged social situations, though, and reduce the frequency of conflicts. This kind of story is very helpful to review when your child is calm, and no longer in "Hulk Smash" reactive mode.

Social Stories

This idea of using a story format to help deal with kids' interpretations of social situations and provide an overall context for kids to understand their own and others' behavior was originated by autism consultant Carol Gray in her 1991 book, *Social Stories,* designed to help children with autism spectrum disorder.

True Social Stories have a very specific outline that is followed to help explain and respond to a problem that a child is experiencing. Social Stories are designed to further explain the "why" and "how" of social situations. Social Stories are created to give examples of appropriate responses and help more literal children by providing a clear but flexible road map to deal with challenges in interpreting social information. The overall tone of these stories is positive, individualized, and specific to only one situation at a time and gives a concrete example of solutions.

Given that Social Stories can help with decoding social situations with peers, their benefit is not limited to children with autism. Modified Social Stories and variations of these types of explanations help all children understand their own and others' behavior and plan what they can do during challenging circumstances.

Social Stories can be used for children with language delay, children who have challenges with flexibility and need things to be "just so," children who may react quickly and with heightened emotion to social situations, children who feel more secure with a plan in place, and visual learners who simply understand and remember better when they can see the words in action (e.g., with photos, pictures, words).

Using Visual Supports to Help with Transitions and Sudden Changes

Ariana, first introduced in chapter 4, was a little girl who sometimes had trouble with changing activities during her swim class. The well-meaning but inexperienced teenaged instructor for the little dolphins' class was at his wits end trying to get her to follow the routine of the class. When all of the little dolphins were practicing dives, Ariana didn't want to get out of the pool. When she was finally encouraged to start diving, she didn't want to get back in the pool to practice with the flutter board. Finally, when the lesson was finished and it was time to dry off and get dressed, Ariana was, of course, more than a little reluctant to leave the water.

The instructor was ready to boot Ariana out and insist on one-on-one classes instead, but her parents were keen to keep her in because she needed work on friendship building as well. Her parents decided to create a photo schedule for Ariana to help prepare her for what she was supposed to do, give her a framework to better understand her routine, and keep her focused on the task at hand. They began by taking photos of the changing room, the pool during warm-ups, diving practice, flutter board practice, free swim, the changing room, and then their car.

Her parents reviewed the schedule with her every day before bed for the week leading up to the lesson. After every activity, her parents reviewed what they had done and what was coming. Ariana would "swoosh" the picture away when she had completed a task and verbally tell what was coming next.

The transformation at Ariana's next class was remarkable. This challenged little girl changed from shark to very cooperative little dolphin in just a week. The teacher didn't have to correct her all of the time and was no longer drawing her peers' attention to her for negative things.

When there were challenges and misunderstandings with peers, her parents again made little books with photos that they reviewed with Ariana every night before bed and immediately before going to swim class. One night during swim practice, the diving board wasn't open because it needed repair and was unsafe. The diving board sadly was Ariana's favorite part, so she was of course very upset. The thing about Ariana at this stage of her life was that she seemed to get upset more easily than other children; her outbursts were louder and lasted longer.

Her parents wisely rode out her tantrums and decided that during her meltdown was not the best time to try to teach her to be flexible in her responses to disappointment. However, they took a few choice photos using their cell phones and came up with a little story to share with her at bedtime and right before class to help prepare Ariana for unpleasant, unexpected surprises at swimming. The story went something like this:

The Diving Board at Swimming

I love jumping off the diving board so much! [photo of Ariana diving]
It is my favorite part of swimming class.
Sometimes the diving board is closed because it is broken. [photo of broken diving board]

I feel disappointed when the diving board is closed.

Tim [the instructor] will find something else that is special to do that is super fun. I could ask for pool noodle fights instead or flutter board races. Those games might help me feel better and stop thinking about the diving board.

Mom and Dad can take me to the school pool on the weekend to use the diving board there instead too.

Maybe the diving board will be open next week.

I can find something else to do that is fun, and then maybe I won't feel so disappointed.

The End.

Going over the story really helped Ariana figure out other options and helped her come up with a repertoire of more positive strategies that she could draw from when she was upset in the moment.

These "stories on the fly" offer an excellent tool to help your child better understand her feelings and other peoples' feelings and reactions, organize her world, and plan her activities and responses. They are kind of like little guidebooks to self-regulation and social perspectives of others.

Young children benefit most from simpler stories with only one or two lines of text per page and picture support. There are now many wonderful apps, such as Pictello, that allow you to move photos into a book format. A slide show on your computer will work just as well and is simple to do.

If that seems a bit much, then simply drawing the pictures for or with your child achieves the same benefit and can be a lovely activity to share. As an added bonus, when you create stories together, you and your child can describe a wanted behavior, model options of responses, personalize the story, review it before situations arise to help prepare your child for situations, and look at it over and over again.

Wrap-Up of Part 1:
Social Skills for the First Seven Years

Here is a summary of the major skills kids need to be successful with interpreting social cues appropriately from infancy to about seven years. These skill categories constantly support each other, and are continually developed throughout a lifetime. As we mature, we accumulate experiences in attending and using all of these skills, which leads to wisdom in our interactions with each other.

From earliest to latest, these are the major skills:

1. Joint Attention:
This term refers to the preference for attending to faces rather than objects, which begins in infancy. You know your child is developing joint attention skills when he or she actively includes you in an activity by looking at what is happening and checking back with you to make sure you are looking at the same thing.

2. Emotion Recognition/Identification:
This set of skills includes 1) recognition and understanding of facial expressions and nonverbal body language, such as shaking your finger or head to express disapproval and 2) identification of simple emotions.

3. Imitation and Turn Taking in Play:
Young children first imitate others' body movements and sounds; later they are able to imitate words and sentences. Turn taking provides the op-

portunity of shared experience that is needed for imitation to develop. It helps increase the amount of time a child spends doing the same activity in the same way together with another person, which directly supports imitation development.

4. Pretend Play: Flexible Thinking

For toddlers and preschoolers, engaging in pretend play is key to developing flexible thinking. In the kindergarten and primary years, dramatic play helps children become more flexible in their thinking.

Signs that your child is developing flexible thinking include the realization that different people like and dislike different things and will act on those preferences. At this stage, your child can recognize that others don't necessarily want the same thing he or she does (toddler years and ongoing).

Other signs of flexible thinking include development of a thinking vocabulary. Your child understands and uses words like *idea, know, think, remember, guess, wish,* and *hope.* This develops in preschool through early kindergarten years (Sussman, 2006).

5. Theory of Mind:

When children develop theory of mind, they understand that not everybody knows the same things as they do. They also understand that everyone does not necessarily think about the same things in the same ways. Children start to develop theory of mind at around age four and up.

6. Narratives:

Narratives involve telling another person about something that happened. Ideas are organized, and the story has a beginning, middle, and end. Children with narrative skills lay out who the main characters are and can presuppose what the listener needs to know. Narratives become the internalized mental voice that we all use to think through complex situations. This develops in the kindergarten years and on throughout childhood.

7. Conflict Resolution and Pulling Together Executive Functions:

Combining executive functioning skills with a child's narrative abilities is what is required for children to "use their words" during conflict resolution. Executive functions are the thinking skills that enable us to plan actions appropriate to a situation, predict the possible outcomes of our actions on others, and to control impulses that may not be well-received by another. The foundations of executive skills begin early in life when parents say things like the following to curious toddlers: "Don't touch!" (inhibition), "Put on your boots and then you can go outside," and "You need to share your ball." Executive functions continue to develop into adulthood until around the late-twenties (or early thirties for late-bloomers).

It is important to remember that for all children on these rungs, we can support their learning to coordinate their thinking, feeling, and behavior. We can do so by: 1) talking about what is happening and 2) providing structure, routine, and extra visual support in the environment to help remove barriers to learning and facilitate executive functions.

Books to Help Illustrate Skills for Different Rungs on the Social Skills Ladder

Here is a list of books that can provide a framework to help your child develop one or more of the items on the social skills ladder. The list begins with younger children's stories and leads up to stories for children up to seven years of age. Of course, age guidelines are simply suggestions. All of these books can be adapted up or down for each child's actual level.

■ *Hug,* by Jez Alborough

Sometimes the simplest stories pack the most punch. This book only has one word, *HUG,* but tells a big story about feelings, perspectives, and problem solving in a very organized, sequential manner. Great first book for story retelling.

■ *Fast Food Vegetable (photography),* by Saxton Freymann and Joost Elffers

These beautiful photos of vegetables carved and modified to look like all kinds of different things encourage flexible thinking, as in things aren't always how they appear to be.

■ *Do You Like Ketchup on Your Cornflakes?* by Nick Sharrat

What's fun about this book is that it makes absurd pairings and encourages discussion about likes versus dislikes and about flexible thinking. Great activity to try for real: Does your child like to eat ketchup on cornflakes?

■ *Boo Hoo Bird,* by Jeremy Tankard

This bird has wonderful friends who literally bend over backward for him to try to solve his problem. The story touches on emotions, problem solving, and flexible thinking.

■ *Harry the Dirty Dog,* by Gene Zion

It really is Harry, but his family doesn't know it because he is so dirty. Provides lots of examples of different people who know different things (theory of mind), feelings, and flexible thinking.

■ *Goodnight Gorilla,* by Peggy Rathman

A simple story with an excellent framework for practicing story retelling/narratives. Also, the cheeky little monkey tricks people, which highlights theory of mind—the zookeeper doesn't know that the gorilla is behind him.

■ *The Gruffalo,* by Julia Doaldson and Axel Scheffer

This book is so wonderful, as it can be interpreted on many levels. If your child can pick up on all of the nuances, understand the tricking and theory-of-mind situations, you can be confident that he is well on his way to being able to put himself in someone else's shoes.

■ *Mmmmm...Cookies,* by Robert Munsch

The boy knows that the cookies he is giving out are made of play clay, but everyone else doesn't. When the teacher figures out what is going on, she turns the tables on the little boy and resolves the issue. Excellent book for exploring that different people know different things and act on what they know.

■ *That Is Not a Good Idea,* by Mo Willems

Fox knows that what he *really* wants to do is lure the mama duck so he can have her for dinner. Plot twist at the end: mama duck knew all along what the fox was up to and tricks him instead. Targets theory of mind and perspective taking.

■ *Knuffle Bunny,* by Mo Williams

A wonderful, simple but powerful book about differences in perspective between a baby and a dad. How does Trixie feel? How does Dad feel? What is Trixie trying to say? Why doesn't Dad understand her? There are also opportunities to explore theory of mind: Trixie knows the Knuffle Bunny was left in the dryer, but Dad doesn't.

■ *Stella and the Sea,* by Marie-Louise Gay

Stella the big sister sees the same situation differently than her very anxious little brother does. Encourages perspective taking and flexible thinking.

- *Rudolph the Red-Nosed Reindeer*
  This classic story covers feelings of exclusion, loneliness, perspective taking, and conflict resolution.

- *Not a Box*, by Antoinette Portis
  A box is so much more than a box. It can be an airplane, a car, etc. The book encourages flexible thinking and pretend play. Reenacting pages from the book with a real box would be a great activity to encourage these skills.

- *Scaredy Squirrel* books, by Melanie Watt
  The little squirrel is initially anxious about everything, but finds out the world is not as scary as he thought. Encourages perspective taking, problem solving, and more complex emotions.

- *Chester,* by Melanie Watt
  This super funny book engages Chester the cat and the author in an epic battle of who gets to write the book. Excellent for perspective taking and conflict resolution.

- *A Bargain for Frances,* by Russell Hoban
  Frances's friend manipulates her and tries to trick her, leading Frances to discover what a real friend is and isn't.

- *Anansi* books
  In these books, which are based on African folklore, the main character, Anansi, is involved in situations in which what people say is not always what they really mean.

- *Trouble Talk,* by Trudy Ludwig
  An excellent book that focuses on how gossip can be hurtful.

Summing Up

And there you have it: seven rungs for seven years. Each rung, however, is not an annual rite of passage. Sometimes kids have one leg on one rung and the other on the next. Classrooms, with their significant social demands, can sometimes make a child's abilities seem lower than they actually are. In other words, your child may be socially stronger and higher up on the ladder at home or with specific play partners. Children's development is not always so linear. The important thing here is to be able to understand how all of these skills are needed and interrelated to create friendships in the early years of school, and how these skills build upon each other as the child gets older.

Important adults in these kids' lives need to explain, interpret, and act as a "nonjudgmental GPS" (Cooper-Kahn, 2014) or "portable frontal lobes" (Greene, 2005) to help their kids navigate their social environments. We can do that by modeling good social examples, using words to support children's interpretations of social situations, and by putting concrete and visual compensatory strategies in place.

Let's move on to the schoolyard and put this all together.

Part 2
Taylor-Made Tools for Recess Success

CHAPTER 9

Getting Ready for Recess

At Thornhill elementary, a little boy in grade two had cancer. This class of seven-year-olds had, for the most part, been together since junior kindergarten—so, about four years. The kids knew each other well, and there was a strong sense of community within this group. Nurses came into the class to explain what chemo was and how it would affect Steve and to answer any questions. The classmates listened earnestly and were empathetic.

Steve was tired a lot and sometimes "spacey" because of the drugs, but he was still a happy, little seven-year-old boy. He wanted to be like all the other boys in his grade and to be included in around-the-world soccer at recess and play Beyblades. The boys would give Steve extra turns when they played these games, carried his sled up the hill without any grown-up telling them to do it, and decided to let Steve be the judge for races when he was too out of breath to run.

Some of these same boys stole things outright from each others' backpacks, pulled their friends off the monkey bars roughly enough to make them cry, and swore regularly—and Steve did some of these things too. These same thoughtful boys openly criticized and excluded each other frequently. Physical roughhousing gave way to uncontrollable laughter in the space of five minutes.

Recess can be crazy. It's free time with countless opportunities for stealth cruelty and beautiful kindness. There are so many different kids with different perspectives bumping up against each other. For better and for worse.

The world's stage is played out during every recess at every school.

Creating a Climate of Empathy

Author Barbara Coloroso, an expert on bullying, says this about the schoolyard: "We don't get a hate crime all by itself; we have to be taught to hate. The schoolyard can be the beginning of verbal bullying which dehumanizes."

Think about that word *dehumanize*. It means that one child sees another child as less than human. Once a child views or is viewed through that lens, the bully-bullied dynamic takes root. This dehumanizing is an alarm-blaring emergency, and we adults are called upon to be frontline responders in this crisis of spirit. We can do that by demanding a radical insistence on a classroom culture of empathy and perspective taking as *the* most important aspect of curriculum.

Several formal programs have been developed to help make classrooms empathetic. These programs are unfortunately not in widespread use, so your child is unlikely to encounter them at school. Why have we not, as a society, prioritized these programs more in our classrooms?

According to the UN convention on the rights of a child, article 19 promises children, "You have the right to be protected from being hurt and mistreated, in body or mind."

Every time we knowingly place a socially vulnerable child (and the incidence is at least three children per classroom) in an environment that cannot ensure their emotional, let alone physical safety, we bystanders contribute to a human rights violation. Children who are chronically ostracized, emotionally and physically shunned, or tormented in overt or covert ways are being mistreated both by their peers and the teachers we entrust to care for them. Teachers and parents need to be educated about what is out there that can better inform our policy positions and insist on better treatment for our children. But we can't advocate for what we don't know about.

Mary Gordon began her career in 1981 as a kindergarten teacher in Toronto, Canada. Early on, she grew alarmed by the gap between young children who entered kindergarten equipped with confidence in their ability to navigate the classroom community and those who, for a variety of underlying reasons, were already defensive or apprehensive in their approach. To reduce this disparity, she created an internationally recognized program called *Roots of Empathy*. The program is so successful that she has been asked to present at the World Health Organization, has won the Order of Canada and multiple prestigious teaching awards, and has had an audience with the Dali Lama himself, who stated, "Programs such as Roots of Empathy have the capacity for building world peace."

Boiled down, her program includes bringing a real newborn baby into a classroom weekly until the infant is about a year old. A relationship between the students and infant is fostered and a positive model of nurturing is demonstrated by the parent and explored by the teacher. By bringing a vulnerable baby into the classroom regularly, Gordon actively challenged the students to "learn about their own emotions, the perspectives of others, understand the power for resolving conflict that lies in being able to see a situation and the world from another person's viewpoint" (Gordon, 2005).

Programs that were originally designed to help children with specific challenges have also been used to increase empathy in classrooms. For example, a study completed by psychologists in British Columbia and Virginia (Mikami et al., 2013) compared two programs for school-aged children with ADHD. One program called COMET (Contingency Management Training) trained the children with ADHD to behave in a way that was more socially acceptable. The other program, called MOSAIC (Making Socially Accepting Inclusive Classrooms), provided behavioral training for ADHD kids, but also included training for peers and teachers to be more socially inclusive.

The results indicated that especially for boys with ADHD, both programs worked equally well for improving behavior. What was significant, however, was that peer ratings were much more favorable after MOSAIC training, and there was a carryover effect of more inclusiveness in general. It would seem that the training may not just benefit the targeted classroom. Students without ADHD seem to have internalized inclusiveness—which may lead to increased tolerance and acceptance in future classrooms with other students with challenges.

Only by making kindness cool and teaching children how to see the world through others' eyes at as early an age as possible can we offer up a hopeful alternative. If we want to teach respect and collaboration, we adults must also become more mindful of how often we subtly and not so subtly lead with intimidation and domination. If we want to teach children not to dehumanize, we adults also must be mindful not to cultivate an "us" (good kids) versus "them" (bad kids) mentality.

As Mary Gordon says on classroom inclusiveness and the importance of fostering it, "Making room for those who have been excluded, with all their needs and aspirations, takes nothing away…The reverse is true. We are all enriched" (Gordon, pp. 160–61).

Bullies and the Bullied

We know that it is usually the child who overreacts or lacks friends who seems to be a beacon for children who are looking to gain or maintain power, often through aggression and force.

Bullies have been described as kids who take pleasure in dominating others, chronically place their own concerns above others', and are more likely to transfer blame to others. This approach can trap children into focusing only on their own perspectives.

Children can become bullies as a response to having been bullied by adults—including adults in the school system or by other children who are more socially insecure and explosive. Some bullies have been shown to have stronger-than-average social skills, but without the empathy to build healthy relationships.

Whatever the reason, there are kids who are vulnerable to being exploited and kids who are vulnerable to doing the exploiting at every school. And that bullying can be subtle but insidious, as shown in this next example.

It was at the school barbecue that Jackson's dad saw firsthand the complexities of the kindergarten social hierarchy and power structure. Parents were standing around talking about summer plans and the prices of summer camps, handing out popsicles to over-excited kids, and simply enjoying the late spring afternoon.

Jackson was waiting for his popsicle with his buddy "Don" (as in the Godfather) when Taylor ran up with a huge smile to say hi. Don looked pointedly at Jackson and said, "Don't say hi to Taylor." Jackson's dad, watching all of this, was waiting for his son to greet Taylor, who had just said hello to his son for a third time. Jackson turned his back to Taylor and told Don, "C'mon, I don't want a popsicle anymore…let's go on the monkey bars" and ran off. Taylor looked crushed.

Jackson's dad, feeling terrible, tried to repair the situation. He told Taylor, "I don't think Jackson was paying attention. I'm sure he didn't hear you." Taylor mumbled something unintelligible to the grass, both of them knowing that that just wasn't true.

Jackson's dad then went over to his son, pulled him aside, and asked why he didn't say hi to Taylor. Infuriatingly, his son had apparently suffered from unexplainable amnesia. When his dad reminded him of the multiple times Taylor had said hi and how Jackson had then run away without responding, Jackson explained, "Everybody thinks he's a loser."

And he was. A loser in the social lottery.

But Jackson was also a "loser." He had "lost" the opportunity to demonstrate empathy, social perspective taking, and being courageous in the face of wrong. In fairness to Jackson, he was more than a little afraid of Don. He was rightly afraid of committing social suicide by aligning himself with the outlier and, as a result, becoming an outlier himself.

Don was also a "loser." It would be easy to cultivate a real dislike for this child, but he was not an evil little boy, nor did he have terrible parents who should be blamed. His truth was that he was born to lead. He was gregarious, funny, intelligent, and getting drunk on power. His "powers" needed to be quickly directed to include empathy, or there would be a great deal of kindergarten carnage before the year was through. Also, with some empathy development and focus on understanding the impact of his actions on others, he could become a strong force for good in the lives of his classmates. Children left to their own devices will not necessarily choose a path of goodness: think *Lord of the Flies*.

This is, of course, a simplistic synopsis of a complex dynamic. The bottom line is that there really is no one-stop solution if we are to really put a dent in this issue by building skills on both sides of the bully/bullied equation.

What Can We Do to Make Bullying Boring and Kindness Cool?

We are failing our children with simplistic responses like the antibullying strategies of having kids just ignore bullies or "walk away." Let's get real. It is simply asking too much. Would *you* be able to walk away and just ignore a boss who berated you, isolated you, or assaulted you almost daily? Would you have the courage to stand up to defend someone else if it could make you a social outcast?

Before you think, "Of course I would," ask yourself if you stand up against malicious gossip when you are invited into the inner circle at work. Do you speak out when given an opportunity to belong by participating in scathing gossip about a weaker coworker or social outlier? Are you able to resist the temptation to participate in mean gossip that puts down others to build you and peers up, especially when you are feeling as if you are powerless and want to fit in?

Many adults—like kids—fail those tests every day. When faced with the ugliness of human nature, we adults can be sanctimonious in our positions, but often we don't practice what we preach. Just look at some of the bullying that goes on during political campaigns and in the reality TV shows we watch to "relax and be entertained." We adults need to be mindful of the meta messages we subconsciously send to our children about power and relationships.

If we agree as a society that we want bullying to truly end, we must also agree on the fundamental need to strengthen *all* of our kids. The bullies and the bullied are both struggling to be valued and looking for strength in all the wrong places. Our children should not go through their school years just trying to survive and minimize damage.

We need to increase supervision and engagement from adults and older kids on the playground and in the hallways. We must advocate for the right to emotional and physical security of our kids at school. Increased security should be combined with an unwillingness to tolerate physical or verbal abuse among peers as well, especially since most bullying is covert and occurs when watchful eyes look away. But that is only going part of the way.

Do we need to step in? Absolutely. Do we need to step in more often? Of course. However, and this may be where things get stirred up a bit, it is important to consider that no formal adult-formulated social program, bullying program, recess program, etc. can *really* penetrate this wild territory called recess. Because these are kids we are talking about, and we are not kids.

This is not to suggest that we throw our hands up in despair and leave our most vulnerable children to fend for themselves. It is important to consider that every time a grownup steps in, we are imposing adult perspectives into a child-led world. As much as we think we "get it," it is impossible to go back and to think like a kid. Every time we try to remember what it was like, we remember from the framework of our adult maturity and experience.

We can and we must instead do our best to be social anthropologists in the schoolyard. That means that we need to accept that each class has its own hierarchy, sets of norms, values, expectations, and culture.

Before we ever enter this class culture and attempt to evangelize, we need to accept that it is right and good for kids to participate in and develop their own communities. That doesn't mean that we don't have valuable insight and wisdom to impart; it's just that we need to pause and reflect on what our grownup track records are when we blindly enter a foreign culture and then impose usually unwelcome "wisdom."

If we want to have respect from the kids we want to help, we have to lead by giving respect. Let us begin by not assuming that kids are doing it "wrong." Instead, let us observe the culture unfold and think about how to build *all* of the kids up from their positions of need as *they* define them.

If we do this, it means that the kid who is repeatedly rejected learns how kids in his culture enter into play that is already in progress and how to be accepted by the group. It means that the kid who is rejecting others in his culture learns better empathy and perspective taking. It is an acceptance that we are all weak and strong and have something to learn and teach. So with these notions in mind, let's think a bit about how to navigate the social jungle of recess at your child's school.

What's the Culture Like in Your Child's Classroom?

Consider these questions as you observe the culture of your child's school and classroom:

- Do you know the kids your child spends most of his day with at school?
- Who does your child like? Who does he not like and why?
- What do the kids in your child's class like to play at recess?
- Who plays with whom?
- Who hates whom and why?
- What does your child like to do at recess?
- Is it with the same kid(s)?
- Who gets teased? Left out? Who doesn't play?
- Does your child like recess?
- When your child gets into arguments or even physical fights, what's it usually about? How does it end?
- Who is the silliest kid in your child's class?
- Who goes to the thinking chair the most?
- Who is the nicest boy in your child's class? Girl?
- Does the teacher know what the kids in his or her class like to do at recess?
- Can the *teacher* answer these sorts of questions?

In other words: "Who's hot…who's not? What's hot…what's not?"

You can drill your kid with questions after school, but it is most likely that he will either be unable or unwilling to answer these questions.

If you've ever asked a five-year-old while driving him home what he did at school that day, the answer was most likely "nothing." Or when you animatedly asked, "How was school today?" you received a cryptic "fine."

School for young kids is a lot like the scene in that movie *Fight Club* where Brad Pitt utters the famous quote that goes something like this: "What happens in Fight Club, stays in Fight Club." Translated for seven-year-olds, it goes, "What happens at recess, stays at recess."

The reality is that the "What did you do at school today?" question is so broad-based for young kids that they probably don't even know where to begin to tell you. Usually when you actually get news, your child will report exceptional things like this: "Joey peed his pants at circle" or "The teacher brought in her parrot today."

Volunteering and Observing at School

So, if you really want to get insight into what happens at school, you need to go on a cultural expedition and voyage into your child's world. You can do that by volunteering *in* your kids' class, instead of just reading to children in the hallway. Volunteer to be a teacher's helper in the corner of the classroom, cutting out alphabet letters or whatever, so that you can quietly see how your child is *really* doing in school.

If the volunteering is a fairly regular thing, kids will begin to normalize your presence and it will not throw off the typical dynamic. You will also begin to gain insight into the social dynamics of the group and how your child fits into it. If you absolutely can't free up a couple of hours to volunteer due to work commitments, you may want to enlist the help of a trusted parent who does volunteer or enlist a grandparent—anyone who has your child's back and is a reliable observer

A word about possible problems with volunteering: some teachers do not welcome parent participation. That in itself should ring alarms. Given how much society expects from our teachers these days, you would think they'd love some help. A teacher who appears insecure about having parents in the classroom raises questions, especially if your child is having trouble in that class. If your child is struggling, there is no one who is more of an expert on your child than you, and no one better able to provide insight into who your child is. Those insights should be welcomed and incorporated into your child's school experience to make things better.

It can also be very helpful to pick your kids up from school regularly, even if it's once or twice a week. This after-school time will give you a chance to inconspicuously see with whom and how your child interacts, to get to know some of the other parents, and to establish a network for playdates.

If you are fortunate enough to live in a neighborhood where the kids go to school and play outside together regularly, then count yourself blessed. The reality for many children today is that they are scheduled with extracurricular activities and live in different neighborhoods. They just don't play outside after school on the street like children used to.

Figuring Out Who's Popular

We can also learn to support our children by identifying the social Olympians in their classrooms and learning from them how to prop up the kids who need extra support.

When you think back to your primary school days, do you remember who the popular kids were? What do you think made these kids top dog in the classroom?

While every class has its own culture, the characteristics those cool kids possess tend to be repeated across preschools, kindergartens, and early primary classrooms across generations and communities.

In general, popular kids know how to enter a play situation in progress, don't draw negative attention to themselves too much, and, while they aren't afraid to defend themselves, can let conflicts go. They can come up with compromises, and once they have a posse of friends, they are more shielded from bullying, which is often only successful when the bully can isolate and then attack. Not being a target of bullying automatically ensures raised status and power in the classroom hierarchy.

Social success is also attained differently at young ages depending on gender. Let's take some time to explore how the boys and girls who are strongest socially relate. This can help us learn how to prop up the children who are struggling.

The Most Interesting Man in the World at Recess

(Boys: bravado, posturing, bragging, to be able to create a persona in boy world…)

Do you know the advertisement for beer in which the debonair, worldly man flanked by beautiful women says, "I don't always drink beer, but when I do, I prefer Dos Equis"?

What makes him so compelling, beyond his handsome face and worldly expression, is how he speaks so matter-of-factly about his outrageous experiences and triumphs. The most interesting man's typical day includes freeing angry bears from painful traps, riding camels in the Sahara, and bench pressing beautiful women to keep fit.

If we were to remove fifty years or so, what would the world's most interesting *boy* look like at recess? The tagline for his commercial might go something like this: "I don't always play soccer, but when I do it's World Cup." He can steal the girls' jump ropes, make funny faces without getting caught, win an arm-wrestling match against a kid in sixth grade, and complete a 10,000-piece Lego death star by himself.

In competitive boy world, this kid gets points for simply being the best at everything and on the edge of challenging authority. Macho comparisons happen between boys in every schoolyard, every day. After school, watch just how often boys compare who has the best Pokémon or who can run the fastest.

There is a boundary between the socially desirable amount of comparing and posturing and what will be perceived as too much. Most boys figure out what the right amount is by violating the unspoken rule and learning from it. In other words, boys have to walk a fine line, and they usually find out how much bragging is okay through trial and error. Figuring out these rules is sort of like trying to avoid setting off invisible laser security lines at the Louvre. Boast too much, and the boy will be rejected, especially if he doesn't have the skill or résumé to back it up. A bit of lying is expected, with inflation rates roughly estimated to be about 10 percent on average based on informal observation. If a boy doesn't boast, the other boys won't respect him as much. The most successful boasting appears to have an appropriate amount of inflation and builds up the other boys around him too.

Ian, surrounded by his buddies at recess, demonstrates his mastery of embellishment. He says, "I can lift maybe fifty pounds—you know, with those metal weights—and Ethan can lift like seventy or eighty pounds because he does gymnastics." (Bear in mind that Ethan probably weighs seventy pounds soaking wet.)

Carlos responds, "No beepin$%$$ way! That's so heavy!"

Ian, sensing that he may have inflated a bit too much says, "Yeah, well, I can do it when I've been working out a lot."

What Ian did so eloquently was inflate himself just the right amount while boasting about his best friend Ethan. By making Ethan even better, he has doubly raised his status by elevating himself and the person who likes him best.

Carlos, sensing power, raised himself right along by inserting a juicy expletive and complimenting Ian and his friend.

Helping Kids Who Aren't the Most Interesting Boys/Girls—Yet

For children who may be more literal-minded, this kind of posturing may feel false and unnatural. The need to compliment or even rank peers may simply not be on their radar. Complimenting and telling "white lies" to make someone else feel better requires a child to recognize 1) what another person would like to hear to feel good, and 2) how the need for the lie outweighs the need to stick to the facts.

Intense, active children may lean toward exaggerating too much, stretching the lie too far, or being too hurtful in their putdowns. These kids also need to be better at putting themselves in others' shoes to understand what reaction their words will have. It can help to teach them to stop or pause, think about the effects their words might have on the listener, and then speak. These more passionate little people may also swear and cuss too often or not in the right context. These dynamos need to further develop perspective taking, planning, and learning when, where, and with whom to engage in this type of communication.

I am not suggesting that parents practice this stuff at home. Rather, you might want to relax a bit and not freak out too much if you hear swearing in the yard. You might actually quietly celebrate knowing that what your child is doing is normal.

When your child comes home talking about what so-and-so can do, be sure to talk about the reality of the assertion. Help raise your child's awareness of what lying is, in different contexts. Point out when you think that someone is lying, talk about white lies and exaggeration, and talk about the effect of lying on others. You can draw on real-life situations and use movies and books to highlight examples of what a lie is and the ramifications of lying.

There are some excellent games that teach and develop the flexible thinking required to be able to lie effectively. Games like Fibber, Telestration, and Malarky can help build children's skills in a fun, supportive way.

Even though boasting is part of typical boy development, too much bragging, blaming, and generally being a poor sport is frowned upon. Kids learn through competition how to cope with their disappointment and frustration when they lose. Losing helps them be better winners too. When they experience failure themselves, they can apply that experience to teams that lose to them. The "good game" high fives become much more sincere when teammates can recognize how hard it can be to be on the losing team. In this way, children learn empathy and how to win graciously.

To not be a sore loser, your child needs to be able to recognize the following:

- that someone always loses, and sometimes he needs to lose;
- that it won't always be his turn to lose;
- that no one likes to lose;
- that it is okay to lose because it makes winning feel even better;
- that he can make the loser feel better by saying something kind;
- that he can comfort himself by using reassuring self-talk.

Some children feel that they have to win no matter what, even if that includes cheating. But that makes everyone feel bad. The person who wins knows that he didn't really win, and his competitors just dismiss the cheater as dishonest.

Your child needs to understand what cheating is and why people do it. Children are not born knowing the rules for fair play, and, for most, it does not come naturally. Adults and other role models teach through example and can provide more support for children struggling with social rules by reading books and watching movies that deal with these issues during calm times when a child is freed up to attend to new concepts.

Here are some good books/movies that deal with sportsmanship, cheating, and lying:

- *A Children's Book about Cheating,* by Joy Berry
- Any movie about superheroes and bad guys—the bad guys often cheat and do unfair things and can provide an excellent springboard for conversation around what was wrong about the bad guy's choice and the effect on others
- *Have You Filled a Bucket Today?* by Carol McCloud
- *Tyrone, The Double Dirty Rotten Cheater,* by Hans Wilhelm

Help Your Child Find a Role Model

With his wild hair, flat cap, and slouchy jeans, Jamal was cool. Three boys had been hanging out with him regularly for the past four years, and many of the other boys in his class hovered around the edges to see what games Jamal was playing at recess. They all seemed to want to run around where he was, and started bringing their basketballs to school too after he started playing "bump" in the yard.

Jamal, plain and simple, had a charisma that drew his peers to him. He was a strong soccer player. Not the best, but close. He was also quick to tell his buddies when he made a great shot: "Did you *see* that one?! Up in the corner and knocked the net down! Oh yeah, oh yeah, I rock!" He was also quick to compliment others who played. When his buddy kicked it next, he said, "Oh man… great shot." He was also fair in waiting his turn. When one of the kids butted, he spoke up and said, "Hey. It's Michael's turn!" He didn't get aggressive; he just stated it with an expectation that the other kid would do what's right.

Jamal didn't insist on doing what he wanted to do all of the time. He often asked what his friends wanted and was heard asking, "Do you guys wanna keep doin' this or do you wanna go get the girls?"

When the other boys indicated that they didn't want to change the game, Jamal did not whine or complain. He seemed to mull over their responses and replied with another fun option for them to consider, such as this: "Yeah, but Anita is pretending kittens again and I'm a German shepherd with rabies" (doing a ninja kick attempt while growling). The other boys laughed good-naturedly but still wanted to stay with what they were doing. Jamal was sensitive to their perspectives and flexible enough to agree to stay with what the majority wanted to do although he wanted to do something else.

When Michael later spoke up and said, "Hey! Amar has a beach ball! C'mon!" Jamal had no trouble switching gears and did what the other boys wanted, even though he still wanted to be a German shepherd.

What Jamal showed in this short, after-school exchange was an ability to compliment his peers appropriately, boost himself up, play by the rules, not cheat, be appropriately funny, and be flexible when his friends wanted to do something else.

Role models are an important component to helping your child develop social skills. Your child can benefit significantly when given an opportunity to spend time with strong social examples and to learn to channel his own, inner Jamal.

To create opportunities for your child to spend time with another child who finds social interaction easy, try to arrange for a playdate with a planned, very interesting activity such as a water balloon fight on a very hot day, or a super fun craft. Try to choose an activity that will entice both children to want to spend time together and does not last very long. If the short playdate is a success, it may lead to more opportunities for the children to spend time together.

What about the Girls? Hot/Not in Primary School

Mei Lyn was easily the "it girl" of her first grade class. She loved her teacher, her class, and her best friends.

After school she was observed sitting on the pavement in the corner of the yard with her little buddies, heads bowed, looking down at something in a circle. "Okay, little kitties, it's time for your milk. Meow, meow, meow," said Mei Lyn in kitten language. She then rubbed up against the "mommy" and started purring in English, "I love you, Mommy."

Mommy Kitty said, "I love you too" in a mixture of meowing and English. She then instructed the little kitties to snuggle in and go to sleep. She was ridiculously sympathetic to her kittens' concerns that they might have bad dreams.

Mei Lyn Kitty, making herself even more vulnerable, pretended to shiver and insisted that she and all of the other kitties were very frightened. Soon, all of the baby kittens were shivering, whimpering, and mewing pitifully.

Mommy Kitty, with a loving sigh, said, "Okay, little kitties, you come and sleep close to me." (They all scrunched up.) Smiling, Mei Lyn said, "Mommy Kitty, you are so beautiful and nice. I love you."

Whew! Gender difference alert! Mei Lyn and her friends are all about the dramatic play, conciliatory language, and cooperative play.

This was an actual exchange on the same day, in the same schoolyard as the lifting weights exchange with Ian. Of course, not all boys and girls play in such obvious gender-specific ways. But there are some generalized differences between sexes that are important to point out here. A number of studies (Killen & Naigles, 1995; Leaper, 1991; MacCoby, 1998; Miller, Danaher & Forbes, 1986) found that boys, in comparison to girls, tended more often to brag, engage in friendly, competitive language exchanges, use profanity/inappropriate language, tell jokes, top each others' stories, give direct orders, interrupt, threaten, argue, and call each other names.

In contrast, language samples obtained in play with groups of young girls showed more use of conciliatory language, expressed more agreements, took turns when speaking, compromised, and talked about emotions (McGillicuddy & Richard DeLisi, 2001).

Not surprisingly, schoolyard dynamics between young girls can be quite different than those between boys.

Mei Lyn talked about her feelings a lot, was not afraid of behaving in a vulnerable way, and allowed the other girls to nurture her. The game was cooperative and collaborative, and the girls shared the conversational floor. Mei Lyn was also profuse in giving compliments and chose to compliment Mommy Kitty's beauty and kindness.

In contrast, Ian bragged but not too much. He boasted about his friends' abilities as well. His compliments centered around accomplishment and physical prowess. He came up with active games and participated successfully in active games. There was some swearing and good-natured teasing.

There was also competition between the girls that day in the schoolyard, but it was more understated and implied. Akira and Vanessa were both hanging upside down by the legs on the climber. The girls were putting on a pretend "show" and were demonstrating various ridiculously flexible tricks on the bars. "Can you do this?" asked Vanessa, looking like a twist-tie gone wrong. Akira tried and couldn't do it. She replied, "That's so good. We didn't do that in gymnastics yet. I can do this, though." And she catapulted off the bars, just missing a concussion.

The girls swapped compliments while deliberately trying to outdo each other. They then collaboratively choreographed a dance routine that was a combination of the Nutcracker ballet and gymnastics.

There was certainly the same amount of competition, posturing, and comparing going on between these two girls, but it was less obvious and more implied than between boys in the yard.

Akira and Vanessa then moved to doing gymnastics on the grass. Vanessa went first, saying but not really meaning, "I can't really do a front walkover very well yet." She then executed a perfect walk-over. Although she wasn't angry, Akira replied in an outraged voice, "You can so do a front walk-over! It's way better than my cartwheel" (not really meaning it). She then did an awesome cartwheel. Clearly, these two girls were engaged in competition, but high priority was placed on ensuring that neither was perceived as conceited and that both presented themselves as "nice" while they tried to outdo and show off to each other.

The Secret Social Language of Girls

Being nice, showing off but hiding behind false modesty, and being included are the social currency for primary-aged girls in the classroom. In other words, power for girls in the early grades resides more in who gets to play and who doesn't. Gossip is a weapon used often for social leveraging and is used to lower girls who do not agree with the dominant choice of activity, do not engage in a lot of collaborative play, or do not participate in the obligatory promotion of the other girls (e.g., "Ingrid is soooo nice…").

At Mei Lyn's school, every recess, some small group of girls whispered to each other and then stopped when another girl arrived to join in. Loyalty was a prized commodity. If one girl "hated" another girl because she said Lauren was ugly, then to stay friends with Abby, you'd better agree that Fiona is mean and that actually Fiona is the ugly one and Lauren is pretty. The underlying anxiety resides in the secret place that you know you could very easily be next on the "not" list.

So much subtext and unspoken code goes on in girl culture even at young ages. This can make it very difficult for some girls, especially those who have difficulty attending to or interpreting nonverbal communication, to pick up on all of the subtle unspoken communications and expectations.

The only way to stop these negative bids for power and control would be to build empathy and perspective taking and to help the girls prize honesty and authenticity. Young girls who struggle to recognize some of the less straightforward types of social communication can be helped by being explicitly alerted to the more subtle verbal and nonverbal communication she is dealing with everyday. Specifically, parents can help their daughters by 1) practicing interpreting verbal and nonverbal communication with them and 2) helping them understand that sometimes people say one thing but actually mean another.

Key Elements for Boys and Girls

We just highlighted some key differences between the skills of socially successful boys and girls. But they have things in common too. Here are the skills shared by Mei Lyn, Ian, and Jamal:

1. They played the same games in the same way as their friends.
2. They came up with interesting adaptations to games but always checked with their friends to see if they were interested in playing that way first.
3. They complimented their friends.
4. They knew how to successfully enter into play already in progress.

To be able to support children who may, for a variety of different reasons, find playing with friends difficult, we must first ensure they practice and are exposed to these concepts at home, with trusted adults. The next level is to try to incorporate these emerging skills with a play partner at home, with a helpful adult nearby to step in and help if needed.

In other words, it is time for Operation Playdate.

CHAPTER 10

"Speed Playdating" and Other Tools to Help Make Friends

Chloe was seeing a social worker once a week. She was a smart, funny girl who, by December of first grade, had been late thirty times and had already switched schools three times. She had nightmares, recurrent stomachaches, and migraines. Every morning was filled with yelling, crying, and constant nagging by her parents to get her in the car for school. Never mind the bus—she would have missed it every day. Each time she changed schools, she left behind a trail of bad experiences and teachers who were reportedly "stupid" and "hated her."

Besides being smart, funny, and creative, Chloe was incredibly anxious—about germs, about being away from her parents, and especially about social dynamics in the classroom. She had made some friends, but none with any staying power. Every other week, she seemed to have a new best friend with last week's model tossed and described this way: "I hate her. She's mean."

Trying to figure out why Chloe seemed so black and white in her thinking about friends, and why they only lasted a week or two, her parents set up a meeting with the classroom teacher. It would seem that Chloe was always ready for things to go wrong with the other kids. If a friend was a bit tired or cranky, Chloe assumed that the friend didn't like her anymore, so she preemptively wouldn't like the other child.

Despite her problems with friends, Chloe was slowly making progress with her separation anxiety, and her parents were working hard to help her develop outside interests that she was passionate about. Their goal was to provide her with some positive experiences to counteract her serious struggles with school.

Chloe's greatest passion was for horses. Her parents signed her up for riding lessons, and invited another little girl from class along. The two girls slowly but surely began to get more comfortable with each other. After about a month of regular classes and rides together, Chloe's parents invited the other little girl over for a very carefully orchestrated playdate that involved pony figures, a toy barn, and very little stress.

The playdates became a regular occurrence and soon led to Chloe being invited to a birthday party and then sleepovers at her friend's house. The teacher also set up some horse books in the classroom and allowed the girls to work together to make a presentation to the class on their riding school. Soon Chloe was viewed as being more socially attractive to the other kids, and, armed with one good friend, she was able to establish a place for herself in the classroom. Her overwhelming persecution perception diminished as her perspective taking had an opportunity to grow with more playdate practice.

The social worker helped Chloe gain control of her fears and gave her an emotional regulation vocabulary and self-awareness that she was able to apply to making and keeping friends.

Emotional Regulation refers to:

- being aware of our emotional responses to situations

- being able to identify how we feel in different situations

- being able to recognize the true size and scope of problems

Emotional regulation begins in infancy and is shaped by relationships and the responses of caregivers. Children who are comfortable with, and in control of, emotional responses have an easier time in building and maintaining friendships and mental health in general.

By the time Chloe was in second grade, her anxiety had lessened significantly. She was now waiting for the bus with a few other kids and had kept her friend for more than a year.

But the path to something resembling a normal social life began with a couple of playdates.

The Benefits of Playdates

Playdates help children develop friendship skills in a familiar and safe environment with support as needed. They help you better understand your child's strengths and weaknesses in being a friend and give you insight into your child's friendship choices, for better or worse.

Playdates also provide outside experience and depth to classroom relationships. These experiences are crucial to helping develop deeper friendship bonds and moving beyond being simply classroom acquaintances. Socially vulnerable children need at least one or two real friends who will care enough to put themselves on the line and be willing to speak out on your child's behalf if others are putting her down. These one or two close friends act as a protective shield that travels with your child everyday into the classroom. At-risk kids need peer protection when the teacher isn't looking, and most school bullying takes place at times like dismissal at recess, during lunch, or during bathroom breaks.

Even if the worst happens, and your child is not generally accepted by his classmates, having just one really good friend and some strong outside interests make not being accepted less tragic. One really good friend matters so much more than twenty-five shallow acquaintances.

Again, this resilience strategy can all begin with playdates.

How Do You Find a Playdate?

First and foremost, of course, ask your child who she likes to spend time with at school and what she would want to do with that person. If no answer is forthcoming, then schedule a time to talk with the classroom teacher to get some guidance as to who might make a good friend and why. You may want to use a "speed dating" approach where a few playdates are scheduled for a short time (60 to 90 minutes) to get a sense of where the "love connections" may be.

Again, hanging around in the schoolyard on a consistent basis will also give your child an opportunity for unstructured time with classmates with you there to pull your child aside and discreetly redirect as needed.

Your child may have different friends for different reasons, just as adults do. You might have a friend that you have great laughs with, a friend that you exercise with, or a go-out-for-coffee buddy.

Your child will benefit from different kinds of kids for different reasons. For example, perhaps after school your child will engage in more physical play, and might get along pretty well with a little boy who she likes to climb and run with. When inviting that boy over, be sure there are lots of opportunities for physical play (e.g., hockey net and sticks, soccer ball, Nerf guns, trampoline, yoga balls outside, opportunities to go to the park). Their friendship may eventually develop to include more elements (e.g., shared love of trains or Wii sports) or not.

Also consider that boys and girls tend to play differently. Mixed-gender friendships can be great, but it is totally normal for kids between the ages of five to seven years old to prefer spending time with their own gender.

Your child may be flexible and lean toward playing a lot of different ways (physical, constructive, dramatic) or not. Being aware of which scenarios bring out the happiest version of your child is the best way to begin to cultivate strong friendships.

A word about mixed ages as well. Exposing your child to others of different ages is a great way to help develop perspective taking. (For example, with a younger child, you may make observations like the following: "Oh, the baby is crying…I wonder why? I think maybe he's hungry." Or, "I'm sorry, sweetie. I know it's not fair that your cousin keeps grabbing your cars, but he's just two and doesn't know better. I wonder what would happen if you offered him a different toy. You might be able to distract him and get your car back.") Opportunities for your child to look at the world through another's eyes will build perspective taking, which is fundamental to building friendships.

While helping your child develop at least one friendship in the classroom more fully is important, you can also be strategic by helping your child develop relationships outside the classroom. By doing this, you will be taking preemptive protective measures should classroom relationships deteriorate. Your child will learn to define her social success by more than just what happens at school. Not trying to frighten you, but sometimes children have bad months or years socially at school, and if they learn to not simply define themselves by their school problems, they will be better able to get through challenging times.

You may want to think about nurturing friendships in dance class if that's what floats your kid's boat, or baseball, or art group. If your child leans toward more individual pursuits such as figure skating or swimming, find a "buddy" and carpool to practices with his parents. Then you can invite that child back to your house to add depth to the acquaintance relationship and to provide an opportunity for it to blossom. If the only thing the two kids have in common is the activity, then find a way for them to spend more time sharing that pursuit together.

Imagine if you were working at a job that just paid the bills, and you really didn't like your coworkers, but you had to stay. How would *you* round out your life to cope?

If your child learns how to separate herself from negative experiences at school and realizes that she is not just the sum of that one environment, she will develop social-emotional resilience. Honestly, some kids need to be more resilient than others. Not fair, but true.

Childhood isn't the easiest time for all kids. We adults often look at it through rose-colored glasses. Socially vulnerable children who have struggled with the feeling of being outliers can be supported to use those negative experiences and gain wisdom. Your child may be more inspired to try to figure out what it *really* means to be a friend and to have a friend, what it is to be a bit different, and ultimately to be happy being who she is.

While it is a natural parental instinct to want to protect and shelter our children, the reality is that angst and friction create some of societies' most interesting and valuable members. There is a strong plus side to having to develop resilience. People who develop depth and strength of character in childhood may be more likely to accept differences, be compassionate, and pursue social justice for others in adulthood.

Let's return back to the idea of the playdate. Imagine that it's on. You've invited Nathan's friend James over, and you and Nathan's mom, Linda, are really getting along. The boys are playing happily in the living room. You're having coffee and commiserating over the fact that you both still break out the maternity pants on occasion even though the boys are now four. You and Linda discover that you are both closet Boys 2 Men fans and have started singing some of their songs when the screaming breaks out.

The two boys are engaged in a grip-to-the-death on a fire truck, and nothing will dissuade them from letting go. Sadly, this is the fifth time this has happened in the last ten minutes. Or perhaps this is how the playdate scenario plays out: your sweet little Nathan has interrupted you *again* to say, "There's nothing to doooooowooooo," or perhaps James comes in and says he wants to go home, or maybe Nathan keeps coming in the kitchen and playing on the floor near you and repeatedly interrupts and asks you to come and play too.

Although these worst-case scenarios can play out under the best of circumstances, there are things that you can do to set up the playdate situation to help prevent problems. It just takes planning.

Here is an organized framework:

- Who to invite?
- What to do?
- How should parents be involved?
- Plan for conflict.

Who to Invite?

Hate to break it to you, but just because you think that Nathan's mom is super cool doesn't mean that the boys will naturally get along.

You know that spark that ignites between adults who have just met? The same can be true with kids. You will want to make sure that the child you invite over will be a good personality fit for your child, especially if social skills are a challenge. Parents may need to be more strategic when you are dealing with socially challenged children and be more attuned to "good chemistry" vibes your child has when meeting potential playmates.

Finding a friend with similar interests is a good place to start. When you pair kids who like the same thing, there is automatically a focus and something to talk about. Temperaments, both those similar and opposite, can be a bit trickier to navigate. If both children are intense and explosive, there will likely be more conflict. However, there may be more opportunities to learn empathy, problem solving, and conflict resolution, which are all important for social growth.

If both children are very independent and tend to not initiate peer interactions, then the challenge will be to get them to engage each other. However, both children may appreciate not having their personal space violated, and might feel more comfortable having an opportunity to get to know each other at a gentler pace.

For children who have challenges with language development, more active games are bonding, fun, and don't require as much chit-chat as pretend dramatic scenarios like reenacting the Lord of the Rings.

There is learning to be gained from all relationships, playdates included. It is important to support any relationship that seems to be working—that is, any relationship in which the children are relaxed enough with each other that they are receptive to learning how to be a friend.

What to Do on the Playdate?

The first step is to find out whether your child knows what her playdate likes to play with. It would also be helpful to have an idea of what the kids play together at school. If at school they play together at the sand table, then it makes sense to give them the opportunity to play in the sand to bridge the awkwardness of trying to get to know each other in an unfamiliar place.

A quick phone call or e-mail to the other parent—or even better, by your child to her new friend—to ask what the kid likes to play will help to set the stage for more opportunities for success.

Be sure to have a play area figured out that is not too cluttered, with a few choice activities accessible. If you have too many toys available, the children may go off in their own directions and not focus on each other so much. If there is too little to do, then they may not know what to do with themselves and may come to you for assistance. Also keep in mind that your child may have strong feelings about some of her toys and may find it very difficult to share them. If that is the case, be sure to put away the items that are special to your child to avoid potential conflicts. A new-friend-in-the-making playdate may also not be the best time to pull out brand-new toys that your child hasn't had a chance to figure out yet or may not want to share.

The first visit to your home should be short and sweet. You want to make it work and claim victory before anything has the opportunity to go wrong. Keeping it short means that there is not a lot of need for the kids to figure out what to do or time to get irritated with each other. You want the children to be eager to play again at another time.

Structuring the kids' time a little may help ensure continued interest and keep things fun. A good structure might be to start with some free indoor play for half an hour, then outside for half an hour, then snack, and call it a day. For more active little people, try starting with outside activity options, then move on to hands-on, busy activities inside, snack together, back outside, and go home.

Playdates for Kids Who Like Things to Be the Same

Some kids need things to be *just so*. If you have a child who lacks flexibility and plays in a particular way, then an even more structured plan is in order to help things go smoothly, as illustrated in this next story.

Alex was a five-year-old kindergartener. He liked to keep to himself for the most part and, during free play, went nowhere but the building center. He was pretty territorial with his structures, and there were frequent conflicts when other kids tried to join in because they did not do things the way Alex wanted them to. Alex liked his world ordered because the classroom usually felt overwhelming and chaotic to him. He often felt bombarded by the noise, the lights, and all of the sudden movements.

Alex was a very articulate little guy and had the ability to express himself to his friends, but he often didn't feel inspired to because his classmates usually irritated him.

Some children, like Alex, are more sensitive and affected by sensory stimulation around them. They may have a more challenging time filtering out all of the tactile input, noise, and sights and may experience a sort of chronic annoyance. Small wonder these children can more easily become overwhelmed by it all. Alex was always aware of the hum of the fluorescent lights overhead, was very distracted when people around him moved, and felt like his socks were too hot, and his pants, especially around the waist, were, in his words, "bunchy."

Besides running around in the park sometimes, Alex hadn't yet been particularly inspired to engage and have fun with other kids. His sensory issues and lack of flexibility acted as barriers to accepting other children in play. So, to help order and make things less overwhelming for Alex, a one-on-one, carefully orchestrated playdate made a lot more sense than trying to start to entice him into playing with other kids in the sensory whirlwind of a busy classroom.

Another way that we can lessen the load for children who are easily overwhelmed, like Alex, is to make playing with other children simpler by making the activities and toys simpler. When your child doesn't have to concentrate very hard to do the activity, he becomes freed up to receive the learning that will take place socially with a playmate.

The formula for frustration goes something like this: difficult game or toy (high cognitive load) + hard-to-learn social skills = frustration, irritation, and minimal learning (Reszka et al., 2012).

Translated into the adult world, for a child to navigate this relationship would be something like a beginner knitter trying to make an argyle sweater while hosting a formal dinner party. It would be much easier if you invited one person over to hang out, just provided a bowl of pretzels, and only knitted one row.

For kids, the easiest activities tend to be 1) physical, social kinds of games such as run and chase, kicking a ball around, jumping on a trampoline; 2) sensory activities such as playing in the sand or water; or 3) cause-and-effect toys such as rocket launchers, Hexbots, and remote control cars.

If your child really isn't yet motivated to play with other children or needs her friend to play the way she wants, you can maintain your child's attention by practicing and role-playing how she will play with a certain toy when the friend visits. Talk about and practice taking turns. Also try to anticipate what might be fun and where things could go wrong and what working through those things might look like. You may be able to prevent potential conflict with this pre-rehearsal during a calm period, talking through potential social land mines, and coming up with options.

By this point, you should have a child in mind to invite, a good idea what the children will be playing, and a space cleared for playing. You should also have arranged for siblings and other distractions to be out of the way. You have set the stage for fun and learning.

Where Will You Be during the Playdate, and What Will You Do?

To answer these questions, it is important to remind yourself of the purpose of these playdates. Your job is to facilitate friendship building and cooperative play. In order to do that, you will need to step in, set up, and then step out (Sussman, (2006).

Here's what that looks like for our friend Alex. He has called a classmate himself and invited him over. He checked to find out what his buddy Devon liked to play and if he has any food allergies.

Alex and his mom then planned out the boys' time together. They agreed that the boys would hang out in his bedroom and the rec room, and spend some time on the trampoline in the backyard. Alex got out his air hockey table, some Pokémon cards, and his Lego racetrack and checked that they had the ingredients for smoothies at snack time. Mom went over what to do if Devon didn't want to play Pokémon and options in case he forgets to bring his Beyblades.

The stage has been set.

Alex is barefoot, feeling relaxed, and ready for show time.

Twenty minutes into the playdate, the boys are playing well while Alex's mom sits in the rec room reading a book. She frequently looks up, talks to the boys, compliments their Beyblade spins, and cheers when one of the boys scores in air hockey.

If you were a fly on the wall, you would see that the boys keep looking over to Alex's mom to see what she thinks when they take a shot. Being a fun mom, she joins in and takes some turns as well. She also makes smoothies with them. What's lovely about this scene is how loving and caring this mom is and how much Alex knows that he can rely on his mom to navigate his social waters. What's nice about this too is how much Devon likes Alex's mom.

What's not so lovely about this is that this is now a three-way playdate, and the boys are denied the freedom to talk the way kids do when adults are around (read: butt jokes). Neither boy needs to dig deep to figure out how to play together, and they are not talking much to each other but rather through a facilitator.

Let's try this playdate again. The set-up works; activities work. Mom is now instead in the kitchen washing dishes out of sight but just within earshot.

She can hear the boys playing air hockey and all is going well until Devon says, "Hey! You tilted the board...that's cheating!!" Alex responds with, "I did not! That goal totally counts." Alex's mom is poised, ready to pounce like a lioness on unsuspecting Devon/zebra. But instead, she waits. The disagreement goes back and forth a couple of times more and then…(cue heavenly music): "Whatever. Take the point. I don't care," Alex says. Two minutes later, both boys are laughing their guts out because Alex, showing his comedic genius, belched.

Alex realized that giving up the goal was more important than having his friend angry with him, so he conceded that maybe in the excitement he did bump the board. This was an excellent opportunity for him to be more flexible and learn to compromise to keep the fun going.

Here's that same scenario, but with Mom immediately going in to remedy the situation before it escalates. In fairness to Mom, her son can be pretty explosive and uncompromising, and she can see that this situation is rife with landmines.

Devon shouts, "Hey! You tilted the board. That's cheating!" Alex, of course, denies it, and the exchange goes back and forth a couple of times with the classic verbal kid dance of "did not… did too."

Mom comes in and asks what is going on.

Alex angrily claims that he didn't cheat despite evidence to the contrary. Alex's mom says, "Well, maybe it's time to do something else. Are either of you two hungry? Or: "Alex, Devon is your guest, why don't you start that point again?" Or: "Devon, is that true?" Do you think that Devon will feel comfortable talking openly with an unfamiliar grownup?

No matter what the outcome, this well-intentioned adult interference undermines the social skill development goals that have been set for trying to increase Alex's flexibility and have him play cooperatively with a friend.

It can be hard to figure out when to step in when children are in conflict. There really isn't a clear, definitive rule—simply some guidelines and your parental intuition.

Let's say your child and his friend are having a disagreement, and things are getting worse, not better. Perhaps the argument is getting hotter, voices are rising, there is name-calling, playing has stopped, or the friend wants to go home. You will want to try and step in to change the focus—perhaps pull your child aside and whisper a reminder, or simply resolve the situation with the kids who are truly stuck and unable to maneuver their way out.

A few more things to consider when stepping in to help during playdate mayhem: It can be embarrassing and even feel devaluing for children when their parents step in to solve problems when friends are over—even in kindergarten. It's more effective to pull your child aside into another room and talk things out.

You want your child to be heard and to help clarify the situation by repeating back his concern, giving another view/ perspective, asking if he has a plan to remedy the problem, and, if not, giving a couple of options. Here's what that might look like with Alex and his mom:

> *Alex's mom:* "Hey, Alex, I can hear that you boys are upset… what's going on?"
>
> *Alex:* "I hate Devon! He says I cheated, but I didn't."
>
> *Mom:* "He thinks you cheated and doesn't believe you when you say it was an accident. That's frustrating. Maybe he got a bit mixed up?" *(gently prompting consideration of another perspective)*
>
> *Alex:* "Maybe he's an idiot."
>
> *Mom:* "I can see that you are mad about this, and I don't blame you. Nobody likes to be accused of cheating. But I did hear you boys playing and having fun. I'll bet that you can turn this around and go back to having fun. Right now it sounds like Devon wants to go home. What do you think you should do?"
>
> *Alex:* "I don't know." *(And he really doesn't—this is not just a give-up kind of answer.)*
>
> **Mom again clarifies the problem for Alex:** "Well, maybe the board accidently got tilted, but Devon thinks you did it on purpose."

Mom then waits expectantly at least five seconds, trying to cue Alex to expand on what she is saying, but he is not taking the bait. His mom then continues with one or two more probing solutions. "Maybe this point isn't that important to you. You could let him have the point and move on."

Alex looks at her incredulously, like she has suggested he amputate his own foot or something.

Again Alex's mom waits a good five to ten seconds to give him a chance to process what she is saying and to formulate a response. Not getting one, she provides one more option: "Or, if you really feel like this is unfair and you are both stuck, you could suggest restarting the game."

She waits, and—bingo—Alex says, "I don't want to play it again."

Alex's mom repeats back what he says to show that she is really listening and to give him more time to think this challenging situation through. She again waits to see if he has an option to suggest. He doesn't, so she gives one more. "Well, if you are sick of playing this game, maybe now is a good time to go outside and show him our trampoline. What do you think would work?"

By this point, Alex's anxiety has lessened, and he is keen to get back to his friend. Giving him some time to cool down and a social vocabulary to help deal with the conflict has significantly helped to deescalate the situation.

Alex's mom puts her hand on his shoulder, and her son says, "Well, I did push the board by accident."

His mom says, "Okay, it was an accident. What will you do to help turn this around so you can get back to having fun again?"

Alex says, "Whatever, Mom. I just want to go. He can just have the point," and he runs back to his friend.

Flexibility experience win for Alex.

Playdates for Intense Kids

At four and a half, Matt has a strong presence in the classroom. He is a fast talker, fast worker, and if you asked him, he would say he was the "second fastest runner in my class."

The other kids think that he can be funny in a silly kind of way, and will play with him outside in the yard. In the classroom, he is often seen sort of circling around what the other kids are doing, frequently causing chaos for attention. He is known for such humor classics as taking the baby doll out of the carriage, throwing her on the floor, and saying: "Call the doctor, call the doctor." Sometimes the kids laugh; sometimes the kids get really annoyed. Matt is okay with his 50 percent success rate.

Outside in the yard, he seems to stand out less than in the contained environment of the classroom, but sadly, he is often at the center of physical confrontations and tends to yell more than the other kids.

It seems that he physically moves faster than the world he is in. His emotions do change faster and are felt more deeply than the other kids'.

Matt's current areas of challenge appear to center around difficulties sustaining play with friends and joining into play already in progress. Matt and his classmates would also benefit if he learned to negotiate and compromise, instead of resort to the use of fists.

It is easier for children to develop social skills with one other friend in the familiar environment of their homes than to try to process the onslaught of rapidly changing input in a schoolyard or classroom.

Matt's mom invited a friend to come over for an hour and a half on a Sunday. Matt's little sister, Ramona, was sent out with Dad, leaving Matt and his mom free to focus on this playdate without distractions. Matt's mom helped organize with him what the boys would do together, explored what Jeffrey liked to do, and discussed which toys Matt would feel fine sharing with his friend.

Matt's mom wisely helped steer Matt's ideas toward outside play to reflect his strengths. She was very motivated to ensure that the boys had a great time so that they would be inspired to play together outside of school more regularly.

It was agreed that the playdate would start outside on the play structure, and then the boys would have a Nerf gun battle, eat a snack, and, if time allowed, build a fort together with spare pieces of scrap wood, a hammer, and nails.

Matt double-checked with Jeffrey that those activities would be fun for him and asked him to bring a Nerf gun and any extra wood he had at his house. Everything was set. The boys were excited and talked about it a great deal in the days leading up to the weekend, and Matt's mom prayed for a sunny day.

On Sunday, Matt greeted his friend, and they ran through the house to the backyard, slamming the screen door behind them. Mom was able to hear bits and pieces of their conversation through the open kitchen window as she loaded the dishwasher.

The boys were whooping it up, performing breathtaking stunts on the slide, chasing each other with handfuls of sticks and leaves to throw, and showing off their various skills on the monkey bars.

Matt ran in breathless, cheeks flushed, and grabbed a handful of dog food, while leaving a trail of kibble as he again slammed the screen door behind him. Two minutes later, he and Jeffrey were back rummaging through the fridge looking for cheese. Slam.

Matt's mom had stepped away from the window briefly but was now anxious to see what was going on, with her mom radar sending out emergency warning signals. Good thing she did. The food was being used, unsuccessfully thank goodness, to try to teach the dog to go down the slide. Dog training abandoned, the boys inhaled a quick snack and were back outside intent on getting a Nerf battle going.

The boys beautifully negotiated rules about who held dominion over which parts of the backyard, made bunkers to hide out, and loaded up on Nerf bullets. The battle was epic, and the boys were having a blast until Matt's Nerf gun jammed and he tried to work out a trade with Jeffrey—his friend's good gun for a really bad one that barely trickled out its bullets.

Both boys, being life-of-the-party types, were growing more and more intense about their arms conflict. As things were escalated to a high level, Matt's mom called him into the kitchen while Jeffrey gathered up the Nerf bullets and started to organize their wood pile.

She began with an open-ended question to get the conversation going, something like: "You both look really mad. What's going on?" Matt, near tears in frustration, shouted out that Jeffrey wouldn't let him use his gun. He felt hard done by and thought that it was unfair that he would be stuck with the "sucky gun."

Mom repeated back what Matt had said, knowing full well that key elements were being left out of the story, and gently stretched Matt's version by asking what had happened to his original good gun.

Matt's response was less than considerate. "It's no fair because I let Jeffrey use my gun. He needs to give it to me—it's mine."

She replied with empathy, "Oh, that doesn't seem fair. You let Jeffrey use your gun and now your own gun is broken. I know that you really love that gun."

Notice that Matt's mom hasn't said anything about how Matt is being unfair, nor is she giving Jeffrey's side yet. She is first establishing a good flow of communication by showing Matt that she is really listening to him (repeating back), not judging him, helping identify how he is feeling, and empathizing. These are all good skills we would like Matt to learn himself in the long term.

Matt, now crying, is truly stuck and is getting more and more upset thinking about his broken gun. He is a little person of extremes. Things can go from AWESOME to HORRIBLE pretty fast. Rightly or wrongly, he now really feels that everything is ruined and, needing to blame someone, decides that it is all Jeffrey's fault. "My gun is broken! My best gun! I *hate* Jeffrey!" He pulls away from his mom, and says, "I'm gonna get that good gun." His whole body is contorted in anger.

Matt's mom gives him a hug and says, "Now hold on a second. It's only fair that you want a good gun that works too. Your game won't be fun if you have a sucky gun and Jeffrey has a good gun. I saw you and Jeffrey playing on the play structure and laughing a lot. I even saw you do an awesome jump from the swing while it was up in the air. How did you do that, anyway?"

Matt is now calming down and being gently redirected away from his catastrophic interpretation of his time with Jeffrey and being reminded of the fun the two of them had. Mom is buying some calmer thinking space by shifting Matt's train of thought.

She waits a bit to see if he has something to say and then ponders, "I wonder if Jeffrey loves the good gun too and doesn't want to use the sucky gun either. He looked really sad for you when your gun got jammed."

Matt is now crying but less angry. "I want a good gun."

Mom says, "I wonder if you just both want a good gun."

Matt has now been redirected to the real problem and away from blaming Jeffrey for his disappointment.

Mom points out that he and Jeffrey only have thirty minutes left to play and wonders if he has done everything that he was hoping to, knowing full well that they still have a fort to build.

Matt recalibrates, and in his exuberant way, jumps up exclaiming, "Forget the Nerf battle—we have to start building the fort!"

Mom gently reminds him to check with Jeffrey to make sure that he wants to build it too.

In this scenario, Matt's mom did a number of things to let some air out of the balloon, to be able to calm Matt down enough to receive her words, and to help him think through an emotionally charged situation.

As Ross Greene says in his book *The Explosive Child,* "An explosive outburst—like other forms of maladaptive behavior—occurs when the cognitive demands being placed upon a person outstrip that person's capacity to respond adaptively." Matt's mom intuitively knew that Matt needed help first to cool down, and then he needed her empathy and support to think through events and help with coming up with next steps. Simply expecting him to work things out on his own was beyond him. To add another great quote by Dr. Greene, "Kids do well when they can."

- Matt's mom began by separating the boys to allow them an opportunity to be away from the situation a bit.
- Knowing that the situation was escalating and appeared to be beyond Matt's ability to turn around, she gave Jeffrey a job to do to allow him to refocus and brought Matt in where they could work this out without yet involving Jeffrey.
- She empathized by repeating back what Matt said. As he was too worked up to be able to participate in the activity that had gone wrong, she helped him change the subject to something that was more manageable emotionally.
- She also gave him some time to cool down and reengage the part of his brain that can receive problem-solving ideas and disengage the flight-or-fight, Incredible Hulk, reactionary part of his brain that was emerging.

Remember that for Matt the goals were simply to have him engage with a friend for a longer time and to help him learn to resolve conflicts using something other than his fists. His mom was able to coach him once his heightened emotional state decreased and then urge him to move on to something else. Also, once Matt was calmer, he was able to see with his mom's help that maybe Jeffrey felt the same way about his special toy, which explained why he didn't want to part with it. That ability to put yourself in someone else's shoes is integral to developing social skills and friendships. Kids who tend to react emotionally before pausing to think things through may initially need more direct interpretation and an opportunity to de-stress in order to receive other perspectives that are presented.

All of his mother's modeling served to teach Matt ways to think through situations. She modeled empathy, respect, and active listening.

Playdates for Kids Who Aren't Very Verbal

What about kids who are as young as three and a half and who have the same goals as Matt, such as playing with friends longer than just a couple of minutes, but who may not have strong language skills to work through conflicts?

Bailey was a little boy who attended preschool full time. He marched to his own drum in class and mostly preferred to play by himself with trucks or trains. He would tolerate a friend playing alongside, but did not appreciate any other kids touching his stuff or adding their own ideas. He clearly expressed this lack of appreciation by throwing himself on the floor screaming when someone tried to add something to what he was doing. He didn't do that all the time, but he had done it frequently and dramatically enough that other kids did not include him in play.

The gap often widens when a child does not know how to interact with other kids or cannot see the value in interacting. Add over-the-top reactions to peers, and classmates will quickly respond by avoiding the child. This lack of opportunity to learn to play with friends just compounds as your child plays alone, not learning social skills while other classmates get more and more adept at navigating relationships.

It is so important to give your child opportunities as early as possible to interact with other children in an enjoyable way. With that in mind, how to help Bailey?

For him, the goals for a playdate were the following:
- including a friend in play over a number of turns
- enjoying interaction with a friend
- developing flexibility/perspective taking
- resolving conflicts

Bailey's mom, Mrs. Wilson, decided that to create real friendships for him, she would need to schedule a regular activity—over a number of weeks with the same friends, to allow relationships to deepen. Also, given Bailey's young age, and the fact that his skills hovered around rungs one to three on the social skills ladder, she wanted to schedule shorter playdates in the beginning (one hour), a couple of times a week. She offered to watch a neighbor's son so that her neighbor could go to Zumba class twice a week and to give her a chance to help Bailey.

Bailey's mom initially adopted a "less is more" attitude. During the first playdate, she just had the boys play in the same room together with their own trucks for half an hour. The boys then made a simple snack together and she chimed in from time to time to cue Bailey to check to make sure that Anthony liked the snack items he was bringing out.

That was it.

At the second playdate that week, Mrs. Wilson had the boys play with their own trucks for about fifteen minutes and gave them a five-minute warning that snack was coming. The boys made the same snack together with Mom on the sidelines supporting only when needed. Then Bailey's mom brought out something new, a high-interest toy that was active and didn't require a lot of conversation.

She had spent an afternoon looking into what kinds of toys are really fun and tend to get a big, enthusiastic reaction. In this case, the chosen object was something called a stomp rocket. She began the activity with the boys to show them how to do it. She modeled how to use the rocket, taking turns jumping on the stomper, and then stepped back once the boys seemed to be catching on and enjoying each other.

Before the boys had a chance to tire of the activity, Bailey's mom invited them outside to throw a tennis ball around for the dog from a "super-powered launcher" and smiled as she saw that the game had changed to chasing each other around. Again she began by modeling how to use the super-cool launcher, showed them how to reward the dog with a treat, and how to take turns. The boys took over and had an absolute blast.

Bailey's mom watched inconspicuously on the sidelines as the boys played together beautifully with the toy and then moved on to a game of tag. She was far enough away that the boys really didn't notice her presence, but within earshot and ready to step in to help advance their play if needed.

Goals for week one were met beautifully. Bailey had moved from playing on his own to taking turns and playing cooperatively with a friend, meltdown free. Bailey now had two excellent play-with-a-friend memories that he could deposit into his experience account to draw from during future playtimes with others.

If you recognize your child in this scenario, consider these fun, high-interest toys:

- stomp rocket
- racetrack with pull-back car (just one) to encourage turn taking
- Hexbot and track
- marble run (already built) with just one marble
- beach ball
- bean bag and target
- water balloons and target
- pogo stick

Remember, the most important goal of these interactions is for your child to share an enjoyable experience over a series of turns. Your child will need practice, coaching, and support. Remember to be sure to fade your involvement as your child's competency grows.

The first place that children learn to play is usually with a parent. The importance of playing with your child cannot be overemphasized. You can teach your child that interactions are fun and to include others, to take turns, to share, and to allow others to also incorporate their ideas.

Playdates for Kids Who Are Overwhelmed by School and Other Kids

Sometimes a child can appear competent during play with an adult but with friends, it all falls apart. Andrew, below, is a case in point.

Andrew was a four-and-a-half-year-old boy who was diagnosed with high functioning autism. Overall, his language skills were age appropriate, but he really struggled to use his language socially and during transitions (changes in places or activities). He was also quite inflexible in his play.

Andrew had spent the better part of a year working with a speech-language pathologist to get his speech and language skills in the typical range. He had also worked on developing better transition-coping strategies, turn taking, pretend play, being silly (flexibility), and playing games with others.

He was doing beautifully. So beautifully that his parents and SLP decided that he had outgrown the need for adult-child therapy. They agreed that more information was needed about how well he was carrying over his progress into classroom interactions with children his age. Based on how socially successful Andrew was during therapy sessions, the SLP expected to provide only minor tweaking of social opportunities and situations to allow for more social engagement practice in the classroom.

But school for Andrew was an overwhelming disaster.

He simply wandered around the classroom, stopping briefly to put a couple of puzzle pieces in. He picked up a book and looked at it by himself for a minute, then wandered over and looked at some farm animals, and then did it all again. He didn't really engage with the activities or people in the room. He was quietly and repetitively occupying space until it was time to go outside.

With the clean-up song completed, kids start chatting animatedly, pushing for the door, anxious to get into their snowsuits and out to the yard. It was a freezing cold winter afternoon that required layers of snow pants, boots, coat, mittens, scarves, and hats.

Andrew looked panic stricken. A kindly teacher came up to him and explained that it was time to play outside and that he needed to get his snow pants. When he didn't move, the teacher distractedly started to take off his indoor shoes and reach for his snow pants. That's when the screaming, kicking, and thrashing began. The kids kept looking over at him worriedly. The teacher was clearly stressed, and Andrew was clearly out of control.

This kind of behavior was happening daily, and everyone had reached their limit. Staff often had to sit with Andrew in the corridor while the other kids went outside, but they felt that they were catering to his behavior and that he was missing out on all the good things that come from friends, fresh air, and exercise. Something had to change. His classmates had become afraid of him, and the teachers were at a loss.

Today was a good day, according to his teacher, because after twenty minutes of wrestling, pleading, and bribery, they managed to get him outdoors. There, he stood staring into the schoolyard, with tears, hiccups, and a runny nose. Andrew then began to purposefully do laps along the fenced perimeter of the schoolyard.

Have you ever been to a zoo and watched a wild animal pace the cage? Miserable Andrew had that same desperate, sad quality. It was cold and wet, and he looked absolutely miserable. Why wouldn't he be? He was probably feeling painfully hot and constricted in his snowsuit. The actions of his classmates most likely made little sense to him, and even if he did want to participate, he probably didn't know how to join in and be included. If he had the ability to reflect philosophically from an adult perspective, he would be justified in surmising that he was experiencing methodical and purposefully unjust punishment. "Success" is subjective and relative.

It was a strange juxtaposition between Andrew's world and his classmates' world. Children were playing happily throughout the yard. Boys were pushing slush with their front-end loaders, filling dump trucks; girls were playing some pretend game under the play structure, and a group of kids were playing with shovels, making big piles.

And there was Andrew circling anxiously, chewing on the collar of his coat, not looking at any of them. He was simply overwhelmed and had no idea that the kids could be fun; the kids had no idea that Andrew could be fun; and neither side had any idea how to begin to bridge the gap. The teachers had tried to make suggestions to Andrew, but they washed right over him. He first needed to develop some skills before their ideas would make sense to him.

Andrew had come far in his social use of language with adults, but what is the point of working on social skills if they aren't generalized so that a child can develop real relationships with other children?

It is absolutely appropriate and necessary to begin work by engaging kids in play with adults who can coach, support, and teach. However, those skills should always be nurtured so that they can be applied to interactions with other children.

Fortunately, all was not lost for Andrew at school. Clearly, he perceived sensation differently, and the snowsuit added to his irritation. Andrew started to receive intervention from an occupational therapist who specialized in helping children with sensory issues. He came up with excellent alternatives and helped to desensitize the snowsuit discomfort for Andrew, which made getting dressed for winter much less torturous.

Andrew also needed one-on-one guidance from the classroom teacher in what was available for him to do, and practice in how to do it in the classroom. This helped him gain familiarity with materials and begin to see the value of playing at school.

The teacher was also encouraged to carefully choose a playmate for Andrew: a little boy who also loved Thomas the tank engine and playing board games. He was paired with Andrew at a special train center in the classroom that was specifically designed just to nurture their shared interest.

Teachers also kept Andrew's mom apprised as to which games and activities in the train center the boys played well with together so that she could provide similar activities at home during playdates. Mom knew just when Andrew needed some support to keep the play fun with a friend and when to step out and let things unfold naturally. Andrew was also taught specific outdoor games like tag at home and at school.

After two months of a focused team effort, Andrew stopped having tantrums. He no longer drew negative attention to himself or intimidated the other children. He had one real friend who shared a similar passionate interest in trains, and he learned how to play chase and to play with trucks in the sandbox.

There were no more laps around the yard either. There were, however, more interpersonal conflicts, but that was actually good news. Andrew was now in relationships with his classmates, figuring things out with and without adult support. He was learning and engaged.

Making Friends Is Not Always Automatic

Many well-intentioned adults hear the message that sending their children to preschool or full-day kindergarten is what their child needs to learn to socialize with other children. Socialization is certainly a crucial component to school happiness, but for some of our most vulnerable children, we are asking them to swim in the deep end without water wings. Maybe even while wearing a hot, itchy, ill-fitting scuba suit.

Many children enter school ill-equipped to manage themselves in a busy classroom. Children often need direct adult teaching of social skills, mindful, goal-based social interaction in the classroom with carefully selected peers, and carryover of the school success into playdates at home targeting the same skills to succeed.

It is not enough to deposit our challenged children into a busy classroom unprepared to make friends, nor is it enough to simply invite friends over and expect that your child will know how to develop friendships successfully.

These children need us and need each other. Especially in the winter in bunchy snowsuits.

CHAPTER 11

How to Make a Better Ant Trap

Entry into Play

Remember Mei Lyn from chapter 9? The sweet kitty at recess? Let's watch her during free play in the classroom as she tries to join in "playing princesses" with some other first grade girls in her class.

There is a small group of girls in an intense-looking huddle around the "creative station" in the kindergarten room. Two of them are wearing high heels, purses, and lots of jewelry. Mei Lyn walks up after coming back from bringing the attendance down to the office.

She stands near the girls, just watching for a minute or so, and she says, "I love your pretty shoes."

Princess #1 says, "Thanks…I need them to go to the ball." Then Mei Lyn watches a little more, before responding: "Can I come to the ball too?"

Princess #2 says, "Sure. You can have the flower necklace."

Now consider Amerit. She quietly rubs her hands together, sneaking glances at the girls from behind her thick bangs. She often wants to join in play, but feels unsure of what to do.

Let's move our lens over to the "dress-up station," which serves as a makeup room for our little princesses getting dressed for the ball. Amerit stands near the girls, pretending to be interested in the puzzle, but really just wanting to play princesses. She stands there silently for five minutes, just watching. She is simply waiting and hoping to be noticed and included. She inches closer and closer until she is well within the dress-up station, but is still not invited into the preparations. Amerit starts to put a necklace on, and

Princess #1 says, "Hey, we need that for the ball!" and takes the necklace back. Amerit walks away and goes back to the puzzle, her shoulders slumped.

Before we get outraged at Princess #1's territoriality or lack of inclusiveness, remember that these girls were engrossed in their activity, and were probably not attending to Amerit's inner turmoil and subtle hints at wanting to be invited. Amerit was in some serious need of understanding the process of how to enter play already in progress and developing the continued courage to do so.

Here's another example of a boy with a problem similar to Amerit's, but who uses a much different strategy in his attempt to be included:

Two little boys are lying on a carpet, building a zoo for their animals to live in with paper towel rolls and masking tape. Their two-foot wall draws the attention of Aidan. He watches from a distance and, impressed with this engineering feat, really wants to join in. Wanting to get the pair to notice him and think he is funny, he shouts "Timber!" and gives the wall a shove. Both boys are understandably upset.

Aidan just laughs, realizing that his joke was not received well, but not knowing what to do next. He makes an unsuccessful bid to repair the situation by trying to explain that the knocking down is the fun part. Much to Aidan's surprise and disappointment, the boys disagree and tell the teacher about the crime against them.

Jessica also wants to be included, but needs a heavy dose of finesse. At recess, she marches up to a couple of kids playing in the sandbox and digging holes for the ants to live in. She sits down and watches for a few seconds. The kids have a little assembly line going: one child does the finger poke, and the other puts the leaves in for softness and sticks for decoration.

Jessica pipes up and says, "That's stupid! The ants are going to climb right out. You have to make a roof like this," and she takes sticks out of the hole and lays them across the top as a makeshift roof. The other kids are outraged, but she keeps doing it, yelling back until one of the kids pushes her and the teacher enters the scene.

Trouble with social entry happens in our adult lives as well. Imagine you are standing in the hallway at work talking to a coworker about a movie you've just seen. Grownup Jessica walks up, jumps in, and says, "That movie is okay, but you know what is a *really* good film?"

Or, you are standing in the hallway at work talking to a coworker about pros and cons of vaccinations. Grownup Amerit walks up and just stands there waiting...waiting... yup, still waiting...until you ask, "What's up?" Amerit shrugs and says, "Oh, nothing, just coming by."

How Do Kids Learn Social Entry Skills?

Children learn social entry skills in play through trial and error. Researchers have found that more than half of children's attempts (53 percent) at gaining entry to a social situation are rejected by typically developing, acquainted children (Corsaro, 1979).

The good news is that as children get older, they get better at joining in, with only 26 percent of attempts being rejected among popular children in second and third grade (Putallaz, Gottman, 1990). The bad news is that all children—apparently even the most socially skilled—experience a great deal of rejection when trying to join in play. There's a lot of rejection in the everyday life of a child at recess.

Sadly, the least socially skilled kids are not allowed entry most often, which means that they have to keep trying. This exposes them to more—you guessed it—rejection. It can become a vicious cycle.

There are a lot of implications to this research. Children, especially socially vulnerable ones, need to be more mindful of how they play and who they play with at recess before even going outside to maximize their chances of success. Further, keeping misbehaving children in for all or part of recess is often a punishment or consequence—call it what you want—used to reinforce classroom behavioral expectations. Children who are kept in for part or all of recess most often tend to be the ones in the class who are having the most challenges with regulating themselves. Those regulation challenges are often not limited to the classroom, but have implications with relationships with other children.

Denying these children a chance to play with peers only compounds with interest the social challenges that these kids face. Keep in mind that it is very difficult to join play that has already started. So, if we let these children outside after paying their debt to society when the other kids have already started playing, they will have an even harder time joining in and will more likely face rejection. This "consequence" often then becomes much more severe than originally intended by the teacher. A good teacher would never justify increasing rejection and social isolation as an appropriate "natural consequence" to being silly in class or not paying attention.

We can also help to better prepare children for the possibility that their attempts at being accepted may be rejected and let them know it happens to everyone. Parents may want to point out to children that other kids sometimes say "no" when you want to join in, but that it is not something to get too worked up about. You may be able to reassure your child by talking about times that this happened to you as child. To take this a step further, you and your child could watch other kids at the park as they try to join in and then figure out what works and what doesn't.

For the 47 percent of entry attempts that are successful among young children, the strategy that works tends to be quite formulaic. It goes something like this: The SSEC (successful social entry child) who wants to play typically walks up to other kids already playing and watches for a minute or two. SSEC then gives a compliment, something positive about the activity, like "Hey, cool ant house" or "I heard that was a great movie."

Then SSEC waits a while longer. Maybe he puts another positive feeler out there, maybe not. SSEC then makes his move with "Can I play?" or "Can I help?" or "Can I come to the ball?" or "Here's another leaf," adding to what the other children are doing.

Why is this approach the most successful? The watching allows the children who are playing to become aware that someone else is interested without interrupting the flow of the activity. Observing helps the new child who wants to play figure out what is happening and how to play. By observing, the child who wants to join is also showing respect to the children playing and sending the message that the wannabe entrant will follow their game and that he finds what they are doing interesting.

Let's be honest: We all love to be complimented. When a watching child compliments an activity in progress, he communicates good will and reduces any concern that he will disrupt the game.

Finally, by asking permission to play or gently adding an element to the game, the newcomer allows power to remain with the kids who are already in the activity. This permits the new person to seamlessly insert himself into the play at hand.

A summary of the steps to successful social entry into play goes something like this:

- Watch.
- Compliment.
- Watch.
- Compliment. Or ask a question about what the kids are doing, or add value to the activity.

When Social Entry Leads to Social Exit

Let's go back to the earlier examples and try to analyze where the breakdowns occurred.

Remember Amerit, whose stealth entry strategy to join the ball was thwarted? She certainly had the watching element down, but she did not compliment the other girls to let them know that she was on board with what and how they were playing, nor did she ask to join in.

Aidan, the boy who knocked down the zoo wall, did not watch or compliment. He simply wanted the boys' attention but didn't know how to get it. He needed some help learning to adapt himself to others' activities by watching and waiting and by imitating their actions.

Jessica, our ant farm critic, needed to realize that when play is already in progress, it is a privilege to be included. She needed to say one or two positive things first and ask to be included. By trying to take over, she was perceived as being too aggressive and a threat.

Helping Your Child with Social Entry

Consider sharing this information on joining play with your child and practice at home. You may try having your child role-play the kinds of scenarios previously mentioned, either with you or with siblings. Again, playing park detective with your child may allow you to explore what worked and didn't for other children. For older children, you may want to expand the activity by asking what advice they would give that child who was rejected (e.g., wait longer, compliment, ask). Practice, practice, practice! You can also give your child more compliments and subtly or not-so-subtly go through the steps to be invited into his play.

You may want to go over social entry strategies with your child in the morning before he goes to school and let him know that you will be asking, for example, about afternoon recess. It might be helpful to write down steps for your child to remember on cue cards or use some sort of picture reminder. You may also want to refer back to chapter 8 and create a social story to highlight the challenges of trying to join in to play and the options to help make joining in easier. After school, you will want to find out how things went at recess. Some questions to guide the discussion include the following:

- Did you try to join in today?
- What were the kids playing?
- How were they playing it? (This will give you insight into whether your child did the watching part.)
- "What nice thing did you say to _____ or about _____ during lunch recess?" (This will give you insight and help remind your child of the importance of saying nice things to classmates.)

It may also be of benefit to bring the teacher on board here. Circle time is a great learning opportunity for children to become kinder to each other. Be brave, teachers! Videotaping kids during free play and showing during circle how to join in successfully is a terrific method of teaching about social entry.

It's also important to raise children's awareness about how it feels to not be included (Amerit) or how it feels when someone barges in and ruins the game (Aidan, Jessica). Role-play with kids in the class or review actual video of classmate exchanges. Just make sure that the unsuccessful entrant is someone whom you know is already socially successful so that he can "take the hit." This is a strategy to use sensitively, sparingly, and with significantly more positive examples of socially successful interactions.

Everyone benefits from putting themselves in others' shoes. We learn to be better people when we deepen our perspective taking.

So, now that we know how to join in, what *are* kids playing in the yard?

CHAPTER 12

The Economics of Ice Chunks

There are recess games that have been played in schoolyards for generations. Of course, sometimes there are modifications, but the heart and soul of the games remain the same. What skills does your child need to understand how to successfully participate in these schoolyard recess staples? It usually all begins with being chased.

Tag and Its Variations

Tag begins in the toddler years when Daddy or Mommy chases a squealing little one with tickle fingers saying, "I'm gonna get you!" Alternatively, it can begin very early with, "Where's _____?" There you are!!! Followed by big giggles.

In the toddler phase, once children get caught, they expect that Mommy is going to chase *them* again. It's all about them at that age. Some kids get stuck here.

To move on, the next step is to understand that once you get caught, it's your turn to do the chasing. It's certainly not as much fun but part of fair play.

If your child is stuck on the being chased part and is older than three and a half, you can challenge her to "try and catch me!" or say "can't catch me!" Make it easy for her initially and then raise the challenge to expand her tolerance for frustration.

Once your child understands the idea of being chased and caught and knows that she also has to do the chasing and the catching, then you can add more complexity by adding another player.

You might have to alert your child to pay attention to the other people playing. You may need to repeatedly ask, "Who's it again?" to keep your child's attention in the game.

Following the rules of tag requires a real cognitive shift in children. You might be surprised to see how many children with social skills challenges get through a full year of kindergarten without really understanding what it means to be "it," as Ryan's story, below, illustrates.

It was mid-May in Ryan's junior kindergarten year. He was running around with a big grin on his face, cheeks flushed with excitement at being four, alive, and in the sunshine with his classmates.

All the kids were squealing and running, so Ryan squealed and ran. The pack of kids ran toward the fence, so Ryan ran toward the fence. Some kids splintered off, and Ryan followed his favorite person, Matthew, toward a tree. Unbeknownst to Ryan, Matthew was "it." Matthew threw himself at Ryan, almost knocking him over and shouted, "You're it!"

Ryan didn't have a sweet clue what that meant, but he saw Matthew running, and so he chased his bud Matthew. Matthew, who had just spent what felt like forever as chaser, was understandably annoyed that Ryan seemed to be going after him. "Get outta here! I was just it!" he yelled over his shoulder.

Puzzled but undaunted, Ryan kept chasing him, thinking that they were on the same side. Matthew was zigging and zagging, and Ryan kept after him. Matthew was getting seriously annoyed at this point. So was Ryan, who was just trying to be with his friend. Finally, Matthew did a break away and Ryan, winded at this point, simply stopped and looked around. He started to run toward Alex, and Alex ran away screaming.

"What the $^*&)?" must have been in Ryan's head. He started running aimlessly and the other kids responded by saying "Can't get me." But he just didn't understand, and his feelings started to bruise.

Kids like Ryan are just missing a social step or two. The best place to practice is at home with some explanation of how and what to do. But lots of games stem from tag:

Blob is one of them. Someone starts off as a "blob," and if she touches you, then you are part of the blob too. You then hold hands and try to add to the blob by touching others.

Sandman is another. Someone is on the ground, the designated sandman. Everyone else is on the play structure, but they have to close their eyes.

(Ridiculously dangerous, but all the kids cheat and peek.) If the sandman touches you, then you're it.

Soccer is a chasing game that kids of all ages (and adults) play. In soccer, one kid has the ball while a group of kids chases it, and then once another kid gets it, he is chased with little regard to whose team he is on. Have you ever seen young children play soccer? They often go after the ball en masse a bit as in the aforementioned game of "blob" but with a ball and two nets.

Hide-and-Seek

Hide-and-Seek is another schoolyard classic. When children are very young, hiding is really very easy—they simply cover their eyes. If the child can't see you, then you obviously can't see her. Young children may also put their head under a pillow thinking they are hiding and that no one can see them. It's really cute when children are two, but not so cute when your child is in second grade. You can tell a lot about a child's perspective-taking ability from how well she understands the game of hide-and-seek.

Here are the skills that your child needs to understand and practice with you before being able to carry out the game with some cred in the yard:

1. Hiding so that another person can't see you. This requires perspective taking. Your child will have to imagine what another person can see to be able to figure out if it is a good spot. To help your child develop this understanding, you could play with another person and point out to your child which hiding spots are good and why.

2. Not hiding in the same awesome spot over and over. You know it—behind the coats in the closet. Yes, it was excellent *once*. Kind of like that joke your child got a laugh from and now tells over and over. Finding a good and different hiding spot each time requires a great deal of theory of mind and perspective taking. Essentially, to be able to find new, good hiding spots every time, your child will need to realize that the other person knows about that spot if he found her there before.

3. Following the rules. These include taking turns being the hider and the seeker (understanding that if you are caught, you are the seeker next time), not peeking while you are counting, and, once you are pretty proficient, adding the element of "home" and trying to run to the home base to be exempt from being "it." Most "good guy" versus "bad guy" games played in the schoolyard are variations of tag plus hide-and-seek.

Ball Games

Ball games are also classic recess activities. Many children love to spend time at recess taking turns taking "shots" at some sort of goal with a moving object, whether it's a soccer ball, a hockey puck, or a basketball. Knowing how to participate in an accepted way in this simple activity not only helps children at recess, but also helps prepare them for gym class and being able to participate fully there too. This simple activity actually requires a great deal of social understanding, as the next story shows:

Some boys were taking turns kicking a soccer ball at a "goal," which consisted of two largish stones serving as goal posts. David took a shot that went wide. No big deal for David. He shook his head and then moved over. Then it was another boy's turn. He scored. Then it was Kyle's turn—his ball missed by a hair. The goalie threw it to the next kid, but Kyle grabbed the ball again and tried to take another shot. The other boys started shouting, clearly outraged. Kyle ignored the shouting and line up his shot yelling out, "I slipped! I get to take another shot." The other boys were irritated and grumbled, especially when Kyle got the next one in.

To be able to participate in these kinds of activities, a child most certainly must have a clear idea of how to take turns, even if her turn winds up sucky and she desperately wants to make a good shot. She must also understand that she will get social points if she knows how and when to give a "cool" compliment.

It also helps raise your child's social standing with classmates if she can make a lousy shot and not make up excuses. Nobody wants to hear that the sun was in your eyes, or that the ball was low on air, or that the goalie moved the rocks.

Kids who are well received in these games are also not afraid to blow their own horns, as discussed earlier, but within reason. Yelling out "Oh yeah, oh yeah!" and dancing around jubilantly is okay in kid culture—just not too often or for too long.

Your child may need to hear other kids boast successfully, so practice at home and watch other kids' facial expressions and body language to give her cues as to when it is okay to brag a bit or good-naturedly rip on a buddy.

So many games find their root in taking turns with a ball or taking shots against a goalie. Here are some variations:

- organized team games such as soccer, volleyball, hockey, basketball, etc.
- handball

- 4 Square
- World Cup
- dodgeball
- horseshoes
- bean bag toss

Play Structure Games

It's important not to overlook the issue of motor skills. Some kids struggle with physically coordinating movements. It might simply take them longer to climb playground structures, plan out how to get that ball in the net, and anticipate where the ball will go next. At a minimum, these sorts of challenges can delay a child's social interaction time, as Sam's story illustrates:

Sam was playing on the play structure in the schoolyard with two friends. They were playing a variation of tag where they were just happily running around the yard away from imaginary monsters. It went something like this, "AHHHH! Monsters!" And then they ran away from the "monster." Leah and Kayla simply ran faster than Sam and were hiding out from the imaginary beast in the tunnel. Sam was totally into the game, but it took him so long to get to the tunnel that Leah and Kayla were already gone by the time he got there.

If your child struggles to keep up with physical activities and this tale resonates with you, a referral for assessment by a physical therapist (physiotherapist) can really help.

There are some practical accommodations that you may find helpful to modify the environment a bit to allow your child to participate more fully and easily:

- When hosting an outdoor playdate, try to choose a park that has a smaller enclosure around the play structure to decrease the ability gap.
- Similarly, you could teach your child to suggest scenarios that limit the play area. For example, pretending that the ground is molten lava, or that there are alligators in the sand. Or your child could suggest to her friends that the only safe spot from monsters is the sand to keep peers close and to put the emphasis on stealth and strategy rather than running and climbing ability.
- Your child could also advocate for games like "capture the flag," or establish territories that you can't leave without being "out" to keep the area smaller.

Physical Dramatic Play

Kids also reenact dramatic play scenarios in schoolyards, which requires the same skills needed to participate in the classroom: pretend-play ability, social perspective taking, and flexible thinking, with a sprinkling of "run around," usually from some sort of enemy or danger involving victims and attackers. Variations of dramatic play most commonly seen in the schoolyard come from action hero movies. Kids play out scenes from movies such as *Captain America* or *Iron Man* or from TV shows, and reenact action scenes from video games such as Minecraft or Skylanders.

If you child finds outside reenactments challenging, you can help by finding out what shows or movies are popular with other kids in the class. Watch those shows together or get books that have those characters in them so that your child develops a familiarity with the characters, situations, and overall vocabulary being thrown around by classmates in the schoolyard.

You can also support your child by getting figures of the characters and reenacting pretend sequences at home. Then you and your child, with or without siblings, can try moving the game outside to get more practice. Finding a super cool prop to help remind your child of what his or her role is will also help provide her with "cred" in the schoolyard (e.g., Iron Man gloves, magic wand, crown, etc.).

Collections

Kids really start collecting items in first and second grade, though if there is an older sibling, this kind of play can occur in kindergarten games. What the children are collecting doesn't matter as much as how they negotiate with each other. In an attempt to control some of the challenges associated with kids trading items from their collections, some schools "ban" collectibles such as Pokémon, Beyblades, or Gogo's, saying that they foster unhealthy competition, stealing, and cheating, and highlight economic inequities.

Before choosing a side on this issue, consider this experience in an elementary school schoolyard during a typically long, cold winter for children in a city such as Ottawa, Canada:

The ice wars occurred every winter for three years for one mom of a very intense and competitive little boy and his sister. This mother frequently had to resort to dragging both of her children home screaming and crying because, tragically, so-and-so "STOLE MY ICE!" That's right—ice. Various sizes of dirty chunks of ice. Apparently in this schoolyard, different groups of kids would harvest ice chunks and build "forts," which were often under siege. The competition got so intense that some kids brought their own "colored" ice from home (aided by food coloring) to be able to brag that they had a better collection.

This mother, pushed into a desperate corner, allowed her semi-hysterical son to put twenty chunks of dirty snow in the back of her van to take home so that they wouldn't get "stolen" before school the next day! She was just so tired and worn down and wanted the screaming to stop.

Kids collect. And they collect at these ages for a reason. Collections force children to deal with others and to learn to do the following:

- *Negotiate and trade:* As in, "I'll give you one questionably yellow, super-rare, semi-slushy chunk for two gravel-stained, largish chunks of ice."
- *Rank and persuade:* "A semi-slushy! Are you kidding!? That's nowhere as good as my round chunk the size of a car tire. A car tire! You could use it for a door for your fort. Act now and I'll throw in a smallish, somewhat-yellow chunk absolutely free."
- *Cooperate and work as a team:* "If we get all the car-tire-sized chunks, then our fort will be the strongest. I'll keep watch while you go find more chunks to make sure that no one takes any of ours." Or, "My mom is picking me up tonight so I'll put all of our chunks in the back of the van."
- *Deal with customer satisfaction:* getting ripped off and disappointment. "Hey!! NO fair!! We said no trade-backs. You can't just say that you want ice back after you made a deal."
- *Problem solve:* "If we leave our awesome ice here, the fifth graders will come out and stomp on our fort. Let's hide them under the bush and bring them out at recess."
- *Know when you are being taken advantage of and grasp fair-play concepts:* "Hey! You guys said that you would give us the yellow ice if we let you hide your ice with ours under the bush!"

It's easy to understand why school administrators might shake their collective heads and want to give up on all of this. There is certainly a lot of potential for conflict.

But it certainly seems to make sense that if kids are resorting to trading *ice* in the absence of other opportunities, then perhaps there is something more going on here than a passing whim. Perhaps this represents a crucial stage of social skills development that helps children better learn to cooperate, problem solve, and negotiate.

There is so much that you can do as a parent to help support your little collector at home. First and foremost, listen to your child. Learn which cards are the most wanted at school, who has the best collection, and who got ripped off today at recess. Specifically, how did that kid get cheated and what does your child think she should have done instead?

If your child doesn't yet have the sophistication to identify when and how she might be taken advantage of, then bring her down to a hobby shop to find out more. You have an opportunity to raise your child's schoolyard cred by helping her understand which cards are worth the most, what a fair trade looks like, how to negotiate a fair deal, and, essentially, how not to get ripped off.

Other ways you can help your child become a better collector:

- Invite the other collectors over and get educated.
- Invite some of those other collectors to go to a hobby shop to talk "shop" with the "experts" in your community.
- Practice trading at home. Get your own collection with some really good and really bad cards. Have your child tell you what to trade with her and why.
- Please consider getting your child some excellent cards or Gogo's or whatever. It may seem shallow, but it just might create an opportunity for your kid to join in with a peer group that was otherwise not available to her before.

For kids who have flexibility as a goal, these rule-based collections and trades are often rigid enough that they may play to your child's strengths, such as need for organization, rules, and order. However, the trading may allow your child to learn to be strategic and realize that others are being strategic too. This provides more chances for your child to work on forecasting what another friend might do or might want that would be different than what she wants.

For our more rigid little people, sometimes taking things not so literally is a goal. Collections and negotiations can help to teach that sometimes people lie, steal, and cheat. You can help your child navigate these social complexities by having your own collection and playing the game with your child at home. Set her up and help her learn how to detect dishonesty and to learn the consequences.

For more impulsive little people, the lesson will be about planning and being strategic. If you impulsively give up a great card, then you might miss out on an even better one you might have gotten if you had waited until the next recess to make a trade.

The Development of Play Skills

Just like with other areas of child development such as language, motor skills, etc., children move through different stages of play. As their understanding of the world broadens, so too does their play. As children's play preferences emerge, they may want to play a certain way longer and in more depth than another child. For example, one child might spend most of her time engaged in dramatic play, while another child spends most of her time engaged in physical games. What is important for children is that they have developed the abilities that are highlighted in each play development stage to be able to support their social interaction skills.

Some of the different levels of play development are described below to allow you to determine where your child is and to plan for what she may be ready to play at recess, in the schoolyard, and during playdates.

When we think about children moving from "me directed" to "we directed" play, this essentially refers to a child moving developmentally from parallel, self-oriented play to cooperative, social play. All of the play types listed below can be played cooperatively, but in general, fully developed cooperative play must be in place for a child to participate successfully in dramatic, cooperative physical games and team sports.

Parallel (Me) Play to Cooperative (We) Play

- **Exploratory play** refers to children simply exploring their environment by picking things up, looking at them, putting them in their mouths, etc.

- **Cause and effect play** begins in late infancy through toddler years. With cause-and-effect games, the child begins to form the idea that "If I do X, then Y happens." For example, "If I push this button, the music comes on."

- **Gross motor and social interactive games** also begin in infancy and the toddler years. Games like peek-a-boo, "I'm gonna get you," "Where's _____?"

- **Relational play** begins early in the toddler phase and occurs when children begin to relate one object to another (e.g., get a drumstick and bang on a drum).

- **Constructive play** begins in the toddler years and involves building or constructing stacking blocks, putting track together.

■ **Pretend rudimentary play** begins around two or two and a half and involves relating one item to another (e.g., relating a cup to a teddy bear to give him a "drink").

■ **Pretend daily living play including more than one step** occurs as your child mirrors activities that she sees in daily living (e.g., get a bottle ready for the baby and feed her; get a blanket and put the baby to bed). This stage begins in the toddler years and continues through the twos.

■ **Pretend play expanded to less common events** occurs as your child begins to understand more and begins to take part in activities that are not necessarily part of her daily routine (e.g., getting her hair cut, going to the dentist). The ages of acquisition of this stage of play vary, but its emergence is typically associated with the preschool years. The amount of time spent engaged in pretend play varies from child to child depending on temperament.

■ **Dramatic play** is what it sounds like—a little dramatic play put on by your child. Dramatic play usually begins around age three and a half, but can occur a bit earlier or later depending on the child. It builds upon earlier forms of pretend play and offers a rich environment for developing social skills and perspective taking. This includes dress-up play with elaborate scripts and play with action figures, doll houses and props, Barbies, and train sets (beyond just building and pushing).

■ **Cooperative physical games** usually begin in earnest around kindergarten with games such as manhunt, blob, tag, dodgeball, and monkey in the middle. Requires agreement and understanding of multistep rules and ramifications for the violation of rules. It also requires understanding and the use of turn taking, fair play, exceptions, and physical coordination.

■ **Cooperative team sports:** While many children play "soccer," "basketball," or "hockey" beginning at three and four years of age, it usually looks like a herd of wildebeest migrating from one end of the field/court to the other. Usually at young ages, if your kid gets the ball, she's not giving it up for anything. The perspective and skills needed to play cooperative team sports typically begin to appear in early primary grades as children become more willing to share the work among a variety of roles in an organized and thoughtful way. In general, children's abilities to participate in cooperative sports such as ballet or dancing that don't involve balls evolve in the same way. At young ages, the children need to focus on their own individual abilities to complete complex physical tasks. As these kids get older and become more coordinated and familiar with routines, they really begin to dance with each other rather than as individuals focused on their own moves.

CHAPTER 13

Shine a Little Light into Dark Places

When You Need More Information

It's 7:30 on Friday night at the suburban community center. There is a major buzz in the air as eleven-, twelve-, and thirteen-year-olds gather in the community center courtyard waiting outside the door for the dance to start. Suddenly there is a rush of movement and a swell of noise.

Ariana, the girl with the sparkly, pink, poufy princess attire from chapter 4, has just been dropped off by her parents. Remember the girl who needed everyone to play the way she said to and the one who tantrummed so dramatically that her parents shut windows when her routine wasn't followed? She has grown to be a dynamic, sassy, beautiful young girl full of enthusiasm and promise. About eight other girls quickly run over and cluster around her, squealing with delight at her presence.

Before they drive away, her parents realize that Ariana still has her big, clunky backpack. They try to shout out that they will take it home for her, but after six failed attempts at calling out from the window, they give up. The squeals and shouts of "ARIANA!!! HI!!! You're here!!! OMG!!! I love your shirt!!!! Where's Claire!!!! Wait……Is Will coming?!!!!!! murmur murmur" drown out any attempt at being heard. There are blasts of laughter and lots of jumping up and down.

Wouldn't we all love a crystal ball? Wouldn't it have been great if Ariana's parents could have glimpsed that scene when they were so worried about her at four? When she couldn't participate in having a classmate over for longer than thirty minutes and had no friends in kindergarten? Wouldn't they have been relieved to see that all of their reading and working with her would lead to this young adult version of their princess?

Kids are resilient. And so are the adults who love them. If your child is currently struggling, know that where your child is today is only one page of a very long story that hasn't yet been written.

There is so much that you can do if you begin by recognizing in which areas your child needs support and then systematically and consistently provide opportunities to help him with those skills.

Is it always easy? Nope, but then nothing worthwhile ever is.

Will it go smoothly, this making and keeping friends? Nope to that too.

Childhood friendships are built, torn down, rebuilt, and abandoned, only to be relocated elsewhere. There will be pain, boredom, happiness, love, laughter, anger, betrayal, and tears. These feelings are real and can be as intense as in our adult relationships.

There is no one book that will get your child's heart through childhood friendships bruise-free, but this business of bumping up against each other while we try to connect needs to be figured out. We are compelled to try. We are all born to be in relationships, to connect, to be part of a community—whatever kind of community your child feels most comfortable in.

It may not be what we thought when we imagined our children into being. There may be more Lego and Polly Pocket in your life than you could ever have fathomed, but there is a place for your child and every child in this world. There is room for your child and every child in this world, and there are people for your child and every child in this world.

We can help our children be in relationships that affirm them, connect them, and give them a sense of belonging. It all begins with the love and connection *we* have with them.

Don't underestimate the power of your daily acts in every moment of every day of love and relationship that you bring to your child:

Every time you put down your phone and sit down to play trains, every time you wake up in the night to put a comforting hand on your child's forehead, and every time you wait expectantly with a wide smile knowing that this is the time your child will get that ball in the basket, you are an ambassador for loving relationships.

Those actions, more than any book with advice on making and keeping friends, teach your child about what it is to be in a relationship with others. This belonging begins with you and the community of your family at home.

You can love your child through these challenges, and with some nudges in specific areas, some practice and information, you can make it easier and better—you've got this.

And if you are worried that there is something going on, something "more" that is preventing your child from being able to learn and connect with other children—you've got that too. When we adults can face those fears, then we can get as much information and the specific tools that are needed to help our children through challenging situations. Going to a psychologist, psychiatrist, or doctor and asking, "Why is my child finding this *so* hard?" can be the first step to empowering all of you.

Sometimes the challenges your child is experiencing with making friends or fitting in at school have a name (see the next chapter) Please try to not be afraid of that. That name can lead to funding, support for you and your family and lend itself to deeper appreciation for what you are all experiencing.

If we can shine a little light on the dark worry we parents sometimes have, it really can lessen the amount of struggle in the long run. Sometimes understanding underlying causes can give us a flashlight and a map to navigate dark paths we find ourselves on.

Ariana quickly grabs her smartphone from her front pocket for the obligatory group selfie, before the girls all crowd around giggling and squealing for another shot. The pulsating beats of a bass guitar then start to drift through the building's front door, which prompts one of the girls to exclaim: "OMG!!!! We have to go in RIGHT NOW!!!! It's started!"

They all run—why would they walk?—through the doors and into the beginnings of being a teenager.

CHAPTER 14

When You Want More Answers
Where to Go and Who to Go To

If you think that there might be "more" happening that is preventing your child from making friends and fitting in at school, check out the following possibilities and resources to help with your investigations. The sources cited are not exhaustive but highlight some basic areas that may be contributing to social challenges.

Professionals Who Can Help

A **psychologist** is a professional with a doctoral degree in psychology who can assess (evaluate) your child and help determine whether your child has challenges in these areas:

- anxiety, depression, or other mood disorder that may prevent her from initiating or maintaining social relationships;
- heightened activity levels, impulsivity, distractibility, attention-deficit disorders (ADD/ADHD);
- interpreting nonverbal communication (such as body language, facial expressions), relating to other people, "reading" or understanding other people (problems that may be signs of an autism spectrum disorder, nonverbal learning disability, or social pragmatic disorder);

- processing words, putting ideas together, remembering what has been said (problems that may be related to learning challenges, difficulties processing information, and executive function issues).

A **psychiatrist** is a medical doctor (M.D.) who can diagnose these same kinds of underlying issues and can also prescribe medication to help your child when needed. A psychologist can offer *nonmedical* treatment for problems connected with these conditions such as individual or group counseling or therapy to learn to manage challenges such as anxiety.

A **speech-language pathologist** is someone with a master's degree in communication disorders and sciences who can assess and remediate problems with the following:
- speech sound clarity,
- understanding (comprehending) words or instructions,
- putting words together in sentences so that they make sense,
- putting sentences together into cohesive narratives,
- social communication with peers.

Speech-language pathologists with specialty training in autism spectrum disorders are able to diagnose in the U.S. In Canada, while speech-language pathologist are not entitled to diagnose autism spectrum disorders, they, like their American counterparts, are often first and front-line responders to issues that affect communication. When autism is suspected, it is always best practice to initiate referrals to include other professionals to provide a team-based approach to intervention.

An **occupational therapist** is a professional with at least a bachelor's degree (in Canada, a master's degree) who has passed a certifying exam and can assess and remediate challenges related to these areas:
- fine motor abilities involving the hands and fingers—e.g., playing with Lego, using small pieces when playing with toys, holding a pencil or utensil—as well as those involving the mouth and face (like chewing);
- sensory integration, such as being extra sensitive to noise or lights or undersensitive to touch (liking to crash into people and things).

A **physiotherapist or physical therapist** is a professional with at least a bachelor's degree who has passed a certifying exam and can assess and remediate challenges related to the following:
- gross motor skills involving large muscles in the legs, arms, and trunk such as sitting, walking, and lifting and carrying objects;

- physical coordination, like climbing play structures, running and catching a ball, and being able to fully participate with peers in physical games.

If you want more information around the "whys" of your child's challenges with keeping up with the other kids at preschool, daycare, or elementary school, there are laws in North America that provide for free assessment of children who may have a condition that would cause significant difficulties learning and participating fully in school. The challenge with getting a publically funded assessment is that there can be the waitlists. If you find the waiting is too long, you can also consult with a specialist privately.

Conditions That Can Result in Social Skills Difficulties

There are a lot of diagnoses that might neatly (or not so neatly) explain some of the kids' behaviors that were presented in this book. These include ADHD, ADD, autism spectrum disorders, executive functioning challenges, social pragmatic disorder, anxiety, nonverbal learning disability, oppositional defiant disorder, or just plain run-of-the-mill social immaturity. Here are some basic descriptions of some of these challenges and resources if you want to learn more.

Is It ADHD? ADD?

ADHD is an acronym for attention-deficit hyperactivity disorder. There are a variety of subtypes of this. Sometimes the term ADD is used for kids who have attention difficulties but not the hyperactivity.

Children are diagnosed with ADHD if they have enough challenges in this area across at least two environments (e.g., at home and at school).

Some possible signs that your child might have an attention deficit disorder include the following:

- constantly in motion
- inability to sustain interactions
- impulsive to the point of not being able to stay and play
- quick to anger/explosive
- not attending long enough to listen to other kids; not attending long enough to notice impact of own behavior on other kids
- not paying attention in class; needing instructions repeated
- not knowing when to stop being silly

- interrupting a lot
- dominating interactions
- possibly destructive tendencies
- "zoning out" (not paying enough attention to notice that the topic of play or conversation has changed)
- appearing dreamy
- not initiating interactions or communicating much or perhaps talking too much

Key Contacts:

CHADD
(Children and Adults with Attention-Deficit/Hyperactivity Disorder)
4601 Presidents Dr., Ste. 300
Lanham, MD 20706
800-233-4050; 301-306-7070
www.chadd.org

CHADD Canada
Box 191
234 - 5149 Country Hills Blvd. NW
Calgary, AB T3A 5K8
info@chaddcanada.com
www.chaddcanada.com

LD OnLine
www.ldonline.org
703-998-2060 (fax)

Books:

For Parents

- *All Dogs have ADHD,* by Kathy Hoopmann (kids like it too)
- *The Explosive Child,* by Ross Greene
- *Late, Lost, and Unprepared: A Parent's Guide to Helping Children with Executive Functioning,* by Joyce Cooper-Kahn and Laurie Dietzel
- *Lost at School,* by Ross Greene
- *Taking Charge of ADHD: The Complete, Authoritative Guide for Parents,* by Russell Barkley
- *The Incredible Years,* by Carolyn Webster-Stratton

For Kids—Some excellent books for young kids where the main characters have ADHD/ADD (undiagnosed):

- *Curious George* books, by Hans Augusto Rey and Margret Rey
- *No David,* by David Shannon
- *17 Things I Am Not Allowed to Do Anymore,* by Jenny Offill
- *Stanley's Party,* by Linda Bailey
- Winnie the Pooh books (character Tigger the tiger), by A.A. Milne

Is It Anxiety?

There are many ways that anxiety disorders manifest themselves depending on what area causes the most stress for a child (e.g., generalized anxiety, social anxiety, panic disorder, obsessive-compulsive disorder). Regardless of the type of anxiety diagnosed, the common thread is that the individual experiences excessive stress and mental anguish when involved in situations that most people don't find distressing.

Some signs of an anxiety disorder include the following:

- avoiding interaction
- clinging to parents
- hanging around adults mostly
- whispering responses
- insisting that things be "just so"
- feeling compelled to repeat the same action (e.g., checking things, washing hands)

Key Contacts:

Anxiety and Depression Association of America
8701 Georgia Ave., Ste. 412
Silver Spring, MD 20910
240-485-1001
www.adaa.org

Kids' Mental Health Ontario
40 St. Clair Avenue East, Ste. 309
Toronto, ON M4T 1M9
416-921-2109
info@cmho.org
www.kidsmentalhealth.ca

Mood Disorders Association of Ontario
36 Eglinton Ave. West, Suite 602
Toronto, ON M4R 1A1
416-486-8046
www.mooddisorders.ca

National Alliance on Mental Illness
3803 N. Fairfax Dr., Ste.100
Arlington, VA
703-524-7600; 800-950-6264 (helpline)
info@nami.org
www.nami.org

The Selective Mutism Foundation
P.O. Box 450632
Sunrise, FL 33345-0632
info@selectivemutismfoundation.org
www.selectivemutismfoundation.org

Books:

For Parents
- *Keys to Parenting Your Anxious Child,* by Katharina Manassis
- *Helping Your Anxious Child,* by Vanessa Cobham, Ronald M. Rapee, and Sue Spence

For Kids—Books for young children where the main character leans toward an anxious disposition:
- *Scaredy Squirrel* books, by Melanie Watts
- *Frog and Toad* books, by Arnold Lobel (it's Toad who works through his worry brain)
- *Stella* books, by Marie-Louise Gay (Stella's little brother Sam is often anxious)
- *Let's Talk about Feeling Worried* by, Joy Berry
- *Mr. Worry* by, Roger Hargreaves
- *Wallace's Lists* by, Barbara Bottner

Is It an Autism Spectrum Disorder?

Autism spectrum disorder or ASD is a general term for a complex disorder with symptoms on a continuum of severity ranging from mild (previously referred to as Asperger's syndrome) to more severe.

Everyone with ASD has difficulty in three broad, general areas:

- social interaction
- social communication
- repetitive or restricted interests

Here are some specific ways these difficulties may be shown:

- difficulties with joint attention and eye contact
- failing to seek out social interactions with others; often on her own agenda, in her own world
- difficulty understanding why other kids act the way they do
- difficulty knowing what to do with other kids
- seeking out much younger or much older kids or adults for interaction
- difficulties staying on topic
- literal interpretation of jokes, teasing
- talking excessively about a personal interest without the insight that listeners are bored or disinterested
- seeking sensory stimulating activities such as repeating the same activity over and over (e.g., lining up toys, hand flapping)
- needing things to be "just so"; inflexible
- really grooving on the rules for games
- not engaging in much pretend play or following a rigid format when pretending

Key Contacts:

Autism Canada Foundation
519-695-5858
info@autismcanada.org
http://autismcanada.org/

Autism Society of America
4340 East-West Highway, Ste. 350
Bethesda, MD 20814
301-657-0881; 800-3-AUTISM (328-8476)
info@autism-society.org
www.autism-society.org

Autism Society Canada
Box 22017, 1670 Heron Rd.
Ottawa, ON K1V 0W2
866-476-8440; 519-695-5858
info@autismsocietycanada.ca
http://www.autismsocietycanada.ca/

Autism Speaks
888-288-4762
familyservices@autismspeaks.org
www.autismspeaks. org

Autism Speaks Canada
2450 Victoria Park Avenue, Unit 120
Toronto, ON M2J 4A2
416-362-6227; 888-362-6227
autismspeakscanada@autismspeakscan.ca

OASIS@MAPP
219-662-1311
info@aspergersyndrome.org
www.aspergersyndrome.org

Books:
For Parents
- *1001 Great Ideas for Teaching and Raising Children with Autism Spectrum Disorders,* by Ellen Notbohm
- *The Complete Guide to Asperger's Syndrome,* by Tony Attwood
- *Early Start for your Child with Autism,* by Sally Rogers, Geraldine Dawson, and Laurie Vismara
- *Essential First Steps for Parents of Children with Autism,* by Lara Delmolino and Sandra L. Harris
- *More Than Words,* by Fern Sussman.
- *Talkability: People Skills for Verbal Children on the Autism Spectrum,* by Fern Sussman
- *Ten Things Every Child with Autism Wishes You Knew,* by Ellen Notbohm

For Kids
- *All Cats Have Asperger's,* by Kathy Hoopmann
- *The Survival Guide for Kids with Autism and Their Parents,* by Elizabeth Verdick and Elizabeth Reeve
- *All My Stripes: A Story for Children with Autism,* by Shaina Rudolph and Danielle Royer
- Amelia Bedelia books by Peggy Parish

Is It Nonverbal Learning Disability (NVLD)?

Nonverbal learning disability is so-called because children with this condition have a significantly harder time learning information that is not verbal than they do with information that is based on verbal ability. So, for example, it is more difficult for them to learn nonverbal communication (gestures, body language, facial expressions) and math than to learn language, reading, and writing.

Children with NVLD have many of the same features as children with Asperger syndrome ("high functioning" autism). That is, they have age appropriate or above average language abilities with difficulties understanding social expectations. However, children with NVLD often have strengths in listening and processing auditory information, whereas children with HFA are more likely to be visual learners. In addition, children with NVLD do not have the restricted or repetitive interests or behaviors that children on the autism spectrum typically do.

For More Information:
- LD Online
  http://www.ldonline.org/indepth/nonverbal
- NLD on the Web!
  http://www.nldontheweb.org

Books:
- *Raising NLD Superstars: What Families with Nonverbal Learning Disabilities Need to Know about Nurturing Confident, Competent Kids,* by Marcia Brown Rubenstein
- *Talkability: People Skills for Verbal Children on the Autism Spectrum,* by Fern Sussman
- *Understanding Nonverbal Learning Disabilities: A Common Sense Guide for Parents and Professionals,* by Maggie Mamen

Is it a Sensory Issue?

Sensory integration refers to how a person's ability to perceive sensory information aligns with the sensations in the environment. For example, someone with good sensory integration is able to tune in to useful visual, auditory, tactile, and other input from the environment and tune out the extraneous sensations. He or she is able to pay attention to the sound of an e-mail arriving, but tune out the sound of the heater turning off and on.

Different people perceive sensory input differently. A child dealing with sensory integration issues may be oversensitive (hypersensitive) to conditions such as noise, touch, sight, movement or undersensitive (hypersensitive) to some or all sensations. Here are some examples of behaviors that may be due to sensory integration problems:

- covering ears or crying at loud sounds (like fire alarms) or sounds that are not overly loud like songs in a minor key
- being distracted or bothered by very slight sounds (like fluorescent lights humming)
- crashing into things on purpose to get more touch input (if hyposensitive)
- flinching or crying as if in pain when bathing in warm water
- being enormously bothered by clothing tags
- craving movement sensations such as swinging or spinning
- closing eyes or not making eye contact when feeling visually overloaded
- turning the lights on and off repetitively to experience the shadows

Key Contacts:

Sensory Processing Disorder Resource Center
www.sensory-processing-disorder.com/

Sensory Processing Disorder Foundation
5420 S. Quebec Street, Ste. 135
Greenwood Village, CO 80111
303-794-1182
http://www.spdfoundation.net/

Books:

For Adults

- *The Out of Sync Child,* by Carol Stock Kranowitz
- *The Sensory Child Gets Organized: Proven Systems for Rigid, Anxious, or Distracted Kids,* by Carolyn Dagliesh

For Kids
- *The Loud Book,* by Deborah Underwood
- *The Very Itchy Bear,* by Nick Bland

Is It a Speech-Language Delay/Disorder?

Children can have delays in understanding and expressing themselves for a variety of reasons. Sometimes speech and language difficulties are a component of one of the other conditions discussed above. But other times a child simply has trouble with one or more aspects of communication. Delays and difficulties with speech and language can lead to problems with social skills as well as behavior issues due to frustration or anxiety at not understanding language or being understood by others. Sometimes it is not immediately clear whether a child has a speech or language delay/disorder alone or whether something else is happening that is contributing to the child's challenges.

Children with speech-language delays or disorders may have some of the following characteristics:
- trouble following instructions
- inability to follow instructions unless simplified or repeated many times
- difficulties asking/answering questions accurately or appropriately
- problems telling a simple story or retelling an event
- difficulties remembering what was just said to them
- using sentences that are shorter than those of other children their age and not expressing ideas as completely as other children
- difficulties speaking understandably
- giving up trying to communicate or getting extremely frustrated because they are not understood

Key Contacts:
American Speech and Hearing Association (ASHA)
2200 Research Boulevard
Rockville, MD 20850-3289
301-296-5700; 800-638-8255
www.asha.org
www.asha.org/public/speech/disorders/ChildSandL.htm

Childhood Apraxia of Speech Association
412-767-6589
helpdesk@apraxia-kids.org
www.apraxia-kids.org

First Words Program
http://www.firstwords.ca/
Hanen Centre
1075 Bay Street, Suite 515
Toronto, ON M5S 2B1
416-921-1073; 877-426-3655
info@hanen.org
www.hanen.org

Speech-Language & Audiology Canada
1000-1 Nicholas St.
Ottawa, ON K1N 7B7
613-567-9968;
800-259-8519
info@sac-oac.ca
http://sac-oac.ca/public/children

Books:

For Parents

- *Childhood Speech, Language, and Listening Problems,* by Patricia McAleere Hamaguchi
- *It Takes Two to Talk,* by Ayala Manolsen
- *The Parent's Guide to Speech and Language Problems,* by Debbie Feit, with Heidi M. Feldman

For Children:

- *Lilly's Purple Plastic Purse,* by Kevin Henkes (main character has trouble listening)
- *The Mouth with a Mind of Its Own,* by Patricia Mervine
- *Talking Is Hard for Me,* by Linda Reinert
- *Hooway for Wodney Wat,* by Helen Lester

Is It a Hearing Issue?

You may want to pursue a hearing assessment if your child has…

- difficulty attending,
- difficulty following instructions,
- a history of recurrent or long-lasting middle ear infections,
- perhaps a family history of hearing loss, or
- a tendency not to respond to your words or noises.

Hearing issues are not uncommon in young children, and it is always a good idea to check it out if you have any concerns.

Although pediatricians can do hearing screenings, and your child's hearing might be screened at school as well, the professional who is best equipped to determine whether a child has a hearing loss is an audiologist. An audiologist has a master's degree in audiology (hearing sciences) and can assess and remediate problems with hearing and processing sounds.

Is It a Vision Issue?

You may want to consider a complete eye exam to rule out a vision problem if your child:

- has difficulty attending,
- may not make eye contact,
- was born prematurely,
- pursues activities on her own agenda or independently,
- seems to move often from one activity to the next,
- bumps into things,
- does not greet familiar people on sight or respond to gestures,
- has difficulty following along when someone demonstrates what to do
- has a family history of visual issues,
- frequently rubs her eyes.

Again, this is something that pediatricians and schools can screen for, but for a definitive diagnosis, your child should see a specialist. An ophthalmologist is a medical doctor who can complete an eye exam and diagnose problems and provide solutions to help remedy visual disturbance. If the problem is just a refractive error (nearsightedness, farsightedness, astigmatism), an optometrist can test vision and prescribe corrective lenses.

References

American Academy of Pediatrics Council on Communications and Media. (2011). Media use by children younger than 2 years. *Pediatrics, 128,* 1–6.

Anthony, M. R. (2013). A randomized trial of a classroom intervention to increase peers' social inclusion of children with attention-deficit/ hyperactivity disorder. *Journal of Consulting and Clinical Psychology 81*(1), 100–112.

Asher, S. R., and Coie, J. D. (Eds.). (1990). *Peer rejection in childhood.* Cambridge, England: Cambridge University Press.

Attwood, T., Grandin, T., et al. (2006). *Asperger's and girls.* Arlington, TX: Future Horizons.

Barkley, R. A. (2011–2013). Executive functioning and ADHD: Nature and assessment. http://www.continuingedcourses.net/active/courses/course069.php.

Barkley, R. A. (1995). *Taking charge of ADHD: The complete authoritative guide for parents.* New York: Guilford Press.

Barkley, R. A. (2014). ADHD, self-regulation, and executive functioning: What it means for management. Webinar.

Barnett, W. S., Jung, K., Yarosz, D. J., Thomas, J., Hornbeck, A., Stechuk, R., & Burns, S. (2008). Educational effects of the Tools of the Mind curriculum: A randomized trial. *Early Childhood Research Quarterly, 23,* 299–313.

Baron-Cohen, S. (1995). *Mindblindness: An Essay on Autism and Theory of Mind.* Cambridge, MA: MIT Press.

Barton, E. (2010). Development of a taxonomy of pretend play for children with disabilities. *Infants and Young Children, 23*(4), 247–261.

Bartsch, K., & Wellman, H. M. (1995). *Children talk about the mind.* New York: Oxford University Press.

Bates, R. P. (2012). Narrative production and the development of executive function: A study of emergent literacy. Thesis.

Bellini, S. (2006). *Building social relationships.* Lenexa, KS: Autism Asperger Publishing Co., 2006.

Bellis, T. J. (2002), *When the brain can't hear: Unraveling the mystery of auditory processing disorder.* New York: Atria Books.

Bergen, D. (2002). The role of pretend play in children's cognitive development. *Early Childhood Research and Practice, 4* (1).

Bernier, A., Whipple, N., & Carlson, S. M. (2010). From external regulation to self-regulation: Early parenting precursors of young children's executive functioning. *Child Development, 81*(1), 326–339.

Blair, C., & Cybele Raver, C. (2014). Closing the achievement gap through modification of neurocognitive and neuroendocrine function: Results from a cluster randomized controlled trial of an innovative approach to the education of children in kindergarten. *PLOS ONE* 9(11), 1–13.

Blair, C. B. (2014). Early communicative gestures prospectively predict language development and executive function in early childhood. *Child Development, 85*(5), 1–17.

Carlson, S. M. (2005). Developmentally sensitive measures of executive function in preschool children. *Developmental Neuropsychology, 28*(2), 595–616.

Centers for Disease Control and Prevention. (March 31, 2015). ADHD data and statistics. www.cdc.gov/ncbddd/adhd/data.html.

Centers for Disease Control and Prevention. (Feb. 26, 2015). Autism (ADDM) data and statistics. http://www.cdc.gov/ncbddd/autism/data.html.

Charman, T., Baron-Cohen, S., Swettenham, J., Baird, G., Cox, A., & Drew, A. (2000). Testing joint attention, imitation, and play as infancy precursors to language and theory of mind. *Cognitive Development, 15,* 481–498.

Cheng, M. (Feb. 2, 2015). Don't let yourself get replaced by screens and technology. Interview. Ottawa, ON: CTV News.

Christakis, D. A., Zimmerman, F. J., DiGiuseppe, D. L., & McCarty, C. A. (2004). Early television exposure and subsequent attentional problems in children. *Pediatrics, 113*(4), 708–713.

Christakis, D. A., Gilkerson, J., Richards, J. A., Zimmerman, F. J., Garrison, M. M., Xu, D., Gray, S., & Yapanel, U. (2009). Audible television and decreased adult words, infant vocalizations, and conversational turns: A population-based study. *Archives of Pediatric and Adolescent Medicine, 163*(6), 554–558.

Coloroso, B. (2002). *The bully, the bullied, and the bystander.* New York: Harper Collins.

Cooper-Kahn, J., & Dietzel, L. (2008). *Late, lost, and unprepared: A parent's guide to helping children with executive functioning.* Bethesda, MD: Woodbine House.

Cooper-Kahn, J. (2015, March 27). *Late, Lost, and Unprepared: How to Help Youth Build Better Executive Functioning.* Autism Awareness Centre Presentation.

Corsaro, W. (1979). "We're friends, right?": Children's use of access rituals in a nursery school. *Language in Society 8*(2–3), 315–336.

Courage, M. L., & Howe, M. L. (2010). To watch or not to watch: Infants and toddlers in a brave new electronic world. *Developmental Review, 30,* 101–115.

Cox, A. J. (2007). *No mind left behind: Understanding and fostering executive control; The eight essential brain skills every child needs to thrive.* New York: Perigree/Penguin.

Dalto, R., & Lamontagne, J. (2014). Developing social and emotional competence and theory of mind in infants, preschoolers and school age children. ASHA presentation.

Davis, J., & Bauman, K. (2011). School enrollment in the United States: 2008 current population reports. Washington, DC: U.S. Census Bureau.

Delaney, T. (2009). *101 Games and activities for children with autism, Asperger's and sensory processing disorders*. New York: McGraw Hill.

Diamond, A., & Taylor, C. (1999). Development of an aspect of executive control: Development of the abilities to remember what I said and to "Do as I say, not as I do." *Developmental Psychobiology, 29*(4), 315–334.

Diamond, A. (2006). The early development of executive functions. In E. Bialystok & F. Craik (Eds.), *Lifespan cognition: Mechanisms of change,* pp. 70–95. New York: Oxford University Press.

Diamond, A., & Lee, K. (2011). Interventions shown to aid executive function development in children 4–12 years old. *Science, 333*(6045), 959–964.

Diamond, A., Kirkham, N., & Amso, D. (2002). Conditions under which young children can hold two rules in mind and inhibit a preponent response. *Developmental Psychology,* 38(3), 352–362.

Diamond, A., Barnett, W. S., Thomas, J., & Munro, S. (2007). Preschool program improves cognitive control. *Science, 318*(5855), 1387–1388.

Dunn Buron, K., & Curtis, M. (2004). *The incredible five-point scale.* Lenexa, KS: Autism Asperger Publishing Company.

Ensor, R., Spencer, D., & Hughes, C. (2010). "You feel sad?" Emotional understanding mediates effects of verbal ability and mother-child mutuality on prosocial behaviors: Findings from 2 years to 4 years. *Social Development, 20,* 93–110.

Ensor, R., Hart, M., Jacobs, L., & Hughes, C. (2011). Gender differences in children's problem behaviours in competitive play with friends. *British Journal of Developmental Psychology, 29,* 176–187.

Frankel, F. (1996). *Good friends are hard to find: Help your child find, make, and keep friends.* London: Perspective Publishing.

Frankel, F., Myatt, R., Cantwell, D. P., & Feinberg, D. T. (1997). Parent-assisted transfer of children's social skills training: Effects on children with and without attention-deficit hyperactivity disorder. *Journal of the American Academy of Adolescent Psychiatry, 36*(8), 1056–1064.

Funk, J. B., Brouwer, J., Curtiss, K., & McBroom, E. (2009). Parents of preschoolers: Expert media recommendations and ratings knowledge, media-effects beliefs, and monitoring practices. *Pediatrics, 123,* 981–988.

Gallese, V., & Goldman, A. (1998). Mirror neurons and the simulation theory of mind-reading. *Trends in Cognitive Sciences, 2*(12), 493–501.

Ganea, P., Lillard, A., & Turkheimer, E. (2004). Preschooler's understanding of the role of mental states and action pretense. *Journal of Cognition and Development, 5*(2), 213–238.

Garon, N., Bryson, S. E., & Smith, I. M. (2008). Executive function in preschoolers: A review using an integrative framework. *Psychological Bulletin, 134*(1), 31–60.

Gitlin-Weiner, K., Sandgrund, A., & Schaefer, C. (Eds.). (2002). *Play diagnosis and assessment.* New York: Wiley.

Gordon, M. (2005). *Roots of empathy.* Markham, ON: Thomas Allen Publishers.

Gray, C. (2010). *The new social story book.* Arlington, TX: Future Horizons.

Greene, R. W. (2008). *Lost at school: Why our kids with behavioral challenges are falling through the cracks and how we can help them.* New York: Scribner.

Greene, R. W. (2005). *The explosive child.* New York: Harper Collins.

Green, V. A., Cillessen, A. H. N., Rechis, R., Patterson, M. M., & Milligan Hughes, J. (2008). Social problem solving and strategy use in young children. *Journal of Genetic Psychology, 169*(1), 92–112.

Hadley, P., & Schuele, C. M. (1998). Facilitating peer interaction: Socially relevant objectives for preschool language intervention. *American Journal of Speech-Language Pathology, 7,* 25–36.

Hallowell, E. M., & Ratey, J. J. (2005). *Delivered from distraction: Getting the most out of life with attention deficit disorder.* New York: Ballantine Books.

Harris, P. L. (2008). Children's understanding of emotions. In M. Lewis, et al. (Eds.). *Handbook of Emotions.* New York: Guilford Press.

Hart, B., & Risley, T.R. (1995). *Meaningful differences in the everyday experiences of young American children.* Baltimore: Paul H. Brookes.

Hodgdon, L. A. (1995). *Visual strategies for improving communication.* Troy, MI: QuirkRoberts Publishing.

Holmes, R. M. (2012). The outdoor recess activities of children at an urban school: Longitudinal and intraperiod patterns. *American Journal of Play, 4,* 3.

Hutman, T., Rozga, A., DeLaurentis, A., Sigman, M., & Dapretto, M. (2012). Infants' pre-empathic behaviors are associated with language skills. *Infant Behaviour & Development, 35,* 561–569.

Iacoboni, M. (2009). Imitation, empathy, and mirror neurons. *Annual Review of Psychology, 60,* 653–670.

Jensen, P. S., Martin, D., & Cantwell, D. P. (1997). Comorbidity in ADHD: Implications for research, practice, and DSM-V. *Journal of the American Academy of Child and Adolescent Psychiatry, 36*(8), 1065–1079.

Kleinknecht, E., & Beike, D. (2004). How knowing and doing inform an autobiography: Relations among preschoolers' theory of mind, narrative, and event memory skills. *Applied Cognitive Psychology, 18,* 745–764.

Kranowitz, C. (1998). *The out of sync child.* New York: The Berkley Publishing Group.

Kuhn, L. J., Willoughby, M. T., Parramore Wilbourn, M., Vernon-Feagans, L., & Blair, C. B. (2014). Early communicative gestures prospectively predict language development and executive function in early childhood. *Child Development, 85*(5),1898–1914.

Kuypers, L. (2011). *The zones of regulation.* San Jose, CA: Think Social Publishing.

Ladd, G. W., Hart, J. M., & Craig, H. C. (1988). Predicting preschooler's peer status from their playground behavior. *Child Development, 59*(4), 986–992.

Laugeson, E. A. (2013). *The science of making friends: Helping socially challenged teens and young adults.* New York: Wiley

Laushey, K. M, & Heflin, L. J. (2000). Enhancing social skills of kindergarten children with autism through the training of multiple peers as tutors. *Journal of Autism and Developmental Disorders, 30*(3), 183–193.

Lieber, J. (1994). Conflict and its resolution in preschoolers with and without disabilities. *Early Education and Development, 5*(1), 5–17.

Lillard, A. (2001). Explaining the connection: Pretend play and theory of mind. In R. S. Reifel (Ed.), *Theory in context and out* (Vol. 3). Westport, CT: Ablex Publishing.

Lillard, A. (1998). Wanting to be it: Children's understanding of intentions underlying pretense. *Child Development, 69*(4), 981–993.

Lillard, A., & Curenton, S. (2009). Do young children understand what others feel, want, and know? *Young Children,* 52–57.

Lillard, A., & Witherington, D. (2004). Mothers' behavior modifications during pretense and their possible signal value for toddlers. *Developmental Psychology,* 40(1), 95–113.

Lillard, A. S., Lerner, M. D., Hopkins, E. J., Dore, R. Z., Smith, E. D., & Palmquist, C. M. (2013). The impact of pretend play on children's development: A review of the evidence. *Psychological Bulletin, 139*(1), 1–34.

Lillard, A. S., & Peterson, J. (2011). The immediate impact of different types of television on young children's executive function. *Pediatrics, 128*(4), 644–649.

Linebarger, D. L., & Vaala, S. E. (2010). Screen media and language development in infants and toddlers: An ecological perspective. *Developmental Review, 30,* 176–202.

Lipnowski, S., LeBlanc, C. M. A, Canadian Paediatric Society, Healthy Active Living and Sports Medicine Committee. (2012). Healthy active living: Physical activity guidelines for children and adolescents. *Pediatrics Child Health, 17*(4), 209–210.

Lorelle Lentz, C., Kyeong-Ju Seo, K., & Gruner, B. (2014). Revisiting the early use of technology: A critical shift from "how young is too young?" to how much is "just right?" *Dimensions of Early Childhood, 42*(1),15–31.

Lowry, L. Classroom features influence interaction in children with autism. Toronto: The Hanen Centre.

McAuliffe, M. D., Hubbard, J. A., & Romano, L. J. (2009). The role of teacher cognition and behaviour in children's peer relations. *Journal of Abnormal Psychology, 37,* 665–677.

Mahoney, J. L. (2000). School extracurricular activity participation as a moderator in the development of antisocial patterns, *Child Development, 71*(2), 502–516.

Meek, S. E., Robinson, L. T., & Jahromi, L. B. (2012). Parent-child predictors of social competence with peers in children with and without autism. *Research in Autism Spectrum Disorders, 6,* 815–823.

Mesman, J., VanIjendoorn, M. H., & Bkermans-Kranenburg, M. J. (2009). The many faces of the Still-Face Paradigm: A review. *Developmental Review.* doi:10.1016/j.dr.2009.02.001.

Mikami, A.Y., & Lorenzi, J. (2011). Gender and conduct problems predict peer functioning among children with attention-deficit/hyperactivity disorder. *Journal of Clinical Child Adolescent Psychology, 40*(5), 777–786.

Mikami, A. Y., Swaim Griggs, M., Lerner, M. D., Emeh, C. C., Reuland, M. M., Jack, A., & Anthony, M. R. (2014). A randomized trial of classroom intervention to increase peers' social inclusion of children with attention-deficit/hyperactivity disorder. *Journal of Consultation of Clinical Psychology, 81*(1), 100-112.

Miller, S. E., & Marcovitch, S. (2015). Examining executive function in the second year of life: Coherence, stability, and relations to joint attention and language. *Developmental Psychology, 51*(1), 101–114.

Montague, D. P. F., & Walker-Andrews, A. S. (2001). Peekaboo: A new look at infants' perception of emotion expressions. *Developmental Psychology,* 37 (826–838).

Neufeld, G., & Mate, G. (2013). *Hold on to your kids: why parents need to matter more than peers.* Toronto: Vintage Canada.

Okuma, K., & Tanimura, M. (2009). A preliminary study of the relationship between characteristics of TV content and delayed speech development in young children. *Infant Behavior and Development, 32,* 312–321.

Over, H., & Carpenter, M. (2013). The social side of imitation. *Child Development Perspectives, 7*(1), 6–11.

Owens, G., Granader, Y., Humphrey, A., & Baron-Cohen, S. (2008). LEGO therapy and the social use of language programme: An evaluation of two social skills interventions for children with high functioning autism and Asperger syndrome. *Journal of Autism Developmental Disorders, 38*(10), 1944–1957.

Page, T. *Parallel play: Growing up with undiagnosed Asperger's.* New York: Doubleday 2009.

Parkes, A., Sweeting, H., Wight, D., & Henderson, M. (2013). Do television and electronic games predict children's psychosocial adjustment? Longitudinal research using the UK Millennium Cohort Study. *Archives of Disease in Childhood, 98,* 341–348.

Pepper, J., & Weitzman, E. (2004). *It takes two to talk.* Toronto: Hanen Centre Publications.

Pierce-Jordan, S., & Lifter, K. (2005). Interaction of social and play behaviors in preschoolers with and without pervasive developmental disorder. *Topics in Early Childhood Special Education, 25*(1), 34–47.

Putallaz, M., & Gottman, J. M. (1981). An interactional model of children's entry into peer groups. *Child Development, 52,* 986–994.

Putallaz, M., & Wasserman, A. (1990). Children's entry behavior. In S. R. Asher & J. D. Cole (Eds.), *Peer rejection in childhood.* New York: Cambridge University Press.

Ramsey, P., & Lasquade, C. (1996). Preschool Children's Entry Attempts. *Journal of Applied Developmental Psychology, 17*(1), 135–150.

Repacholi, B. M., & Gopnik, A. (1997). Early reasoning about desires: Evidence from 14- and 18-month-olds. *Developmental Psychology, 33,* 12–21.

Reszka, S. S., Odom, S. L., & Hume, K. A. (2012). Ecological features of preschools and the social engagement of children with autism. *Journal of Early Intervention, 34*(1), 40–56.

Reuland, M. M., & Mikami, A. Y. (2014). Classroom victimization: Consequences for social and academic adjustment in elementary school. *Psychology in the Schools, 51*(60), 591–607.

Richert, R. A., Robb, M. B., & Smitt, E. I. (2014). Media as social partners: The social nature of young children's learning from screen media. *Child Development, 82,* 82–95.

Rizzolatti, G., Sinigaglia, C., & Anderson, F. (2008). *Mirrors in the brain: How our minds share actions, emotions, and experience.* New York: Oxford University Press.

Rogers. S. J., & Dawson, G. (2010). *Early Start Denver Model Curriculum checklist for young children with autism.* New York: Guilford Press.

Rowan, C. (2010). Unplug—don't drug: A critical look at the influence of technology on child behavior with an alternative way of responding other than evaluation and drugging. *Ethical Human Psychology and Psychiatry, 12*(1), 60–67.

Rubio-Fernandez, P., & Geurts, B. (2013). How to pass the false-belief task before your fourth birthday. *Psychological Science, 24*(1), 27–33.

Salvas, M. C., Brendgen, M., Tremblay, R. E., Vitaro, F., Dionne, G., & Boivin, M. (2014). Friendship conflict and the development of generalized physical aggression in the early school years: A genetically informed study of potential moderators. *Developmental Psychology, 50*(6), 1794–1807.

Schmidt, M.E., Rich, M., Rifas-Shiman, S. L., Oken, E., & Taveras, E. M. (2009). Television viewing in infancy and child cognition at 3 years of age in a US cohort. *Pediatrics, 123,* 370–375.

Seo, H. A., Chun, H. Y., Jwa, S.H., & Choi, M. H. (2011). Relationship between young children's habitual computer use and influencing variables on socio-emotional development. *Early Child Development and Care, 181,* 245–265.

Shanker, S. (2012). *Self-regulation and mental health.* Toronto: York University.

Sims, M., Hutchins, T., & Taylor, M. (1997). Conflict as social interaction: Building relationship skills in child care settings. *Child and Youth Care Forum, 26*(4), 247–260.

Sobel, D., & Lillard, A. (2001). The impact of fantasy and action on young children's understanding of pretense. *British Journal of Developmental Psychology, 19,* 85-98.

Stagg, S. D., Slavny, R., Hand, C., Cardoso, A., & Smith, P. (2014). Does facial expressivity count? How typically developing children respond initially to children with autism. *Autism, 18*(6), 704–711.

Stewart, K. (2002). *Helping a child with nonverbal learning disorder or Asperger's syndrome.* Oakland, CA: New Harbinger Publications.

Stock-Kranowitz, C. (1998). *The out of sync child.* New York: Perigree.

Strasburger, V. C. (2007). First do no harm: Why have parents and pediatricians missed the boat on children and media? *The Journal of Pediatrics,* Oct. editorial.

Stuss, D.T., & Knight, R.T. (Eds.). (2002). *Principles of frontal lobe function.* New York: Oxford University Press.

Sussman, F. (2012). Let's pretend: The relationship between play and theory of mind in typical children and children with ASD. The Hanen Early Learning Program. http://www.hanen.org/SiteAssets/Helpful-Info/Articles/pretend-play.aspxCentre.

Sussman, F. (1999). *More than words.* Toronto: Hanen Centre Publications.

Sussman, F. (2006). *Talkability: People skills for verbal children on the autism spectrum: A guide for parents.* Toronto: Hanen Centre Publications.

Thorell, L. B., Lindqvist, S., Bergman Nutley, S., Bohlin, G., & Klingberg, T. (2009). Training and transfer effects of executive functions in preschool children. *Developmental Science, 12*(1), 106–113.

Tremblay, M. S., LeBlanc, A. G., Carson, V., Choquette, L., Connor Gorber, S., Dillman, C., et al. (2012). Canadian sedentary behaviour guidelines for the early years (aged 0-4 years). *Applied Physiology, Nutrition, and Metabolism, 37,* 370–380.

Ulinger Shantz, C. (1987). Conflict between children. *Child Development, 58*(2), 283–305.

Ursache, A., Blair, C., & Cybele Raver, C. (2012). The promotion of self-regulation as a means of enhancing school readiness and early achievement in children at risk for school failure. *Child Development Perspectives, 6*(2), 122–128.

Vallotton, C., & Ayoub, C. (2011). Use your words: The role of language in the development of toddler's self-regulation. *Early Childhood Research Quarterly, 26*(2), 169–181.

Vandewater, E. A., Rideout, V. J., Wartella, E. A., Huang, X., Lee, J. H. & Shim, M. (2007). Digital childhood: Electronic media and technology use among infants, toddlers and preschoolers. *Pediatrics, 119,* 1006–1015.

Vaughan Van Hecke, A., Mundy, P., Block, J. J., Delgado, C. E. F., Parlade, M. V., Pomares, Y. B., & Hobson, J. A. (2012). Infant responding to joint attention, executive processes, and self-regulation in preschool children. *Infant Behaviour and Development, 35,* 300-311.

Vespo, J. E., Pedersen, J., & Hay, D. F. (1995). Young children's conflicts with peers and siblings: Gender effects. *Child Study Journal, 25* (3).

Walker, S. (2005). Gender differences in the relationship between young children's peer-related social competence and individual differences in theory of mind. (2005). *Journal of Genetic Psychology, 166*(3), 297–312.

Webster-Stratton, C. (2005). *The incredible years: A troubleshooting guide for parents of children aged 2-8 years.* Seattle, WA: Incredible Years.

Weisleder, A., & Fernald, A. (2013). Talking to children matters: Early language experience strengthens processing and builds vocabulary. *Psychological Science, 24*(11), 2143–2152.

Wetherby, A. (July 2009). Improving early detection of autism spectrum disorders in infants and toddlers. Presentation at Florida State University, Tallahassee, FL.

Wiig, E., Secord, W., & Semel, E., (2004). *The Clinical Evaluation of Language Fundamentals—Preschool 2.* San Antonio, TX: PsychCorp.

Williams, J. H. G., Whiten, Z., Suddendorf, T., & Perrett. D. I. (2001). Imitation, mirror neurons, and autism. *Neuroscience and Biobehavioral Reviews 25,* 287–295.

Zimmerman, F. J., & Christakis, D. A. (2007). Associations between content types of early media exposure and subsequent attentional problems. *Pediatrics, 120*(5), 986–992.

Zimmerman, F. J., Christakis, D. A., & Meltzoff, A. N. (2007). Associations between media viewing and language development in children under 2 years. *The Journal of Pediatrics,* 364–368.

Zimmerman, F. J., Glew, G. M., Christakis, D. A., & Katon, W. (2005). Early cognitive stimulation, emotional support, and television watching as predictors of subsequent bullying among grade-school children. *Archives of Pediatric and Adolescent Medicine, 159,* 384–388.

Acknowledgments

Special thanks to:

The parents and caregivers of the children I have been privileged to work with. I continue to be humbled and inspired by your willingness to try anything, do anything, and share everything if it meant helping your children.

The kids on my caseload. The world needs you! You are all beautiful and so much fun and have been the best teachers.

Simon—you are my best friend and "I love your way" (rock quote for you). Without you, this book would be full of inappropriate dramatic dashes—I have been blessed to have you as my partner.

Maya and Elliott, my wonderful kids. Thanks for letting me watch you in the schoolyard while trying to figure out this recess business. I hope it never got weird. Thanks too for your insights, explanations, and teaching me all about Beyblades. I love you both so much and am so proud to be your mom.

To *my* mom—someone who always believed in her kids and did everything to give us a better life.

Dad, for teaching me to think "big" and to help "big."

Taylor, for the idea of even writing a book in the first place and to both you and Dave for all of the encouragement and over-dinner chats.

My editor Susan, who has a real gift for well-placed tweaks and making everything sound so much better.

Jill, my dear friend, the one who never tired of listening to sometimes alarming shifts between self-loathing and hope. You have a real gift for encouragement. Bird-by-bird. Thank you from the bottom of my heart.

My colleagues and supporters in the Ready for Recess and Wanna Play programs: Mary Lynn, Tanya and Mylene. Thank you for being flexible enough to have snack on the floor and rising to unexpected challenges with grace (think watermelon). Thank you for being the special caring, dedicated, and smart women you are.

The rest of the team at CHEO and First Words: Anique, Arlene, Chantal, Danielle, Deirdre, Janice, Jenn, Karine, Karrie-Lynn, Kim, Laurie-Ann, Laurice, Marie-Andree, Marie- France, Maureen, Nicole, Sarah, Seana, Sherri, Sophie, Sussie, Sylvie, Tammy, and Tiffany. Thank you for taking the time to listen and share your wonderful insights. It is such a gift to work with you.

Marcus and Sarah, for your encouraging words and ideas shared over many wonderful meals.

My NYC ladies, Connie and Anne, just because you're awesome.

Carol—I never will be able to understand how you find the time to do so much and so well! Thank you for lending your sharp mind to this text.

Robin—Even with only half of the pages, you managed to provide bang-on suggestions and be so supportive, though text did seem like it was "missing something." Thank you.

Special thanks to Ross Greene for being willing to read chapters of a very rough manuscript and say, "I think there is a book here." I have come to admire your kindness beyond your outstanding professional contributions.

Adele Diamond, for taking time out of a very busy schedule to look over the framework and offering needed insight and encouraging questions.

Scott, for eating all of the centers out of the Oreos. They really weren't good for me.

Last, but not least: thanks, Teddy. Everyone should have an overly extroverted and sensitive golden retriever to rest your laptop on when writing a book.

Index

About the Author

S honna Tuck is a speech-language pathologist with special expertise in early identification and intervention for children who are socially at risk. Her book is based on twenty years of reviewing research, advocacy, and a passion for helping children and their families.